Karl Jaspers

Karl Jaspers. By permission from *Réalités*, French ed., (September 1965)

Karl Jaspers:
Philosophy as Faith

by Leonard H. Ehrlich

The University of Massachusetts Press Amherst 1975

Publication of this book was assisted by the
American Council of Learned Societies under a grant
from the Andrew W. Mellon Foundation.

In remembrance

HENRYK FISCHGRUND

A man of courage in a hostile world
Remembered with admiration by the remnant of his family

Shot by the ss • Warsaw • Spring 1943

DR. LEON EHRLICH

Lost and hapless victim
Remembered with love and pity

In 1939 he taught me Nietzsche • In 1942 he perished in Auschwitz

JOSEPH FRANI

Remembered for his friendship, nobility, and quixotic valor
Shot by a german sniper while giving first aid

Bellevue Ferme • February 15, 1945

Contents

Preface

In this book the attempt is made to give a definitive interpretation of Jaspers's philosophy by combining two approaches. On the one hand, by taking one of the many main themes of Jaspers's philosophy as my vantage point, I try to gain an overview of the vast range and varied content of his thinking. The theme I selected for this purpose is Jaspers's conception of philosophical thought as the articulation of faith. On the other hand, I try to arrive at a clarification of Jaspers's philosophical significance within the history of philosophy. I do this by making critical comparisons among Jaspers and others with respect to some of his most important philosophical achievements.

By means of my interpretation I would like to contribute to the initiation of a phase of Jaspers-interpretation which is less dependent on exposition, on isolated ad hoc topics and on terminological slavishness than previous phases, and thereby to facilitate his entrance into the main stream of philosophical thought. I am also trying to make Jaspers accessible. This does not mean that I can make him easy; it can only mean that if I succeed, then I have shown the effort to understand him and his significance to be worth while and perhaps even of vital importance.

It is with great pleasure that I am able to acknowledge the help and kindness of many persons without whom I could not have written this book; I can mention only some of the many. From my colleagues, Professor Emeritus Shute and also Professor Aune and Professor Chappell, I received needed interest and encouragement; from Ms. Holden and Ms. Rood invaluable secretarial service; from the director of the University of Massachusetts Press, Mrs. Leone Stein, patience and forebearance; and from Ms. Bolster and Ms. Swartz exacting editorial work. Dr. Saner and Frau Jaspers made it possible for me to consult Jaspers's *Nachlass* in connection with my research for these studies. I express my gratitude to Dr. Saner for this and for his work, which has already proven itself indispensable for any serious Jaspers scholarship.

I had hoped to express my gratitude to Gertrud Jaspers by submitting a copy of the finished book to her. This is not to be. A few days ago she died peacefully at home, surrounded by loving friends, in her ninty-sixth year. But she knew and shared the suffering and the memories of her Jewish people. In this way she brought into Karl Jaspers's house and into the realms of his thinking the consciousness of what he called "the profundity of the Jewish soul": the will to live and act in an unredeemed world, and to bring to bear on it an unrelenting sense of truth, a severe sense of justice, faith without illusion, and in despair the guiding beacon of hope.

My wife, Edith, has been the collaborator in the interpretation of Jaspers since the time when we were his students in Basel. Her contribution to this book has been essential in all its aspects. It is proper that I also thank my children, Carl and Karin, for helping with the tedious labor of proofreading.

Materially, I was aided by the University of Massachusetts, which gave me sabbatical leave and some research grants, and by the American Council of Learned Societies, which, under a grant from the Andrew W. Mellon Foundation, subsidized the publication of the book. I express my gratitude to them.

Parts of this book have been published in the *Bucknell Review*, *Massachusetts Review*, *Harvard Theological Review*, and the Acts of the Fourteenth and the Fifteenth International Congresses of Philosophy.

Freiburg and Basel
May 1974

Introduction

Karl Jaspers's philosophical achievement is varied and is presented in many works which differ in size, scope, aim, and plan. The reader, wondering whether the different portions of this achievement are connected and how they are held together, is soon aware of a pervasive unity which binds them, unmistakably, as testaments of a single mind. However, no attempt to articulate this awareness of unity and to indicate basic features unfailingly underlying all his work would succeed. We find that we have entered an open-ended thought structure which lends itself to ever fresh modification. We meet more or less recurring methods and methodologies, concerns and conceptions, distinctions and syntheses which, functioning as sources of disquiet much in the manner of horologic balances, move and direct the structure. We would be incorrect in regarding any one of these impulses as controlling the rest. However, the more prominent of these tend to beat in concert and reverberate on the many levels of the structure: if we focus on one we shall be able to gain and to give a measure of insight into the broad range of Jaspers's philosophy, but there are various approaches to Jaspers, each emphasizing what is in a collateral position and, hence, receiving different treatment in another approach.

Let us look at the alternatives. This will serve to place my choice of Jaspers's notion of philosophical faith in proper perspective and will aid in describing the reasons for this choice. It will also acquaint us prima facie with the recurrent impulses of Jaspers's thinking. The alternatives which seem to me to be of primary importance and which I shall now briefly consider are freedom; the distinction between Being in itself and as it appears, and that between subject and object; methodology and the transcendental method; the cipher; the practical and political import of philosophical thought; the ingenuous synthesis; periechontology; general fundamental knowledge; and philosophical faith.

Jaspers is, first and foremost, a philospher of *freedom*. His spirited promotion of the possibilities of man's freedom, particularly in view of the opportunities and dangers posed by the remarkable development of modern science and its technological utilization, affects his manner of treating philosophical problems. It affects, of course, his philosophy of man. He finds the essence of man in his singular potential for deciding and participating in his own destiny; hence man's essential being transcends the generally determinable dimensions of being human. These dimensions, to be sure, follow their own laws. And they are indispensable forms of the realization and appearance of man's essential being. But by virtue of this function their self-value is highly limited and ancillary to the concern over freedom. The highlights of this aspect of Jaspers's work are his explorations of the fundamental certainty of being which gives rise to the concern over truth; the historicity of man's active realization of truth; unrelenting communication between men as the primary means of a reasoned realization of truth; and the role of situations, particularly of "limit situations," as goads to freedom and selfhood.

Besides affecting his philosophy of man, Jaspers's concern over freedom leaves its mark also on his treatment of modes of reality which transcend man, i.e., the world and God, or, as he prefers, "transcendence." Thus transcendence is the ground of the free man insofar as, being free, he is independent of the world, and, being finite, cannot be the source of his own being. The world, in turn, as the arena of the realization of freedom, is invested with value. However, the world as object of scientific knowledge is admitted to exist beyond man's value interests save that the realization of truth for its own sake is itself of value. The insufficiency of the determinate immanence of the world points to the possibility of freedom beyond the world; and the urge toward the realization of these possibilities, meeting the recalcitrance of the course of the world, requires its knowledgeable mastery in order to succeed. Thus, according to Jaspers, the success of a way of thinking which is particularly attuned to the realization of freedom in the world must, by bracketing this concern of freedom, be more than a philosophy of freedom. Failing that it would be a mere "existentialism," i.e., an attempt to absolutize man's freedom. For Jaspers such an absolutization is unrealistic and neither is required for nor promotes the realization of freedom. An approach to Jaspers that emphasizes his concern over freedom is liable to fail in disassociating this philosopher of existence from existentialism.

Two related pairs of concepts carry a considerable burden of Jaspers's philosophical edifice, namely, *Being-in-itself* and in its *appearance*, and *subject and object*. He holds that Being is grasped in its appearance and, as it appears to human thought, is split into object and subject. Being-in-itself, comprising object and subject, eludes human grasp. These two distinctions show some important features of Jaspers's thought—first, his view that for man reality is fragmented because his thinking is limited in time. Consequently this fragmentation must be taken as a principle of man's philosophical concern to grasp and orient himself in reality and to face the perennial question of the unity of Being. The distinctions show, secondly, his view that freedom and existence transcend the determination of man's thought and that their ground transcends the determinable immanence grasped by means of thought. Finally, the distinctions show Jaspers's affinity with Kant.

Of course, these pairs of concepts are not beyond challenge, as Jaspers himself indicates. Yet he considers them indispensable both for the hypothetical procedure of science and for maintaining the possibility of metaphysical thought in view of the development of modern science. But precisely because these distinctions are subject to criticism, an examination of them is most suitable for a critique of Jaspers. The idealist, for example, cannot accept the distinctions as fundamental because Being is founded in thought and is wholly intelligible; and for the positivist they are dispensable because whatever is can be known scientifically and no metaphysical thought is needed or possible. The realist would consider the distinctions between Being in its appearance and Being as it is in itself to be tentative because for him thought is ontological; and object and subject are, for him, merely two modes in the order of Being which, as such, do not require a distinction between scientific thought and metaphysical-ethical thought. Ontologists and Neo-Scholastics in particular read Jaspers with these considerations in mind. A characterization of Jaspers with emphasis on the range and impact of these distinctions and with reference to related criticisms should prove to be fruitful and ought to be attempted. I have decided against this approach for two reasons: it would be too narrowly technical to be of wide interest, and, since it would stress formal ontological conceptions, it would tend to detract from the wide range of the concrete application of the distinctions to which Jaspers mainly draws his readers' attention.

Methodology is a recurrent theme in Jaspers. And no wonder. Jaspers favors the view that thought is autonomous and freely posits its approaches to reality over the view that thought reflects reality as it is in itself. In his view an ontological cosmos of what there is, is impossible. But there remains, as a principle of organization, the articulation of the different ways of knowing, i.e., methodology. By Jaspersian methodology is meant the disclosure and use of a plurality of methods, the clarification of the relevance, range, and limits of each method, the conception of an insight in consideration of the methods used to determine it, and the

systematic arrangement of results of research according to methods of research. Methodology antedates Jaspers's career in philosophy, having been the principle of order of his *General Psychopathology*, his first major work and his main contribution to psy-
chiatry and medicine. Similarly, a system of all forms of
knowledge according to the different methods of scientific and
philosophical thought was the topic of one of the three projected
volumes of Jaspers's *Philosophical Logic* which were to follow the
one volume which Jaspers actually published in his lifetime, i.e.,
Von der Wahrheit. In these ways Jaspers indicates that methodology is one of the alternative approaches to his philosophical concern.

Philosophical thought proper is, for Jaspers, fundamentally the
exercise of the *transcendental method*. The distinction between
different ways of "transcending" has also served as a principle of
organization in one of Jaspers's works, i.e., the first of his two
main philosophical works, the three volumes of *Philosophie*
(1932). All these facts about the organization of Jasper's works
show that the topic of methodology generally and of the transcendental method in particular is unavoidable even if it is not the
main topic of a characterization of Jaspers's thinking.* The
method of transcending to the indeterminate ground of determinate reality springs, according to Jaspers, mainly from two
motives: first, the insufficiency of all determinate forms or realms
of being and the impossibility of considering any of them to be
Being as such; and, second, the insufficiency of all determinate
modes of being human and the need to bring the indeterminable
possibilities of freedom to bear on these modes.

Closely tied to Jaspers's transcendental methodology is the notion of *cipher*-language, which is one of his most distinct and original achievements in the clarification of the meaning and possibility of metaphysics. It means the following: man seeks to assure
himself of the transcendent ground of all reality grasped by the
determination of thought. Such assurance is itself a matter of
thought because nothing is real for man unless it is mirrored in
thought. But thought, as an act of determination, is inappropriate
for the assurance of the indeterminate ground of determinate
being which, as this ground, transcends determination. Hence the
unavoidable determinacy of the expression of such assurance must
be cancelled, lest it be confused with scientific thought. This confusion can be avoided if expressions of transcendental grounding

---

*I shall have occasion to show the import of the transcendental method in
 this volume, and the role of methodology in Jaspers's conception of scientific knowledge in a projected volume of Jaspers Studies.

are understood as the cipher-script of transcendence, the key to whose decipherment is unknown to man, whose human decoding, therefore, is never achieved with finality and ever remains man's unfinished task and a challenge to his creativity. For Jaspers all expressions of such assurance, many of them supported by tradition, are ciphers, whether they be myths, religious doctrines (the trinity, the redemptive crucifixion of God), general notions (nature, history, evil), metaphysical ideas (God, soul), speculative proofs (of God's existence, of man's freedom, of the oneness of Being, God, the soul), or the experience of art.*

Ciphers lack the sort of concrete, determinate evidence by which they can be given a literal meaning and scientific truth value. Thought about ciphers would be a merely formal operation with empty conceptions if there were no concrete test of their truth at all. For Jaspers such a touchstone of metaphysical truth is the practical life which it makes possible, and the actions by means of which adherents to such truth testify to it. Ultimate philosophical positions and their analogues (e.g., in religion) have *political* implications and consequences, and *practical* affairs of mankind, unless they are devoid of meaning and aim, are the testing ground of transcendent truth and man's commitment to it. The concern with clarifying the political impact of man's vision of the ultimate truth and with confirming the grounding in truth of man's practice and association is the counterpart of Jaspers's philosophy of the cipher-script. It is also another recurrent motive of and a possible approach to his thinking. Indeed, Jaspers's philosophical interest in politics became pre-eminent in the last two decades of his life. Most of his later writings are devoted to the problem of maintaining and increasing man's possibilities of freedom in the face of the double threat of totalitarianism and nuclear war. His political credo is: No peace without freedom no freedom without truth.†

We have still to mention four intertwined conceptions of Jaspers's, i.e., the ingenuous synthesis, periechontology, philosophical faith, and general fundamental knowledge. Aware or unaware, all men face and grasp realities on the basis of a pervasive conception of Being, whether implicit in uncritical usage or elaborated in a philosophical system. This conception is usually rooted in and sanctioned by tradition. Jaspers calls it fundamental knowledge. A characteristic of our historical situation is the acute awareness of traditions and fundamental conceptions of the truth of Being other than our own. The ensuing problem posed for mankind and

---

*Chapter 7 in this volume is devoted to the philosophy of ciphers.
†Jaspers's philosophy of practice and politics will be the subject matter of another project volume of Jaspers Studies.

for philosophy is, according to Jaspers, to come to terms with this multiplicity. Jaspers rejects a relativistic resolution of it. And rightly so. For the cause of truth is not served by denying those who deemed themselves in possession of it and thereby gained fulfillment. And that all human visions are relative can be as little known as the absoluteness for all men of one of these visions. Neither can man rise above humanity in such a manner that he can gain enough insight into all possible human visions of truth to assign each its place in a comprehensive synthesis. The only synthesis which, in Jaspers's view, is possible, is of the modes of truth, their scopes and limits, their forms and possible contents, and their peculiar opposition to falsehood. It would have to open up the regions in which human realization of truth can take place. This would have to be done without adulterating or gainsaying what has been realized by man in the past, and without prescribing or proscribing what may yet be realized. Moreover it would mean recognizing as truth and promoting truth which is not one's own fulfillment of truth.

The need for such an *ingenuous synthesis*, to use Jaspers's expression, as well as the diversity of forms of its possible execution, is underscored by the fact that Jaspers himself attempted two elaborate versions thereof. His *Philosophical Logic*, particularly its first part, *Of Truth*, exemplifies a systematic version of such a synthesis. The historical version consists of his studies of the great thinkers of the past and of recent times, most of which are to be found in his *Great Philosophers*. Jaspers completed neither of these two attempts. This fact may well be an additional index to the significance of the ingenuous synthesis: the attempted synthesis of the possibilities of truth for man remains a fragment even where these possibilities are merely formally conceived. The incompleteness of the execution of the task bespeaks its nature, i.e., the ways of truth transcend the grasp of a single man. The result of the incompleteness is by no means negative. The inherent failure to complete the task can engender the desired openness for truth other than one's own.

But the expression of the concretion of the will to openness is not the only fruit of the ingenuous synthesis. Another is a general conception of Being and its dimensions which is responsive to the diversity of visions of truth and capable of serving as the basis of communication between men who hold to these visions. Jaspers has worked this out in two ways, in his "periechontology" and in the idea of a universal fundamental knowledge.

A conception of Being such as Jaspers's *periechontology*, (i.e., doctrine of the 'encompassing'), has the following features. First, it is drawn from the multifarious experience of human thought by means of a massive incorporation of and a critical reflection on its transmitted testimony. Secondly, it discloses the dimensions of Being in which, or with respect to which, human realization of truth takes place, but without determining such realization. Thirdly, it conceives of Being and its modes as transcending and "encompassing" any human determination or assurance thereof. And fourthly, by upholding in this way the transcendent ground of all human realization of the truth of Being, it assures an openness for such realization other than one's own. Jaspers's elaboration of his periechontology builds on the opposition-pairs Being-in-itself and appearance, object and subject, transcendence and immanence. By means of these he characterizes seven modes of the "encompassing" in their distinctness, their irreducibility, and their relation. Mundane existence (*Dasein*), consciousness-as-such, and spirit are the three immanent modes of subjective being; the world is the immanent mode of objective being. Existenz and transcendence are, respectively, the subjective and objective modes of transcendent being. And reason, driving toward oneness and unity, binds the modes of Being. This periechontology is a very prominent aspect of Jaspers's work, starting with his lectures *Reason and Existenz* (1936). Taken out of the context indicated here it may well be confused with an "ontology." However, Jaspers proposes it in opposition to and in lieu of an ontology, since ontology in his view tends to be a closed doctrine of being rather than a fluid assurance of the dimensions which can accommodate all manner of awareness of Being.

The other consequence of the ingenuous synthesis is the idea of a *general fundamental knowledge*. This may be, but is not here conceived as, the fundamental knowledge of this or that person. Rather it is the project of a knowledge which, in its formal homogeneity, comprises the heterogeneity of concrete fundamental knowledge. It can be the instrument of turning the disparities among believers into a communicative solidarity. Jaspers thinks of the task of a general fundamental knowledge as a continuous project of modification and clarification in accordance with the progressing experience of human thought. This idea does not assume prime importance in Jaspers's writings until about 1960. And, as already mentioned, it is a distinct outgrowth of the "ingenuous synthesis" and a possible approach to his philosophical thinking. But, though distinct, it is closely related to his periechontology, which he offers as a general fundamental knowledge having historical validity. In fact, the two conceptions interpret each other. The periechontology exemplifies the scope of the enterprise of formulating a general fundamental knowledge, particularly insofar as it presupposes knowledge of the experience of mankind. And the idea of a general fundamental knowledge confirms the periechontology as having merely historic significance and not as an absolute doctrine of Being.

No doubt the disturbing juxtaposition of the yearned-for concord in one truth and the actual discord of the many realizations of truth is a basic motivating force of Jaspers's thinking. It is reflected in his ingenuous syntheses, his periechontology, and the idea of a general fundamental knowledge. It is tempting to join him in the odyssey for the ingenuous syntheses, and, humbled by the richness of human visions, seek haven in the port of openness. Or to explore the basis, content, and usefulness of his periechontology. Or to embark with him on the perennial project of a general fundamental knowledge. With such powerful ideas to guide us through Jaspers, the choice of his treatment of faith seems too modest. But there are good reasons for it. First, faith, the risk of thought concerning matters about which man is essentially ignorant, is the basis of the multiplicity of human visions of ultimate truth. Hence the soundness of the broad ideas and enterprises by which one might come to terms with this multiplicity and seek to realize a community of men in spite of it will of necessity be keyed to a critical account of the phenomenon of faith. Moreover, the confirmation of freedom through the confirmation of the plurality of faiths and the founding of human communication and community on this plurality of faiths are, for Jaspers, the main promises of a philosophical reflection on the nature of faith. In this sense, a synthesis which remains ingenuous, or the labor at a general fundamental knowledge, takes as its point of departure, and in turn appeals to, the basic actuality of faith philosophically considered and clarified. These ideas of synthesis can then be seen as desirable instruments of communication between adherents of different faiths and even as expressions of what Jaspers calls *philosophical faith*. The emphasis on his treatment of the phenomenon of faith not only leads to a consideration of its culmination in these grand ideas and enterprises but also affords a latitude for displaying some of the diversity of his philosophical topics and explorations which most of the other alternative approaches to his work do not so readily permit.

Furthermore, his treatment of faith is itself an act of synthetic openness. This can be seen if we consider the following: historical research such as that of H. A. Wolfson shows that the notion of faith as a moment of thought is not only a contribution of the biblical religions but also has its roots in ancient philosophy.[1]

Nevertheless, the articulation of the ways of faith occurred under the auspices of the theological synthesis of these two traditions. In the modern resurgence of independent philosophy the actuality of faith as a moment of thought has usually been recognized, e.g., in Hume and in Kant. However, it was left to Jaspers to undertake a purely philosophical examination of the nature and significance of faith independent of any requirements of revealed faith. And yet, he is, no doubt, beholden to revealed faith as an aspect of the tradition of thought with respect to which he has constantly sought to realize an ingenuous synthesis.

Perhaps the reasons for choosing Jaspers's treatment of faith as the leading idea of my exploration of his philosophical thinking can be illustrated by an experience which germinated this choice. People from many countries came to pay homage to Jaspers on the occasion of his eightieth birthday. One of the speakers at the solemn and festive meeting at the Basel studio of the Swiss Radio was Professor Masao Kusanagi, who had come from Japan. The next morning I had a conversation with him in the room of the Basel Art Museum in which the panels of Konrad Witz's Heilspiegel altar-piece are displayed. I asked what was there in Jaspers that captivated the Japanese philosophers. Professor Kusanagi answered, the idea of the 'encompassing', which, as we have seen, is an important conception in Jaspers's periechontology. We were standing in front of a pair of panels which depict the Church and the Synagogue, a familiar confrontation in medieval art and at the time when these panels were painted (1435). Witz's realism, austere, less subtle and less mellow than that of such great Flemish contemporaries as Van Eyck, leaves little doubt as to the meaning of the panels. Church is presented in an attitude of serenely triumphat piety: she holds the chalice in her right hand and in her left the staff topped by the cross. Synagogue is in an attitude of exposed pride and vanity: her right hand holds the tablets of the law, her left the broken staff. Church is modestly gowned and groomed; her mannerly coiffure reveals a portion of her ear. Synagogue's gown leaves her arms exposed and is taken in to follow the curvature of the bosom; her hair falls loosely over her shoulder and reveals the whole ear. She has turned away from Church, her head and eyes cast down, yet standing upright, alone, shamed, yet proud and vain. Church is turned toward Synagogue but is looking upward with devotion, supported by the staff, and, with a gesture of generosity, she is offering the chalice. The light gown and vague shadows emphasize that Synagogue has been brought to light but the light is not upon her. The dark gown and sharply drawn shadow cast by Church heighten the fact that the light is upon her.

The juxtaposition of Kusanagi's comment and the Witz panels gave me pause. I found it marvelous that a decidedly Western thinker's idea, engendered by his reflection on the experience of the tradition in which he is firmly rooted, should strike a familiar chord in a thinker similarly confirmed in a wholly different and equally profound tradition. Surely Jaspers's interpretation of his tradition as affording a bridging between visions of truth, affirmed in their diversity, in virtue of the insight that truth in its absolute unity is transcendent, has borne fruit. Yet before me I saw depicted another possibility of the same tradition, a more real possibility because it has consistently become fact with grim, unforgettable results: the possibility of the one sister, by force of the humble pride of her faith, humiliating the other and gainsaying the validity of her truth. It is an abuse of the claims of faith if the truth by which a man lives requires the suppression of that of another. Thus Jaspers's clarification of the obligation of testimony and tolerance which faith as expression of human vision of truth imposes could be of inestimably pervasive consequence. In comparison, a conception in the nature of a general fundamental knowledge by which two civilized and learned men, separated by distance, culture, and tradition, can assent to the oneness of the source of human truth seems to be a less accessible means of promoting what Jaspers desires, namely, freedom and communication. I thought then, as I think now, that Jaspers's treatment of the phenomenon of faith, though more humble a theme than his more distinctive and prominent conceptions, is of more urgent and immediate significance.

By virtue of the affinity of certain aspects of this topic with concerns which, traditionally, are mainly theological, Jaspers was bound to become engaged in discussions and controversies with theologians. His public discussions of this nature began with his guest lectures at the University of Basel in July 1947 on the theme "Philosophical Faith,"[2] which preceded his permanent move to that university. His controversy with Bultmann over the problem of demythologizing the Bible continued these discussions. They occupied a goodly portion of his last years as a teacher and culminated in the publication, shortly before his eightieth birthday, of his *Der philosophische Glaube angesichts der Offenbarung* (literally, Philosophical faith vis-à-vis revelation).[3] These writings contain Jaspers's thoughts on the nature and significance of faith, show the intertwining of his notion of philosophical faith with the other recurrent basic motives of his philosophizing which I have mentioned, and attest to the challenge and relation of his thinking to doctrinal theology. Yet two facts are most noteworthy. First, his thoughts on faith and related thoughts on religion and theology which are expressed in these controversial later works were expounded in earlier works and in his teaching. Secondly, Jaspers's realization that his philosophical thinking on these matters was related to and had bearing on doctrinal theology was absent at first and required germination. We can gather this from a passage in his "Philosophical Autobiography":

> At the end of a lecture-course in metaphysics (1927/28), a Catholic priest who had audited it came to thank me and to express his agreement: "My only objection is that most of what you have presented is, according to our point of view, theology." This statement . . . took me aback. Clearly I am speaking of matters which others consider to be theological; yet I do not speak as a theologian but as a philosopher. This called for clarification.[4]

The "clarification" makes it possible to distinguish two major aspects of Jaspers's thought—first, the philosophical conception of faith and some of the various philosophical problems to which this treatment leads or which it clarifies; secondly, the effort to promote truth in religion by means of a philosophical critique of religion and a dialogue with its theologians. Since the distinction between these two aspects is more a matter of emphasis than of clear cut separation, both aspects will be considered in this volume. However, the topics pertaining primarily to the first aspect will serve as the principle for the arrangement of chapters. It is within this framework that the second aspect will be considered, as occasions arise; I am, however, planning to consider this second aspect explicitly in another volume insofar as it pertains to that volume's topic of the political import of Jaspers's philosophical concern.

Chapter One

Testimony of Faith and Evidence of Knowledge

i. Faith and Knowledge: Distinctions and Relations

A conception of faith depends largely on what is thought to be opposed to it, and hence distinguished from it. The list of opposition concepts with respect to faith is large: doubt, mysticism, unfaith, faithlessness, counterfaith, superstition, temptation, despair. All these distinctions can be found in Jaspers in some form. However, as one reads through the relevant material, widely distributed over the large corpus of Jaspers's works, one finds that the fundamental distinction, underlying all the others, is the one between faith and evidential knowledge.*

The distinction of faith and knowledge, each with respect to the other, is a fundamental requirement of enlightenment. However, Jaspers points out, the fact that this distinction is required does not mean that it is a necessary step in human thought. Jaspers says,

> It belongs to man as man to cast his glance into the depth of truth. Truth is present for him at any time and in him through some language be it ever so crude and obscure.[1]

But wherever, in the history of a tradition or in the life of a person, the distinction is made between empirical being and reality transcending such being, the consequences of this "crisis of consciousness"[2] are inescapable. This first step in the process of enlightenment, or any subsequent step, does not give the lie to previous consciousness of truth.[3] Only

> false enlightenment destroys tradition . . . leads to nihilism . . . produces disorder and anarchy.[4]

True enlightenment does not impose limits on thought and questioning but indicates where limits actually exist. For it not only brings to light prejudices and beliefs which were hitherto

---

*Even though the term 'knowledge' is, usually and in Jaspers, used in a much broader sense than 'evidential knowledge', it is here used, for the sake of convenience, in the latter sense, except as otherwise explicitly indicated.

unquestioned but also sheds light on itself. *It does not confuse the ways of the understanding with what it means to be human.*[5]

It is necessary for the modern enlightenment to concede that the empirical and formal sciences, by means of their evidential methods, have preempted the realms of cogency and universal validity. Accordingly, claims of cogency and universal validity on behalf of truths which do not submit to evidential procedures are to be criticized appropriately. Matters of faith cannot resort to such claims, for the personal commitment essential for faith does not exist in the public domain, which is the realm of evidential truth. On the other hand, the search for truth must not be restricted to what can be evidentially known. The reason for this is simple. The pursuit of scientific knowledge and the technological use thereof is open to anyone, be he good or evil.[6] What it means to be human is, however, neither based on nor supported by science. It lies beyond the limits of knowledge in the realm of faith.

For Jaspers this difference between faith and knowledge is dramatically exemplified in the contrast between the situations of Galileo and Bruno. On the surface they are similar: the Inquisition required both men to recant certain beliefs which were considered heretical. Galileo's beliefs were scientific theories; Bruno's were metaphysical. Galileo's refusal to recant would not have made him a martyr; but by his recantation Bruno would have stood before the world despicable, unfaithful to his truth and untrue to himself.

It would be unfitting to die for a truth that is susceptible to proof. But at what point the thinker who believes he has plumbed the depths, cannot retract his statements without harm to the truth itself—that is his own secret.[7]

The truth of knowledge is a matter of methodical verification. Such verification can be repeated by anyone who follows the appropriate method. My radical selfhood is not reflected in my knowledge—only the soundness of my submission to the impersonal, intersubjective criteria of research is reflected in it. What is true by methodical validation is true whether I believe it or not, whether I act upon it or not. The truth of faith is a matter of personal verity. No one can take my place in my commitment; no one but myself can be responsible for my faith. Faith does not exist except through personal commitment.

Unlike faith, knowledge requires no risk. Knowledge calls the intellect into play; faith one's very being. In distinction from knowledge faith means bearing witness.

And yet for Jaspers the relation between faith and knowledge is not one of simple distinction where, as one ends, the other begins. That this distinction cannot be such a radical one becomes clear when we recall that it is consequent upon a "crisis of consciousness" prior to which belief of knowledge and belief of faith were as one. This reminder merely indicates the possibility of the positive relation of the two. We are left, however, with the task of facing the problems attending their relation in consequence of the enlightenment which leads to their distinction. That they are related, Jaspers maintains in both ways: knowledge depends, in some sense, on faith; and faith depends, in certain ways, upon knowledge.

At first glance it would seem that faith is not relevant to knowledge, for cogent knowledge does not require a basis of or justification through faith. It is cogent of its own accord, i.e., by virtue of evidence and its criteria. The content of knowledge evidently can not be considered a matter of faith. On the other hand, this cannot be said of the fact that knowledge is pursued; this pursuit is grounded on faith. According to Jaspers this is a matter of courage to risk what may become of man when he knows.[8] This positive relevance of faith to knowledge, the faith in the value of knowledge is, naturally, not knowable. And to the contemporary mind, usually oriented toward science as the only significant mode of thought, the suggestion that faith activate knowledge seems suspect. Yet this relevance is actual and manifest. It becomes most eminently manifest when strictures are imposed on the relentless pursuit of knowledge.[9] The well-known stories of the early scientists' cautious but determined struggle against and prevalence over the opposition of the church and her spokesmen serve as examples of this manifestation.

In any case, the relevance of faith to the pursuit of knowledge depends on the nature of the faith—or unfaith—which is brought to bear on this pursuit. Thus, "in a positivistic conception of knowledge cogency isolates itself, without knowing what it is about, therefore without understanding itself and hence it is methodically not dependable."[10] For Jaspers himself, pursuit of knowledge is the condition for all other truth. Accordingly, it is a mark of man's dignity as seeker of truth "to desire to know what can be known." From an unrelenting faith in knowledge "arises an atmosphere of reliability, openness, criticism, sovereignty and readiness of a wholly present self."[11] Jaspers would, therefore, oppose an unfaith such as positivism which would deprive the pursuit of knowledge of its substantial founding in the concern over truth and, at the other extreme, a faith which requires for its "beatitude the sacrifice of the inquiring intellect."[12]

Mutatis mutandis, faith is dependent on knowledge but in a different sense, i.e., insofar as knowledge serves as the vehicle of faith. This fact increases the need for caution not to confuse the two. It also intensifies the dual struggle against taking knowledge as absolute and against restricting the pursuit of knowledge. For here we are dealing with a more complicated situation. To this point, faith and knowledge have been assigned their distinct and separate areas of certainty and their positive and negative relations have been defined in the light of this distinction and separation. Now one mode of certainty (i.e., faith) uses the categories, products, and methods of the other mode (i.e., knowledge) as the framework of its manifestation. Specifically, the content of faith is objectified in the form of knowledge. Or, to state this in the form of an ancient, well-known phrase, faith seeks understanding.

"Faith seeks understanding" does not mean that faith requires the underpinning of a proof or argument.

> What I can prove I need not, in addition, have faith in. If I search for the content of faith in the form of objective certainty, I have already lost my faith.[13]

Rather, what is involved here is the requirement that man, as thinking being, express, clarify, and understand himself in thought. But whatever appears within the objectivity of thought is subject to its rules and criticism. Therefore, the expression of faith in the form of thought unavoidably entails argumentation on the plane of knowledge. The use of thought on behalf of faith turns into destructive and self-defeating usurpation if it is meant to signify more than the self-clarification of faith. It is destructive of truly cogent knowledge, with which it is bound to conflict.

The opposition of the church to Galileo's confirmation of the heliocentricity of the planetary system can again serve as a case in point. Though their conflict was factually real enough, it need not have been. The conflict was, after all, not logically real because each spoke on a different plane, and only apparently of the same thing. A view opposing Galileo's theories did not disturb him because he was the spokesman for implacable, impersonal evidence. Even a contradictory theory which is equally well substantiated does not disturb the scientist; contradiction spurs the researcher on to a renewed appeal to nature as the court of decision.

One cannot avoid expressing matters of faith in the language of knowledge. If, however, such expression is taken literally, the inevitable vitiating result is the assertion of one truth at the cost of another. And subsequently the equally inevitable result is the self-destruction of the truth of faith. For any expression of faith, particularly in the form of an argument, can be countered with a refutation or an argument for an opposite position. There is no evidential court of appeal—only authority and, in the end, force. The 'argument' of true faith is not subjection but a summons.[14] Kant was by no means the first to discover that arguments concerning matters transcending the evidential scrutiny to which only determinate reality is subject, come in contradictory pairs although his "antinomies" are the most famous examples.[15] According to him such "antinomies" do not signify real conflict because they constitute neither reality in itself nor our knowledge of reality. They are matters of faith, or, as he would say, they are ideas invoked to "regulate" our diverse relations to and orientation in reality.

Faith, in order to avoid its self-destruction, must not be confused with its objectification in thought. To be sure, objectification is unavoidable because whatever is for man appears within the framework of the distinction of object and subject. But the reality of faith is lost where the existence of the self is suspended in favor of an impersonal intersubjectivity. This suspension is required in knowledge. Faith is real only where the "objective" content of faith, i.e., "faith in something" is as one with the "subjective" "faith as which one exists."[16] Faith can remain vital only as long as it is not abandoned to cognitive verifications. It would be convenient and comforting if decisions about the truth of faith could be left in the arena of objective verification, but that is an impossibility. It would relieve the person of the risks attendant on his own commitment.[17] The objective aspect of faith, "faith in something," requires as its counterpart the subjective aspect, the proof of deeds. From the viewpoint of faith, an assent to an objective "credo" which is analogous to cognitive assent and not a contemplative articulation and self-assurance of one's faith is hypocritical adherence to the outward form of faith without selfhood. Faith is active or it is not at all.[18] The circumstance that faith precipitates action and therefore expresses itself in terms of objective obligation and value constitutes a distinct problem which must next be treated as such.

ii. Objectification of Faith: The 'Ought' and Tradition

Activity occurs within the objective world of human affairs. As a function of faith, action is faith in its objective appearance. In this

way faith is subject matter of the knowing *intellect*.[19] More particularly, it is subject to evaluation in accordance with principles
of purposiveness and obligation. For the intellect, order and justification are possible only through an appeal to a universal 'ought';
from this viewpoint any human choice which is not the fulfillment
of a duty, i.e., which is not determined by the principle of obligation, appears to be capricious. Certainly, then, faith, expressing
itself in human activity, seems exposed to the scrutiny of such
principles. From the viewpoint of its own logic, however, faith is
the wellspring of a person's justification, and not itself subject to
justification. Though exposed to the public domain in which the
intellect reigns supreme, faith withholds its homage to the latter as
the court of universal decision. It seems inevitable, then, that a
conflict should arise between the call to order based on customs,
law and morality, and the seemingly capricious adherence to a
faith.

However, there are strong indications that Jaspers thinks otherwise.[20] Of course conflicts between faith and the objective 'ought'
exist,[21] and they are not lessened by clarifying the relation between them. However, such clarification can reveal the contending
parties in such a conflict. The cogency of the 'ought' is of the
same order as that of logical and empirical inference: given these
purposes, and those conditions under which they are to be realized, then such an obligation ensues. Yet immediately we see the
difference between the pull of the 'ought' and that of faith. The
'ought' is cogent, but precisely because it is conditional upon the
presupposed purposes or claims upon us. The certainty of faith is
not cogent—it has no recourse to principles of evidence and universality, much less to evidence and universality proper. Its claim
upon us is unconditional. For the 'ought', the individual person is
merely a case exemplifying its universality. For faith, the person
animated by and animating faith fulfills the requirements of the
'ought' by transcending it.

The 'ought' is, after all, a claim which is purely formal and remains empty and unfulfilled unless embraced by an existing person. The person can withhold his compliance or choose to act in
accordance with a contrary 'ought'. This does not mean that the
existing person would withdraw his loyalty to an 'ought' or oppose it at random. Objectively there is no difference between the
various realities which lie outside of the 'ought'; they all seem to
be instances of caprice. There is, however, a marked difference
between the unconcern of psycho-biological vitality and the existential concern rooted in a realm of possibilities which not merely
incorporates but reaches beyond that on which a specific 'ought' is

based. I do not have a stake in complying with the 'ought' by virtue of my vitality, though out of fear I may be compelled to do
so.[22] The existing person, on the other hand, does have a stake in
the 'ought'. He comprehends his own unconditional activity,
which is the expression of his faith, in the form of the objective
'ought'. Moreover, only the existing person has a stake in the
'ought'. If the 'ought' were obeyed without existential commitment, it would be either the instrument of a dehumanized mass
apparatus, or it would be obeyed without conviction, participation
or risk.

The genuine being of the 'ought', according to Jaspers, is

> the being which finds itself in the ought . . . and this being
> which is its own ought is Existenz. It *understands* as an 'ought'
> what it *does* unconditionally.[23]

Hence, a person would disobey the 'ought' at the risk of being
untrue to himself. And yet he must not confuse the cogent though
relative 'ought' with the unconditional demands of his faith which
may require him to act beyond and against the 'ought'. Such an
opposition can in turn be expressed in the form of an alternative
'ought'. It is therefore not identifiable with what Kierkegaard
called the "teleological suspension of the ethical." Kierkegaard's
example is to be understood as a conflict between ethical formal-
ism and the unconditional demands of faith. Yet genuine ethic is
never without its animation by a faith, and there is no conscious
faith without its expression in the objective concreteness of action
and, concomitantly, in the intellectual form of an 'ought'. Jaspers
maintains that

> existential possibility, when it is actualized, is more than ful-
> fillment of duty, while license is less; but objectively the two
> are indistinguisable.[24]

Only a positivistic intellectualism, insensitive and indifferent to
the distinction of modes of reality which defy objectification,
could lead to confusing the two and to subsuming both under the
common category of the 'emotive'. Complying with as well as
stepping beyond the 'ought' is attended by the risk that attends an
active faith.

Jaspers is without doubt painfully aware of the discomfort such
thoughts cause the members of a civilization whose goodness—
such as it is—and betterment, they believe, depend on bringing the
rule of law to bear on human affairs. The struggle to maintain the
rule of law is real and vital in his eyes. For him the struggle would
be doomed to failure if it were to be carried out between the soul-

less forces of law and the blind adherents to an obscure faith claiming to be above the law. The rule of law is relative to what is posited as its basis. But even if a specific rule of law were deemed absolute, this absoluteness would be relativised by the temporal nature of the realm in which it is realized by man. For man, the absolute rule of law is an abstraction against which he measures his temporal actions. Perhaps the only absolute which the rule of law can claim without contradiction is the "law of the rule of law."[25] The struggle, then, is not one between the universal appeal to law and the capricious appeal to faith. It is rather between faith and faith, where both, insofar as they are clarified, express themselves in the form of a universal 'ought'. Faith is blind without the articulation of the universal 'ought'. And the law is empty without existential commitment. Argument for law for its own sake can be a matter of intellectual virtuosity but does not involve obligation. And who, in the light of our century's experience, would deny that any position whatever can be dignified by its formalization as law?

Below the surface of argumentation on the subject of rule of law versus rule of law lies the deeper struggle between the different possibilities of being, whether positive or negative, love or hate, faith or nihilism. The real struggle is a matter of understanding, of self-understanding and mutual understanding, of pointing out and summoning the positive possibilities of being, in short, a matter of what Jaspers calls 'communication', and not merely one of scoring points in argumentation or of backing up argument with force. This struggle is man's way of realizing truth, with freedom and in time. He loses his way if he mistakes the cogency and universality of the 'ought' for the unconditionality of the faith which is expressed through it. A faith objectified in a universal 'ought' for all to see and understand in the same way is a great convenience. But it is lost if the 'ought' shatters against recalcitrant realities, if it is confronted with other objectifications which are more persuasively or more forcefully argued, or if a believer is separated from or abandoned by the community of fellow believers. The test of faith occurs precisely at the moment when its objectifications fail, collapse or in some way perish, and where faith cannot be tied any more to an object of interest.[26] There, in the radical absence of objective guarantees, is the extreme moment of truth for faith, a truth which depends essentially on the risk of personal commitment and testimony through action.

While action is the test of faith, the underpinnings of the objectifications of faith are strong, particularly in the form of the heritage of cultural goods in art, religion, education, literature, lore, and tradition. Without this heritage faith is almost unthinkable. Our heritage determines our faith rather than merely channeling it. Before we are aware of our faith it is formed by our heritage. Thus formed, we function as the instrument of the formation of those who come after. We realize that the objective heritage is indispensible for our selfhood. On it we nourish the truths we hold without question and which fulfill our being. And without upholding and involving the objective heritage in the upbringing of the new generations, we would deprive them of what we can recognize as humanity. The objectification of faith in the form of fixed traditions and the authoritative guardianship of our heritage is necessary for the communicative bridging of the time and space by which existing persons are separated from each other. But objectification is merely the meeting ground, and the fixed solidity of language, images and tradition merely the means of the meeting of Existenzen which as such transcend and do not appear as determinate objectivities. Hence, the actuality of the existing person and of his faith are not identical with his objective testimony, whether it is original or a confession to a well-established creed. The actuality would be lost if the fact of tradition, seemingly self-perpetuating beyond human design—whether it is in its favor or directed against it, were taken as a cognitive form and objective guarantee of the truth of one's faith. The solidity of the transmitted heritage must not be thought to constitute the jelling of faith into knowledge. This would again subject faith to criteria of truth which are not relevant to it, and would lead it into conflict with truths to which alone these criteria appropriately pertain. The objectification of faith in a form which can be transmitted is a personal confession and an act of communication. Confrontation with "the objectification of the contents of faith in the cultural heritage" can be taken "as preparatory to the possible adoption" of this faith. It is not the occasion for "taking an obstinate hold of" it.[27] The objectification of faith, unavoidable as a vehicle for faith, necessary and desirable as a means of communication and transmission, does not render its contents objective.

In Jaspers's view the confusion between objectification as the vehicle for and expression of faith and cognitive objectivity leads to a needless conflict between faith and knowledge. Concomitantly, it tends to cloud the truth of both. By virtue of this confusion one would submit to evidential demonstration what is not demonstrable, e.g., the existence of God or the immortality of the soul. One would also curtail the critical exercise of the intellect regarding matters which, by the same token, are not subject to evidential refutation. The result of such confusion was behind the condemnations of the "Latin Averroists" at the University of Paris during the last third of the thirteenth century. On the other hand, one would withhold certain statements from evidential scrutiny which, by the nature of their contents, are subject to such scrutiny, or else impose restrictions on the pursuit of evidential truth. Jaspers, in the tradition whose most eminent spokesman for the British and American public is Hume, considers statements of faith taken as literal statements about happenings in the world, i.e., miracles, incapable of holding up when faced with the question of the reliability of the relevant testimony.[28] And, similarly, he agrees with Buri that, if one embarks on the enterprise of demythologising, there are no logical limits beyond which contents of faith may not be demythologized.[29]

Jaspers's most severe criticism, however, is reserved for restrictions on the pursuit of evidential truth out of piety toward a faith, particularly as imposed by institutionalized faiths which exercise authority and have recourse to means of enforcement. A content of faith which is supposed to be cogent will, in time, lead to a conflict with knowledge. The result will be suppression of the pursuit of knowledge and of knowledge itself, which, by virtue of its objective evidence is, in fact, cogent. Jaspers maintains that

> there has never been, nor is there today, a socially powerful religious faith in which the "sacrifice of the intellect" does not have to be made in fact.[30]

Jaspers demands and uses the appropriately radical methods necessary to resist the suppression of what is actually cogent knowledge by a faith which poses as cogent knowledge. With regard to knowledge, he demands free research wherever it may go and however far it will go. The possibilities beyond the limits of research can indicate themselves only through an articulation of these limits. And these limits are not really indicated by a reflection on principles in the suburbs of research but by the labor of actual participation in and active incorporation of research. "Experience in the sciences . . . [is] the indispensable presupposition for veracity."[31] With regard to matters transcending objective determination, the objectivities through which they are expressed, particularly the quasi-knowledge of discursive expressions, are to be brought to their foundering point if they are to reveal what they mean. The non-literal, mythological, analogical, symbolic, or metaphysical character of such an expression has to be brought to consciousness, or, if it has the formal structure of metaphysical argument, it is to be pursued until its inherent paradox, contradiction, circularity or tautology is shown. Only at these extreme limits of thought can metaphysics reveal itself radically in its true nature, i.e., as the congealing of a faith out of a nebulous ground of being transcending human comprehension and by means of an invocatory activity of thought. For Jaspers, as we shall see in the next section, skeptical relativizing of propositions about ultimates is an inescapable function of man's concern over ultimate truth.

It can be readily seen that Jaspers pleases neither positivists nor traditional metaphysicians nor theologians by comprehending metaphysics as the expression of faith and by contrasting the validity of both with the objective validity of scientific cognition. The positivist demands objective verification, and, finding that metaphysics fails to measure up to this standard, dismisses it as meaningless or else trivializes its significance. Jaspers agrees that metaphysics is not objective but upholds its significance as an expression of faith.

The traditional metaphysician would uphold the significance of metaphysics by claiming for it the objectivity the positivist demands but sees lacking in it. Jaspers considers such claims not only impossible and futile but also unwittingly destructive of metaphysics and, therefore, a function of the dehumanization of man.

The theologian agrees that the dignity of man and the worth of a person is firmly tied to his faith. To him the metaphysical pursuit of ultimate questions, whether conceived as cognitive inquiry or expression of faith, is only of ancillary and preambulatory value. Beyond this scope he deems metaphysics to be aberrant and a folly, a folly confirmed for him by the divergence of systems and the failure of objective metaphysics. Against such tenuousness he upholds the firmness of scripture and its interpretation. His theology claims not only historical objectivity in the usual sense but the support of the authority of God's revelation. Jaspers agrees that all thought is rooted in some faith but considers the jelling of a faith into an exclusive credo to be subject to criticism no matter what such a credo may base itself upon. Accordingly, the concept of revelation merits an elaborate philosophical criticism, particularly in the light of the distinction between faith and knowledge.

However, it is important to note in connection with what has been presented here that for Jaspers the issue is not one between philosophy and science, philosophy and objective metaphysics and philosophy and theology severally. The aim is to face all these issues on the same basis. This basis is the distinction between knowledge and faith in the light of man's experience with philosophical thought and the development of modern science.

iii. Doubt As Substrate Of Faith

The preceding demonstration of relations between faith and
knowledge, and of various modes of their mutual dependence does
not detract from the fact that for knowledge the actuality of faith
seems questionable. For whatever is not or cannot be validated,
and therefore does not merit cognitive assent, is subject to doubt.
And whoever is not in a position to assent, or not to assent cognitively, with respect to an object of thought is in a position of ignorance. From the standpoint of knowledge, faith, being other than
knowledge, is a matter of doubt and ignorance. A characterization
of faith which is offered in distinction from knowledge must,
therefore, show the positive content of cognitive doubt and ignorance. We find, however, that in order to understand how Jaspers
treats the relevant aspects of the significance of doubt, we have to
start with the converse problem, i.e., his examination of how
knowledge is itself subject to doubt.
  Matters of faith are subject to cognitive doubt; this seems incon-
trovertible. The question raised by this circumstance is whether it
permits a positive determination of the extracognitive realm of
faith. Jaspers sees no reason why the response to this question,
asked from the perspective of knowledge, cannot be affirmative.
This is indicated, first of all, by his treatment of the fact that
knowledge itself is subject to question. Here all depends on how
knowledge is brought into question, namely in alliance with or in
opposition to knowledge.
  In commiting ourselves to knowledge as a way of truth we must
still question knowledge on the basis of principle. Jaspers sub-
scribes to the insight that no knowledge is sufficient unto itself,
that knowledge is relative to chosen presuppositions and methods
of validation, to evidence and the correlative criteria of evidence.
Moreover, the process of cognition is activated and guided by actualities which are themselves, ultimately, not objects of knowledge.
The values which are actually placed upon knowledge, the interests which determine the direction of inquiry—all these may be
known; but the value of knowledge is, from the standpoint of
knowledge, a precondition of knowledge, and, as such, not subject
to inquiry. Ultimately the process of cognition issues from a commitment the most pure form of which, leaving the process free of
suppositions which prejudice inquiry, is an original will to know.
  The fact that the actuality of knowledge points to actuality beyond itself, that cognition is enacted by an option of faith, is

borne out by the possibility, and by historical actualities, of opting against knowledge. In this connection Jaspers discusses and rebuts some familiar oppositions to knowledge:[32] that it is fraudulent; promises certainty and leads to nihilism; deprives life of joy and hope; by means of its method of analysis, nullifies whatever it analyzes. Jaspers's responses are instructive for our problem. In essence they are as follows: knowledge leads to nihilism only if one opts for knowledge with demands of absolute and unconditioned certainties which knowledge cannot satisfy. The demand for such certainties requires ways of truth other than knowledge. Knowledge requires that its devotees bracket such demands which in its view are false demands. The despair of knowledge is not the result of inquiry but of that false demand on knowledge.[33] Also, since knowledge is not absolute and only probable, it never impinges with finality upon the realm where hope in alliance with faith may prevail. The mode of being which is deemed to be threatened by knowledge is intensified by the burden which knowledge places upon the powers of hope and enjoyment. In the end it is an existential decision whether to

> have the peace of ignorance or run the risk of extreme boundary situations. No man is to be expected to do so, no man is to be forbidden to do so.[34]

Finally, only deceptions are nullified by analysis. Beyond those the reach of knowledge is limited to generalities and to evidential appearances. It neither penetrates nor lends the support of objective certainty to man's freedom and to what can be actual only through freedom.[35]

For our topic the upshot of these considerations is as follows. To question the value of knowledge in opposition to knowledge is itself questionable. For we mistake the cognitive mode of certainty for the certainty of a faith, of conviction, of personal commitment. The result of this mistake is, on the one hand, that knowledge is expected to yield certainty concerning those fundamentals upon which we seek to ground our lives, and on the other hand, since the ways of knowledge do not lead to these fundamentals, we fall into despair over the loss of certainty concerning fundamentals. Faith in the possibility of knowledge is a false faith if the ways of knowledge are extended beyond their proper limits. However, the fact that knowledge is questioned through opposition on the basis of non-cognitive concerns heuristically serves to relativise the fact that whatever is not knowledge is a matter of doubt. While it is that, it is therefore not devoid of significance.

For, as we have seen, knowledge is itself, in some way, founded on what cannot be subject to knowledge, namely the *sapere aude*. In this "odd pathos," as Jaspers calls it, he sees an indication of the "unconditionality of the will to know that cannot be adduced from the validity of [cognitive] accuracy." The positive and not merely heuristic significance of past oppositions to knowledge lies in the fact that it reminds us that "the original will to know is a risk because it is attended by the peril of despair."[36]

In his *Philosophie* Jaspers touches upon a theme which is now, in the atomic age, of universal concern, and which is the subject of Dürrenmatt's play *The Physicists*. In words used almost verbatim by Dürrenmatt* Jaspers reminds us that "it is our fate to be able to know, and to know. There is no reversing this fate [*Es ist nicht rückgängig zu machen*]. We only have the choice to fulfill or evade it."[37] If we are pursuing Jaspers's thinking correctly, the fulfillment of the fate to know presents us with the task of drawing on the resources of faith concerning matters subject to cognitive doubt whence springs the will to know. By evading this fate we are burdened with a pre-critical state of mind where, together with the rejection of the risk of knowledge, we are liable to risk our being for faiths unworthy of such risk. The sound alternative, then, is to accept cognitive doubt as the condition of faith.

Doubt as a condition of faith is not only a characteristic of the supracognitive nature of faith. Phenomenologically Jaspers points out that faith proves itself as genuine precisely when it stands the test of doubt, when it maintains itself in the face of cognitive doubt.[38] Such doubt is the touchstone of faith. For this reason also, Jaspers holds, faith exists only together with unfaith. For whatever is a matter of faith is subject to doubt, and doubt allows for opposite options. Thus every possible faith, particularly in its rational formulation, carries with it the possibility of its opposite possibility against which it must maintain itself if it is at all actual. It is precisely in its confrontation with doubt that one can fully understand faith as risk.[39] According to Jaspers's extreme, though by no means hyperbolic, characterization of this aspect of faith, "Utter objective uncertainty is the substrate of faith proper."[40] Doubt is the "spur"[41] of faith which is nourished by the unceasing choice between the "either/or" which only doubt provides.

For Jaspers the explication of the significance of doubt, particularly for faith, is connected with the problem of the possibility of

---

*Towards the end of the play Möbius says: "Was einmal gedacht wurde, kann nicht mehr zurückgenommen werden."

dogmatism. The opposition of dogmatism and skepticism may remind us of Kant, especially of the introduction to his first *Critique* and the preface to the second edition. This is not inappropriate, for here is one of the topics whose treatment by Jaspers is fully in accordance with the intentions of the thinker from Königsberg to whom he owes so much. Indeed this portion of Jaspers's thought can be taken as an interpretation of what Kant stated in this famous sentence:

> It is knowledge, therefore, that I had to reduce in order to gain room for faith, and it is the dogmatism of metaphysics, i.e., the prejudice to proceed in it without critique of pure reason, which is the true source of all the unfaith which stands in opposition to morality and which is always very dogmatic.[42]

For Kant the "despotism" of dogmatism and the "anarchy" of skepticism are suspect. How do they arise? The very beginning of the first *Critique* is the index to the answer:

> Human reason has this peculiar fate that in one species of its knowledge it is burdened by questions which, as prescribed by the very nature of reason itself, it is not able to ignore, but which as transcending all its powers, it is also not able to answer.[43]

The "species of knowledge" whose main topics are God, freedom and immortality and to which the main and major portion of the first *Critique* is devoted has a general fundamental problem which reason can neither "ignore" nor "answer." The problem recurs in the "Transcendental Dialectic" where diverse aspects of it are discussed. In the second edition it is announced in the new preface Kant prepared for it:

> What necessarily forces us to transcend the limits of experience, and of all appearances is the *unconditioned*, which reason, by necessity and by right, demands in things in themselves, as required to complete the series of conditions.[44]

The topical similarities between Kant and Jaspers are striking. There are also, however, important differences. In Jaspers's thinking, dogmatism and doubt, far from being merely suspect, became significant moments of transcendental thought. This is germane to his argument because critique, particularly of reason, is a mode of doubt. Also, Kant saw the fulfillment of the "peculiar fate" of human reason in inquiring "whether, in the practical knowledge of reason, data may not be found sufficient to determine reason's transcendent concept of the unconditioned, and so to enable us

. . . to pass beyond the limits of all possible experience."[45] While for Kant the "practical knowledge of reason" is conceived primarily in purely moral terms, Jaspers speaks of broader and more diverse dimensions of human existence. In one respect Jaspers follows Kant fully, namely in the main features of the Kantian critique of cognitive thought, i.e., that it concerns reality in its appearance and that it reaches its fulfillment in the empirical. Where Kant speaks of the unconditioned ground of all conditioned insights that the mind produces in its encounter with reality as the ultimate task of reason, Jaspers speaks of the concern over the one and absolute truth encompassing all particular and relative truths.

The problem, in Jaspers's view, is, simply, as follows. Whatever is couched in the form of human thought is determined in accordance with relevant criteria. All such thought is, then, relative to some posited absolute enabling this determination to be made. The one truth, however, cannot be relative, or a postulated absolute, or determinate, or particular, i.e., a truth amongst many truths. It must simply be the one truth comprising absolutely all specific truths, determinations, relativities and postulations. Considering the indeterminacy of the one truth and the determining agency of human thought, the one truth is said to transcend human thought. Both are unavoidable, then: thought directed toward the one truth and the adulteration of the one truth in the form of human thought. The task is to direct thought toward the one truth critically and without permitting a human thought to take the place of the one and absolute truth. A thought in whose form the ultimate concern over the one truth may be expressed, if taken literally in the manner of cognitive thought, constitutes an anticipation of the one truth. Determinative thought, no matter whether it assume the form of a myth, a metaphysical theory or a religious dogma, is not capable of such an anticipation, and neither is it given to man, existing and thinking in time, to anticipate in this manner. It is not that the positing of presuppositions is to be shunned or outlawed on any level of discourse. This is impossible. Indeed, Jaspers's approach to the problem of the significance of metaphysics is particularly attuned to the phenomenon that "thinking man is bound to the inevitability of positing something as absolute." Moreover, Jaspers maintains, the result of a deliberate attempt to avoid this inevitability will be that "against the will and without notice something will take the place of the absolute at random."[46] Particularly when it comes to ultimate questions, the necessity of positing a comprehensive presupposition as absolute leads naturally to dogmatic fixation. Human thought concerning the absolute, if dogmatically conceived, may be possessed and submitted to as if it were an item of knowledge. However, insofar as the concern over the one truth is rooted in the temporal movement of human existence, historical selves "participate in deciding and bringing forth"[47] conceptions of the one truth. In the apt Kierkegaardian phrase, often considered, injudiciously, suspect, an element of such conceptions is the leap into faith. To be guided by such conceptions is, as Kant would say, the "task" of man; but to consider such human conceptions to be the one truth itself turns such conceptions into falsehood. In Jaspers's view, the overturning of dogmatism is a task necessitated by the inevitability of positing something as absolute particularly with regard to ultimate questions. It is also an expression of the concern over the one truth as transcending human conception. Since doubt is the method of counteracting uncritical assent, it is in this light that Jaspers understands it to accompany dogmatism. All depends, however, on how this method is conceived and employed.

When the pursuit of the one truth arrives at generalities which are too obtuse to fit specific cases, or unique situations lead to a plethora of particular truths, doubt arises to overturn them and to uphold the one truth as transcending the grasp of human thought. With reference to Nietzsche Jaspers writes that unlimited doubt is the passion for truth. "Faith in truth *begins* with doubt in all hitherto believed truth," he quotes Nietzsche as saying.[48] Jaspers saw that, for Nietzsche, the relentless exercise of the will to truth must, in the end, question itself and may, perhaps, even invalidate itself. But Nietzsche's aim, according to Jaspers, is not nothingness but genuine Being.[49] Nietzsche's radical movements of doubt and extreme formulations, such as the well-known dictum, "nothing is true, all is permitted," are, accordingly, designed to force us to find the fulfillment of truth "in our own historicly present existence."[50]

Jaspers's encounter with Nietzsche's thinking on the problem of truth and with two opposing extremes of erroneous interpretation of Nietzsche—one tending to trivialize him, the other seeing him as the apostle of nihilism—gave added impetus to the clarification of the role of doubt in faith. Equally compelling to him is the fact that "skepticism" is an age-old invective used especially by the religious believers in reference to philosophy.[51]

In addition, Jaspers traces the history of the moral condemnation, logical refutation and *ad hominem* confutation of skepticism within the confines of philosophy itself.[52] None of these procedures grasps the full significance of skepticism and therefore does not succeed in the desired overturning of skepticism.

Jaspers sees that for Nietzsche the relentless exercise of the will to truth will in the end question itself. Doubt, as we have seen, is for Jaspers the primary means whereby the concern over truth breaks through the wall of cogitative fixations of the truth. The necessity for thinking in terms of absolutes may lead to the untruth of dogmatism. However, a radical doubt, in opposing the untruth of dogmatism, may itself get stranded in untruth, if it becomes fixed and ceases to be a moment of the concern over truth. Traditionally such fixed doubt has been called skepticism in the narrow sense, and Jaspers distinguished two kinds: namely dogmatic skepticism and indecisive skepticism. Cicero, denying all certainty in acknowledging only probabilities which he accepts as tentative guidelines and without obligation, serves Jaspers as a typical example of indecisive skepticism. For Jaspers, a man who, when faced with the insight of the impossibility of ultimate certainties, does not commit himself, is a nonentity. And a dogmatic skeptic, in denying that anything can be known, knows too much. But to condemn the skeptic or to oppose him under the banner of dogmatic assent is not the truthful or fruitful way of overcoming skepticism.

Jaspers considers the movement of skeptical relativising to be the alternative to both dogmatism and skepticism. Such a skeptical movement is a third step in carrying the concern over truth beyond the steps of assent and of doubt, where, if this concern gets bogged down, it turns into dogmatism or skepticism. The movement of skeptical relativising is, in a way, Jaspers's own program of philosophy. This sort of philosophical doubt would explore or at least grant each position its range of significance, would give each position free play as a way of truth unhampered by other positions and other ways, and would preclude the usurpation of the one and only truth on the part of any position by means of a movement of absolutization and anticipation. This approach is intimately tied to the postulation of the transcendence of the one truth. On the one hand it does not permit any man to speak with superhuman authority so that what is absolute for him is held to be absolute for all. On the other hand, it upholds the possibility that, in the disparity of their visions and ways, men are united in a common task and a single goal. For in Jaspers's view one can neither maintain that there are as many truths as there are persons, nor can one maintain that there is one truth for all persons. As to the latter, no truth known to any one person, no truth upon which any one person bases himself, can be so comprehensive that it comprises the truths of all others. As to the assertion that there are as many truths as there are persons, Jaspers points out that these truths stand together but not next to one another. Even in mortal combat with a fellow man

> I recognize something like truth in him which is not truth for me, which is not my truth, but something which limits and questions my truth.[53]

Even as he upholds the skeptical movement, against the philosophical dogmatist and nihilist, as an "indispensable way of philosophizing" so Jaspers also means to meet the challenge from the side of revealed faith. From this viewpoint, skepticism consists of the refusal to confess to revealed dogma. To Jaspers such confessing seems "ominous," for

> it is divisive, and opens the abyss of noncommunication when together with a confession it is demanded that others participate in it as the language of absolute truth.[54]

Confession of faith opposes skepticism and considers itself opposed by skepticism. But it is not skepticism which turns against confession of faith, but that sort of faith "which proceeds skeptically on the path of its verbalizations," and which stresses confession in deed over confession in word.[55]

iv. The Fulfillment of Ignorance

Jaspers's clarification of faith as requiring the substratum of doubt is closely tied to the critique of the range and limits of knowledge. *A fortiori*, the location of faith within the region of ignorance involves him in a characterization of ignorance in relation to knowledge as its polar opposite. We can therefore reject as irrelevant for our discussion thoughtless and naive ignorance which is prior to knowledge and the critique of knowledge. Similarly, we can reject the kind of ignorance which results in "opinion" and "conviction" as, for example, Marcel conceives of them in distinction from "faith." In Marcel's conception "opinion" is

> lack of knowledge [which] is not self-evident or self-admitted. . . . Opinion is a seeming which tends to become a claiming. . . . The more information one has . . . the more impossible it is to form a unilateral judgement . . . and opinion is, by definition, unilateral.[56]

In distinguishing "conviction" from "faith" Marcel bases himself
on his teacher Bergson's discussion of the open and closed moral-
ities in the second part of *The Two Sources of Morality and Religion.* Accordingly, conviction is a "believing that," a response to
ignorance by "putting up a sort of barrier."[57] Faith, on the other
hand, is "believing in": "it means that I place myself at the disposal of something." This "existential index" is "completely lacking in conviction."[58] This conception of opinion as assertion without knowledge where knowledge is possible, is of course in
accordance with Jaspers's thinking. Even though he uses the term
"conviction" (*Überzeugung*) as meaning the expression of faith, he
would also agree that faith differs from what Marcel calls "conviction"; Jaspers would call it "dogmatism." This is not a confusion
of terminology, however. For Marcel points out that faith, in its
expression, uses the language of conviction. He points out that

> To the extent to which I am concerned to account for my
> belief, I am obliged to treat it as a conviction. . . .
>   If I believe in God and I am questioned or I question myself
> about this belief, I shall not be able to avoid the assertion that
> I am convinced of the existence of God. On the other hand,
> this translation, which is in itself inevitable, misses, I think,
> what is essential in the belief and is precisely its existential
> character.[59]

In Jaspers's thinking the critically deduced fact of ignorance
becomes a principle of the characterization of transcognitive
thought and faith. In this conception, ignorance goes hand in hand
with knowledge. Knowledge and ignorance have a common origin
and they are acquired together. Both arise from the will to know
in which Jaspers sees a metaphysical impulse to reach the limits of
knowledge.[60] Ignorance in this sense is not merely the privation
of knowledge; it is acquired in concomitance with knowledge,
and it is measured by the range of actually acquired knowledge.[61]
So far, Jaspers's treatment of the meaning and significance of ignorance vis-à-vis knowledge is quite traditional, and reminiscent of
"Socratic ignorance." Accordingly, he speaks of the "guilt not to
know what could be known"[62] and considers ignorance acquired
in the pursuit of knowledge as the impulse toward further knowledge and certainty.[63] Of special significance here is that, like Socrates, Jaspers upholds the relationship of ignorance to knowledge;
for both Socrates and Jaspers the realization of ignorance at the
limits of knowledge does not call for an acquiescence in the
"knowledge that one doesn't know" but a relentless effort "to
know what can be known."[64]

A new aspect of the meaning of ignorance arises at those limits of knowledge which cannot be overcome by further inquiry. Such ignorance can, first of all, be viewed as the essence of a tragic situation. Ignorance concomitant with tragic knowledge is, then, an openness for what may be mythically called the unfathomed and implacable direction of tragic events.[65] In this vein Jaspers interprets Shakespeare's *Hamlet* as "knowledge concerning Being within the framework of ignorance."[66] But, as Kierkegaard sees the movement of faith beyond the movement of tragic resignation and God as teacher beyond the merely maieutic function of the Socratic teacher, so Jaspers sees the tragic as pointing beyond itself. However, Jaspers considers even the "leap into faith" which may occur at the unbridgeable ultimate limits of knowledge to be engendered by a relentless will to know. What can be known may be limited but the will to know is unlimited. If it is relentless then "Even where I cannot know anymore I cannot stop wanting to know."[67] If it suffers shipwreck on the rock of the unknowable, it is not by its own choice but because it must. Such deeper ignorance engendered and intensified by the pursuit of what is knowable can be the source of freedom and of faith. It can be the source of freedom because it is precisely by virtue of my ignorance that I am confronted with the necessity of choice.[68] And it is nothing other than the risk and tentativeness of faith that can fill the void left by the impossibility of the steady finality of knowledge concerning the absolute. Faith is not indifference to ignorance nor the indifferent acceptance of it; faith means, beyond mere "endurance" of ignorance, "welcoming" it as the chance and task to maintain oneself despite and against ignorance.[69] But by risking one's selfhood in faith, one also gains oneself. For the alternative to ignorance, and its fulfillment by a realization of truth which requires the participation of one's choice and responsibility, is the objectivity of knowledge and the submission to what it brings to light. If the possibility of faith at the limits of knowledge would disappear, or if human existence would be restricted to what is knowable, then human existence, in Jaspers's words, "would be a puppet show, with those objectivities pulling the strings."[70]

As in many other connections, Jaspers's key to a genuine fulfillment of ignorance by faith is an enlightened critique of the limits of knowledge and the actual pursuit of knowledge to these limits. For not only is knowledge pursued for its own sake but these limits indicate the "infinite weight" of the pursuit of all that is knowable "as our indispensable way to enter into the substance of what we cannot know."[71] On the other hand the more acutely we are aware of the limits of knowledge the more successfully will we resist accepting as knowledge what is no more than a speculation concerning the unknowable. "The philosopher knows that he does not know and he strives to know," and philosophy traditionally means the search for truth and not the possession of truth.[72] In this light scholasticism and ontology are for Jaspers aberrations of philosophy, and the main lesson to be learned from the history of metaphysical speculation is that speculations do not endure the test of cognitive critique. For him the significance of speculations concerning Being and its aspects is that they illuminate our ignorance concerning such matters.[73] In their positive significance as fulfilled ignorance they are, like myths and metaphysical experiences, a form of the 'cipher language' by which the transcendent ground of being may intimate itself as the object of faith. The further significance of speculation, particularly in its proliferation, is, therefore, that it guards against taking for knowledge what can be only a matter of ignorance and against confusing such pseudo-knowledge with genuine knowledge.[74] For Jaspers theological orthodoxy and philosophical ontology are instances of such pseudo-knowledge. Genuine knowledge is binding on all. But even if faith is expressed in the general terms of speculation, it is absolute only for the individual who opts for it. By virtue of the concomitance of the acquisition of knowledge and ignorance, faith as the fulfillment of ignorance and knowledge impel each other. But both are concretely unique in the individual: the certainty of actually acquired knowledge, and the faith by which the will to know comes to terms with the limits of this knowledge.[75] For Jaspers faith is sound and true to the extent that it coincides with actual cognitive ignorance; and this depends on whether what can be known is actually known.

The confrontation with unbridgeable limits of knowledge can but does not necessarily lead to faith. Either the limit of cognitive thought is not recognized; but this is uncritical. Or, where this limit is recognized, it is treated with the sort of indifference which Kant called "the mother of chaos and night" and against which, together with dogmatism and skepticism, he turned in the name of critical philosophy. Jaspers considers the agnosticism of positivistic ignorance to be typical of such indifferentism. In so far as the positivist does not attribute to the totality of reality what can be said only of a specific aspect of it, in which case he does not even recognize the limits, or considers ignorance to be a merely temporary gap in knowledge, recognition by him of limits of knowledge in principle is of no further consequence: "What we cannot speak about we must pass over in silence," as Pears and

McGuiness incorrectly translate a famous sentence in Wittgenstein's *Tractatus.* The possibility of such unfaith stands in polar
relationship to the possibility of faith.

> Where agnosticism will not let me rest, because a relation to
> the unknowable keeps goading me, my positivism has an
> end. [76]

Chapter Two

The Alternatives to Faith

We have traced Jaspers's philosophical characterization of faith as distinct from knowledge to the point of locating it within the region of learned ignorance. Knowledge is thought conditional upon evidence and criteria of evidence. By way of distinction, faith is consciousness of unconditional truth intimated at the limits of what can be known.[1] We shall now turn to Jaspers's characterization of faith on the level of thought where faith is one among other possibilities. We shall concentrate again on the contrasts and polarities which he brings to light. After distinguishing, in this chapter, faith from unfaith and lack of faith, from superstition and mysticism, we shall speak of the actuality of faith. Subsequently we shall turn our attention to Jaspers's treatment of the combat between faiths and the role of authority in faith. Finally, by way of a summary and a prelude to the problem of the content of philosophical faith, we shall consider Jaspers's concept of philosophical faith.

i. Unfaith

If faith is consciousness of absolute truth intimated at the limits of knowledge, unfaith is the denial of such truth. Scanning the history of thought, Jaspers notes that, like positivism and naturalism in the twentieth century, there have been in many places and at many times different forms of explicitly stated unfaiths. For him the fact that more or less elaborate and potent forms of unfaith have arisen wherever systematic thought developed to a high degree does not seem coincidental. In this connection he discusses the skeptical doctrine of the Carvakas of ancient India, the "indignation" of the Preacher in Ecclesiastes, and the ancient Greek philosophies of materialism, hedonism, and skepticism.[2] He concludes that faith and unfaith are "poles of selfhood" where neither persists without its polar opposite as a constant possibility. We have had occasion to mention that for Jaspers faith is actual only where it must maintain itself against the challenge of unfaith. *Mutatis mutandis*, unfaith is nourished by its opposition of faith. But Jaspers does not only consider them to be concomitant in their mutual provocation but sees a modicum of each carried by the other.[3] Faith, as the experience of Augustine and the writings of Kierkegaard have shown, is the more genuine the more intimately it is acquainted with the 'either' in confrontation with which it opts for the 'or'. And unfaith, in its negativity and as a basis for life, maintains a minimum of faith, not without truth and dignity, albeit dogmatic in form and largely unfruitful. It will be recalled that, according to Jaspers, in thinking, man cannot avoid positing something as absolute. Thus the materialist posits matter as the minimum of concrete objectivity, the hedonist pleasure and pain as the vital minimum basis of valuation, and the skeptic the relativity of all that is objective and subjective.[4] The positivist posits only that as significant which can in some way be reduced to the empirically verifiable.[5] Jaspers does not consider the well-known refutations of the positive minimum in these different forms of unfaith to have any significance beyond their liberating effect. As such these refutations are negative and not the source of faith which is, in its nature, positive. He also cautions against obscuring the fruitfulness of unfaith. Just as Plato considers "contradiction" and the "opposition of unity" as the incitement to thought, so Jaspers considers the possibility of unfaith, particularly in the form of skepticism, to be the indispensable spur of faith and thus also of philosophizing. Besides that, the positive minimum of each unfaith has most likely something fruitful to offer. Thus, according to Jaspers, even though the "inquiry and mastery over nature was, historically, based on other faiths," the ontological theories of materialism served as the indispensable presuppositions for this inquiry.[6] Largely however, Jaspers considers unfaith to be essentially fruitless. Citing Goethe he maintains that

> in the conflict of unfaith and faith all epochs in which faith reigned supreme are brilliant, uplifting and fruitful in their time and for posterity. On the other hand, all epochs in which unfaith gained a wretched victory disappear from memory because no one likes to torment himself with knowledge of the unfruitful.[7]

Faithlessness[8] is quite different from unfaith. The latter is negative faith and stands in polar opposition to faith. In the case of faithlessness the tension of the polarity is absent. It may be the neutrality of the uncommitted spectator, or a readiness to compromise out of a lack of obligation. It may be the hyprocrisy of 'both/and', or the fruitless surrender to chance or the powers that be. It may be the suicide's realization of the nullity of self and the futility of all,[9] or passive submission without confidence.[10]

ii. Superstition

Man is caught in a paradox. He invokes or perceives the intimation of truth at the limits of what he can know, and expresses it in forms appropriate to the immanent mode of man's being but inadequate to truth in its transcendent fullness. He is torn between the critical injunction not to make graven images and his desire to have a golden calf as concrete object of veneration. The reason for this paradox is simple:

> When we do not bind ourselves to finitude we remain, empty and ungrounded, in mere possibility. . . . But what speaks through finitude becomes lost in it insofar as a finitude is taken as absolute.[11]

To have faith means to risk being guided by the truth while not knowing the truth, as philosophy means the search for and not the possession of truth. But man's mode of thinking and doing prefers possession to search and concretion to intimation. The determinate mode of thought and the concreteness of acting and making serve as the indispensable vehicles of faith and philosophy. Hence a persistent and intense critical awareness is required not to mistake the presence of the immanent vehicle for the presence of transcendence, and not to substitute the "authority, idol, cult, rite, confession, law or doctrine,"[12] for what may intimate itself through them. Failure to maintain such critical posture leads to the aberration of faith, to superstition. It is the objectification of faith in the form of a knowable determinate content.[13] It is the fulfilled will to possess transcendence in the immanent object,[14] be it in a concrete thing or act in the empirical world or, at the opposite extreme, a fixed, even if abstract, thought or doctrine.[15]

Most forms of superstition result from the attempted materialization of transcendence;[16] magic is therefore one of its frequent expressions. What transcends determinate and concrete objectivity is treated as such and is supposed to be at man's disposal in the manner of other real objects. Far from being merely the harbinger of reassuring news, Jaspers shows himself in the following passage as siding with the empiricists' critique of the aberrations of faith: "There are no objective miracles . . . no ghosts, no clairvoyance, no magic."[17] He counters the old objection to the empiricists' critique of miracles, recently reiterated for the English-speaking world by C. S. Lewis, in his *Miracles: A Preliminary Study*, according to which the impossibility of miracles cannot be demonstrated on purely logical grounds. This impossibility is indeed not logically grounded, according to Jaspers, but is based on the commitment to the conditions of empirical cognition. He sees how this commitment and the concomitant certainty of the impossibility of what is affirmed in superstition can serve as the basis of positivism. However, he also sees that commitment and the certainty of this impossibility as the condition for a genuine relation to transcendence. For superstition and the unfaith of positivism are on the same plane insofar as they detract from such a genuine relationship, the latter by relegating it to the realm of illusion, the former by materializing transcendence. But in the enmity between superstition and positivism Jaspers sees in the latter the always-justified victor.

This does not mean that the commitment to empirical cognition cannot turn into a form of superstition. Certainly, some of the most forceful passages in Jaspers's critique of modern times are devoted to his exposure of what he calls, with provocative candor, the superstitious belief in science. One of his many characterizations of this superstition goes as follows:

A misleading consequence of the false conception of science that the world can be known in its entirety and in principle has been to consider it as already fundamentally known. The opinion arose that it is now only a matter of good will to establish for mankind the right world order on the basis of knowledge and thereby make possible a permanent condition of wealth and happiness. In its wake . . . a new phenomenon entered history. . . . The will . . . to order the whole . . . through knowledge of the whole.[18]

In his political writings Jaspers maintains that this will to mastery over the whole on the basis of supposed insight into the ultimate principles of being—a procedure entrenched in modern times since Descartes[19] but related to the claim of exclusiveness on the part of the Biblical religions, and on the side of philosophy to the tradition of constructive ontology—is at the root of broad social planning and reaches its logical extreme and ultimate actualization in the totalitarian form of government. His characterization of the superstitious belief in science continues as follows:

> This typical modern superstition expects what science cannot render. It accepts supposedly scientific total views of things as conclusive knowledge. It uncritically accepts results without awareness of the ways in which they were methodically gained and of the limits wherein a scientific result is valid. It considers all truth and all actuality to be at the disposal of our intellect. It has absolute confidence in science and, without question, follows its authority wielded by official bodies of experts.[20]

It will readily be seen that the error on which the superstitious belief in science rests lies in the false interpretation of the presupposition that the world can be known. A proper understanding of this presupposition enables us to gain insights into particular aspects of the world; we understand this presupposition wrongly if we take it to mean that the world as a whole is subject to cognitive certainty.[21] It is perhaps somewhat more difficult to see in what way all this can be called superstition which, in Jaspers's use of the term, means the putative possession or recognition of the transcendent in the immanent, that is, either in the form of a concrete object or of a determinate thought. This problem is clarified if we recall that for Jaspers, in agreement with Kant, the world and the realm of what can be known in their totalities are "transcendental ideas" and not "empirical realities," and thus evade being objects of knowledge. The superstition in question consists in treating the idea of the world and the ideals of science not as transcending and defying, though, as the case may be, animating knowledge, but as if they were actual items of knowledge.

Jaspers's frequent criticism of the superstitious belief in science indicates that he considers superstition to be a perennial possibility for mankind. A person living in an age which prides itself in upholding the ideals of the Enlightenment may be taken aback by Jaspers's remark that "the Middle Ages were hardly more superstitious than the age of Enlightenment."[22] For Enlightenment, "the emergence of man from his self-inflicted tutelage," about which Kant wrote, serves as a shield against superstition only if it is the genuine and not the false Enlightenment. The mark of genuine Enlightenment is self-criticism to the extent of not permitting anything that man can know and think and do and meet as being absolute for all or a guarantee of the presence or actuality of the absolute.

Accordingly, one might consider revealed faith to be an example of superstition. After all, it is a faith whose authority rests on the revelation of God in time and at a place. To be sure, the very concept of revelation and the actuality of revealed faith present a special problem for philosophy and for Jaspers. According to Jaspers's analysis of the problem, revealed faith can be genuine if, in the manner of genuine faith, it is "trust without guarantee." It turns into superstition if the believed revelation is thought to provide an objective and therefore cognizable guarantee for the diverse contents of this faith, such as redemption or immortality, an objectification which serves as the basis for an institutionalization of the faith.[23]

In many respects Jaspers feels two ways about the institution of the church and the fact that it appears to be founded upon a superstition. However, in appearing as such the church can be a shield against rampant superstition. Jaspers characterizes this particular role of institutional authority as follows:

> The faith of the crowd desires the object. . . . It wants to have, touch, see, and know what it believes. . . . It drives toward superstition. . . . Authority safeguards against superstition by preserving the profundity of the secret of the incomprehensible of what must be accepted with silence; and yet it also satisfies the impulses which lead to superstition. . . . There is no efficacious faith without a church or its analogue.[24]

Ultimately the antidote against superstition, including the superstitious reliance on science and the materialization of transcendence, consists of the critical distinction between what is known and what cannot be known and the illumination of the role of freedom, of choice, and of responsibility, with regard to matters which transcend knowledge.[25]

iii. Mystery and Mysticism

a. Mysticism and Faith

At the limits of the reach of knowledge, thought turns toward reality transcending cognizable immanence. Here arises the possible polarity of faith and unfaith, of invoking or rejecting transcendence. In either case superstition, the putative presence of transcendence in time and space, is deemed to be a false possibility. But faith, in polar relation to unfaith, is not the only positive possibility. Mysticism is another. The mystic, though he is a being in time and space, is in possession of transcendence. However, he differs radically from the believer in superstition. The latter possesses transcendence by materializing it; the mystic, in confrontation or union with transcendence, transcends his own temporality.

Jaspers's characterization and criticism of mysticism as distinct from faith is offered from the standpoint of faith. Yet he upholds mysticism as compossible with faith. He maintains that "what mystics have described without being able to describe it is . . . an experience which it is impossible to doubt."[26] In particular, he holds that ordinarily dubitable claims of mystic union are credible by virtue of the fact that throughout history such extraordinary experiences had been decisive for men of undoubted quality.[27] Moreover, how intent this Frisian thinker is on the possibility of mysticism can be gleaned from a passage which, in its near rhapsodic character, does not fail to ring true:

> Standing on the shore of the North Sea in a thunderstorm I see only the glaring then fallow and eerily fantastic light in the clouds and sea, wander in storm and rain, becoming almost one with the elements. When the soul of this landscape speaks this is, to be sure, objectively nothing, but in its experience it is the concrete presence of something which Rembrandt and Shakespeare knew. It is like a revelation of Being. I feel as if the most magnificent of man's creations—the Parthenon and the Strasbourg Cathedral, Chartres and the ceiling of the Sistine Chapel—could be lost for me but not this. From this nature . . . one can live. Here is . . . experience of infinity. Here is an efficacy which makes me independent because it maintains my tie to the ground of things. . . .
> Together with Plotinus, Eckhart, and Cusanus, I think the sublime thoughts in which all determinate objectivity is lost but in which music of abstraction seems to convey the most profound manifestation of Being. Mentally disciplined speculation brings the mystic experience of the one in all. Infinity becomes present in a way in which nothing palpable remains at hand.[28]

It would be a mistake to take this passage for more than a formal recognition of the possibility of mysticism in the form of an empathic characterization of the outward setting and the manifestation of the mystic experience. Whatever the many contexts in which Jaspers has the occasion to discuss the possibility of mysticism, he discloses ever new facets of its contraposition to philosophy and to faith, and the recurrence of the questions philosophy poses as to its genuineness and truth. Characteristically, therefore, the cited passage continues as follows:

> But infinity eludes the concrete form [*Gestalt*]. It is manifest precisely in the dissolution of all that is formed. It seduces to extinction in nothingness. It deceives in arousing a fantastic mood of enjoyment of nature and mystical joy. . . . Finitude as historicity, i.e., in union with its eternal ground and not as isolating finitude of mere immanence, is the form of being without which I cannot be certain of any being. The unhistoric experience of the infinite ground . . . requires the fulfillment and supplement in historic concreteness of something finite in order to gain speech.[29]

In Jaspers's treatment the incompatibility of faith, philosophically considered, with mysticism, rests on a twofold basis.

First, philosophy radically accepts temporality as a condition for man's search for truth, while for mysticism the voiding of time is the condition for truth. This does not mean that in Jaspers's view time is not acknowledged by the mystic. This would be as incorrect as it is to maintain that the philosopher does not acknowledge certain modes of atemporality. What is characteristic for the mystic is that time is not of decisive significance; this is typically expressed in this epigram by Jacob Boehme:

> Wem Zeit ist wie Ewigkeit
> Und Ewigkeit wie die Zeit
> Der ist befreit
> Von allem Streit.[30]

More than that, temporality is for the mystic "ruinous, veiling, narrowing, and deceptive."[31] But time is not an accidental concomitant but an essential constituent of the movement of thought; therefore, even though thought may aim at surmounting the vissicitudes and manifold of time, and to fulfill itself in the universal and the One, it cannot extingush time. We can speak "as if" time were extinguished.[32] The extinction of time would mean the extinction of thought. The tranquility of the transtemporal eludes thought and man the thinker. In the experience of union with eternity it moves the mystic insofar as he thinks it. As a rational proposition the mystic insight is subject to criticism and thus relativized.[33]

Therefore, secondly, philosophy accepts the radical split between subject and object, while mysticism seeks to transcend the split in mystical union of subject and object or in the immediate confrontation of one with the other. From the viewpoint of philosophical thought, mystical thought is an attempt which is doomed to failure. So also is a not purportedly mystical conception of human thought according to which it is gifted with intellectual intuition. According to Jaspers, philosophical thought is historic and mediating. Historicity means active decision which is in time but of eternal validity. Eternity is mediated through time but is not present as such. It is in this sense that Jaspers agrees with Kant in gainsaying intellectual intuition by restricting intuition to the sensuous. For Jaspers, the denial of intellectual intuition and the affirmation of philosophical faith become compelling when we consider that God's thought is usually held to be intuitive. To have seen God, to have been one with God, to think like God, enables the mystic to be, together with God, master over the course of events.[34] This is an extreme action and according to Jaspers, an overweaning one; but as we shall see, the road to it is cleared by granting the intellect the power of immediate insight. In this connection, we can also see how Jaspers, by his criticism of mysticism in the name of philosophy, parts company with strong traditions of Christian theology. According to the latter, the mystic vision of God is not incompatible with faith, but is a promise, a moment, and fulfillment of faith.[35]

b.   Intuition and Mediation

Precisely this theological promise served Duns Scotus as a basis and goad for supplementing the Aristotelian epistemology of abstraction with that of intellectual intuition.[36] The introduction of intellectual intuition into Western thought served many purposes. It served to accommodate philosophical thought to dogmatic requirements. It simplified the theorizing on how thought represents existence. It provided the atmosphere for the many forms of ecstactic mysticism which appeared in the later Middle Ages and in modern times and which were, for the most part, far cries from the *logos* mysticism of Origenes, Plotinus and Pseudo-Dionysius. It opened the door to gnostic visions. And intuition is the last resort of the proponent of truths which are not only necessary but also held to be absolute, as with Descartes, Leibniz and Locke and, more profoundly, with Spinoza. We do not wish to imply that mysticism and rationalism are similar. However, they share the principle that immediate insight, particularly into absolutes, is a moment of human thought.

Distinct from this conception, Kant, and with him Jaspers, draw the radical consequence from the phenomenon of the synthetic (Kant) or mediating (Jaspers) function of human thought. Existence—of self, of the object, of God—transcends human thought. Though thought is directed toward and by existence, existence is independent of thought and defies thought. An intellect which is intuitive, according to Kant, would be one "through whose representation the objects of this representation would at the same time exist."[37] The phrase "through whose representation" suggests that Kant considers that any intuiting intellect would, by its act of understanding, bring about the existence of the object of its understanding. Such a creative act of intuitive understanding is traditionally thought to be God's mode of understanding, as Kant himself points out.[38] Does this mean that the alternative is, either non-intellectually intuiting, i.e., only sensibly intuiting human understanding, or divine, creatively intuitive intellection? Not necessarily. For as Kant himself points out, "We cannot judge in regard to the intuition of other thinking beings, whether they are bound by the same conditions as those which limit our intuition."[39] By the "conditions" to which our intuition is bound and with respect to which Kant raises the question of sameness in the case of other thinking beings, he seems not only to mean those of time and space as forms of our sensible intuition, but also the condition of sensibility as such. It is, after all, conceivable that minds other than God's intuit intellectually. Such a mind, in intuiting, would at least require the existence of its object without necessarily producing the existent by its intuitive understanding. Such requirement of existence was an important point in Duns Scotus's distinction of intuition vis-à-vis abstraction.[40] He attributed to man the power to intuit intellectually providing that the object of such intuition be both existing and present.

A problem suggested by some critics of Scotus is relevant to our examination. While conceding that the object of intuition must exist, they raised the question whether God cannot cause us to intuit objects which are not present.[41] And, of course, God, by virtue of his omnipotence, could cause this. The problem, then, which is raised by conceding human intellectual intuition is, at first, not that of arrogating powers which are thought to be God's. Rather, an intuiting intellect which intuits only receptively and not creatively could be certain of the existence of the object of its understanding even without the certifying presence of the object. Unless an intuiting intellect would be, and would be known to be, restricted in its thinking to the intuition of existents which are actually given, it would not be able to distinguish between thoughts concerning existents and thoughts concerning non-existents; it would have to think all its thoughts under the aspect of existence. It could not account for nor even consider the possibility of thought extending beyond the understanding of actualities. And in this way the attribution of intuitive intellection to man leads to the notion of man's likeness to God and the illusion of his participation in or recourse to divine power. For the only intuitive intellect for which the existence of what is understood is certain to be given, is the *intellectus archetypus* postulated by Kant.[42]

Such a mind and only such a mind would be unencumbered in its understanding by the categorial and methodical apparatus of synthesis and mediation which are constitutive of the phenomenon of human thought. Typical, for Kant, are these passages from the "Transcendental Deduction":

> Our understanding can only *think*, and for intuition must look to the senses.[43]

> Were I to think an understanding which is itself intuitive (as, for example, a divine understanding which should not represent to itself given objects, but through whose representation the objects themselves be given or produced), the categories would have no meaning whatsoever in respect of such a mode of knowledge. They are merely rules for an understanding whose whole power consists in thought, consists, that is, in the act whereby it brings the synthesis of a manifold, given to it from elsewhere in intuition, to the unity of apperception. . . .[44]

Seeing thought as mediating and therefore the postulation of transcognitive ideas as tasks actively realized in time, particularly by means of cognitive and moral activity, Kant rejects mysticism with cutting impatience:

> Now, whether wisdom is *poured into* man from above through inspiration or is *scaled* from below through the inner strength of his practical reason, that is the question.

> He who maintains the former as a passive means of cognition entertains the chimerical possibility of a supersensuous experience which is self-contradictory in representing the transcendent as immanent. It bases itself on a certain secret doctrine, i.e., mysticism, which is the opposite of all philosophy. Precisely this he, like the alchemist, deems to be his big discovery, and, being relieved of all the rational but arduous research into nature, he dreams blissfully in a sweet state of enjoyment.[45]

Clearly the old Kant had not forgotten his piece on Swedenborg three and a half decades earlier.

We see how Jaspers's Kantian conception of thought, which is attuned to the historicity and mediativeness of thought, precludes mysticism as one of its possible moments. Yet he deems mysticism to be a human possibility, and endeavors to place it as such, particularly with respect to philosophy. It will be recalled that mysticism and philosophy share a directedness towards transcendence at the limits of knowledge. It would therefore seem that both stand in polar opposition to unfaith in its many forms. In principle this is, of course, correct. But the matter appears in clearer perspective if we focus on the immanent which alone is knowable and the purported transcending of which is at issue.

In this manner we find faith standing in a mediate position along a line one of whose polar extremes is mysticism, the other positivism. All three are confronted with the same human condition. But each assumes a different position with respect to it. We may characterize the condition as that of historicity. Man is immanent in the world, in nature, a being in space and in time. If he lives his mundane existence naively then he is not confronted with the possibilities of his historicity. But if by a "crisis of consciousness" he erupts from such naiveté by posing questions with respect to his mundane existence or even fashioning it in the light of supra-mundane truths and values, then such critical awakening brings forth an "insoluble ambiguity." On the one hand he is "not any longer only" a mundane being. Indeed, one who subjects his mundane being to his decisions and assumes responsibility for it is essentially more than it. And yet "he exists only insofar as he appears" in his mundane being.[46]

According to Jaspers, both positivism and mysticism attempt to resolve the ambiguity of man's historicity by relinquishing one of its constituents. The positivist would regard himself and all human beings exclusively as mundane beings, and deny the significance of the transmundane. The mystic would renounce the world and his own mundane being and become one with the transmundane. It seems that both will fail. The positivist, at a moment of truth, must choose, and, in choosing, reawakens to his transmundane selfhood; and the mystic, when faced with a similar necessity, will relate the two realms of his experience which otherwise have no mutual relevance: the shadowy realm of his moribund earthly being, and the genuine transmundane reality with which he is united in states of ecstasy.

The third way, besides these poles, is the way of mediation. Here we may speak of more than one possibility if we consider revelation in accordance with theological traditions, as a form of mediation. But for Jaspers mediation proper is philosophy. Vis-à-vis our polarity it may be characterized as follows: it is thought which neither restricts itself to what can be known nor seeks to force its way to a premature realization of the one and ultimate truth. It is the *risk* of faith within the world and the *love* of wisdom, rather than the *possession* of transcendence beyond the vicissitudes of the world. It is the partaking rather than the fulfillment of being.[47] Possession and faith are irreconcilable.[48] And love requires the relative distance of its object from the lover. There is no love where the distance is absolute, as in positivism. And there is no love in mysticism where the distance is removed.[49] For philosophical thought, transcendence is distant, infinitely though not absolutely distant, and God is hidden, though he may be intimated in an endless array of ciphers, none of which lend themselves with finality to human decoding.

Philosophical thought with its moment of faith neither abandons man's mundane existence, since it is the only arena of man's realization, nor abandons man to his mere mundane existence. In distinction from both positivism and mysticism, neither of which acknowledges the dialectical tension of man's historicity, philosophy mediates transcendence in the temporal movement of active thought. It is itself mediate between these poles as the recognition of man as being "more than the understanding intellect and less than divine thought."[50]

c. Anselm versus Thomas

Jaspers's critique of philosophical faith vis-à-vis positivism and mysticism offers some noteworthy historical sidelights. In his interpretation of Anselm's *Proslogium* argument for the existence of God he considers the significance of Thomas Aquinas's 'refutation' of it. Behind their disagreement Jaspers sees a fundamental difference in the conception of human thought. Both accept the validity of the understanding, particularly in its empirical employment and, accordingly, propose cosmological arguments for the existence of God. Both accept the truth of the Christian faith, and, accordingly, uphold the authority of the Church in teaching this truth. But here they part company. Anselm exercises the philosophical freedom to explicate his faith speculatively by means of the dialectical use of discursive thought. His program is avowedly a *quaerere intellectum fidei*, where the 'conclusion' of a sequence of thought is not a new, universally verifiable insight but cogitative assurance and clarification of a faith which for such a sequence is always already presupposed. Hence his *Proslogium* argument for the existence of God, a "meditation on the grounds of faith,"[51] hence his speculative explication of the atonement and redemption in *Cur Deus Homo?*, hence also his metaphysical writings on the trinity. The distinction between theology with its tenets of faith and philosophy with its contemplative freedom and rational rigor does not exist for Anselm. But this distinction is all-important for Thomas. He restricts human thought to the intellect. Here it may range freely, unencumbered by the requirements of faith. But matters of faith are matters of the authoritative teaching of the Church, which means acceptance without understanding and without the search for understanding. Hence the trinity, the redemption, and the assurance of God's reality by contemplating Him as "the being than which none greater can be conceived" are beyond the proper, natural and legitimate reach of man's mind. Hence Thomas's restriction, in his 'refutation' of the *Proslogium* argument, to its purely formal aspect, and his utter disregard of what, by the nature of the matter, is the important aspect, namely that speculative thought is a *fides quaerens intellectum*.

Jaspers characterizes the difference between Anselm and Thomas as follows:

> Thomas thought with the natural understanding, which for him was empirical and rationalistic. Or in receiving revelation, he thought mystery. Anselm knew no such cleavage. Because he understood revelation with reason, he was able, in his fundamental thought of certainty of God, to exercise pure reason even without revelation.[52]

In this contraposition the ascription to Thomas of the alternative 'either the intellect or mysticism' may give us pause. For in an age when Thomas is vaunted for being the teacher of scientifically rigorous thought in the name of the Christian faith, attention is not ordinarily paid to this aspect of Thomas. But it is of great importance to him, if for no other reason than to account for the revelation through the prophets.[53] In Thomas's words,

> Since man can only know the things that he does not see himself by taking from another who does see them . . . the knowledge of the objects of faith must be handed on by . . . God. . . . But, since the things that come from God are enacted in a definite order . . . some persons had to receive them directly from God, then others from them, and so on in an orderly way down to the lowest person.[54]

Hence,

> there is a twofold way of knowing things, one by means of abstraction . . . the other . . . by the infusion . . . by God.[55]

Such infusion occurs in a state of rapture.[56] That Thomas understands rapture to mean mystical ecstasy and that he conceives of it as an alternative to and vis-à-vis the natural intellect can be seen from his characterizations of rapture:

> Such transport takes place through the divine power, and then it is properly an elevation. For, since the agent makes that which is passive like itself, the transport which takes place by the divine power, and which is above man, has an ordination to something higher than that which is natural to man.[57]
> When however, this takes place, the mind must leave off that mode of knowing in which it abstracts. . . . They are said to be in a state of rapture, as if by virtue of a higher power they were separated from that which naturally belongs to them.[58]

Jaspers is probably correct in surmising that Thomas's opposition to Anselm's "profound trust in the unity of thought and faith in the source of reason, that is, of philosophy"[59] was political. In explanation he correctly points out that one of Thomas's primary tasks was to "conjure" the "danger of thought for authority which had become far more evident in his own day than in Anselm's day."[60] But whatever the motive, the implied principles are clear. On the one hand, the gainsaying of philosophy and of faith, philosophically considered, in the name of the restriction of human thought to the intellect, particularly in its empirical employment, restricts the alternatives of realization on questions which "reason is not able to ignore but which it is also not able to answer" (Kant) to mysticism, be it authoritative, emotive, romantic, charismatic, or even nihilistic. On the other hand, the restriction of thought to the intellect, whether or not it is accompanied by the alternative of mysticism denies the exposure of ultimate questions and putative answers to the critical and public scrutiny of dialectical thought.

d. Mystery and Mysticism in Wittgenstein and Other Recent Thinkers

The alternative 'either the intellect or mysticism' serves many masters. It served Thomas. It served Wittgenstein. This is indicated in some passages in the latter portion of his *Tractatus* over which some of his interpreters despair. Miss Anscombe thinks that Wittgenstein took the term 'the mystical' from Lord Russell.[61] Perhaps she is right but their meanings are not the same. Lord Russell distinguishes mysticism from logic and by his genteel skepticism relegates to the former whatever is not amenable to the latter, thus, incidentally, displaying a curious and telling confusion of philosophy and mysticism proper. This conception does not coincide with that about which Wittgenstein writes. Black quite rightly sees that "Wittgenstein's 'mysticism' is far from being an irrelevant aberration" but "one of the chief motive powers of the book."[62] Yet even Black has difficulty coming to terms with this side of Wittgenstein, imputing to it an "equivocal character."

With respect to 6.522 of the *Tractatus*, i.e.,

> There is, indeed, the ineffable. It *shows* itself, it is the mystical.[63]

Black says,

> On the one hand, it seems clear . . . that he conceives there to *be* the mystical. Yet, on the other hand, remarks like those of 6.5, 6.51, and 6.52 seem to say that any effort to express the mystical, whether by saying or by showing, must result in absurdity.[64]

Now it seems to us that Wittgenstein is neither absurd nor equivocal. A philosophy according to which what can be meaningfully and signifyingly thought and said is exclusively attuned to what is determinately the case in time and space, cannot—if it is consistent—permit the possibility of transcendental discourse and problems within the confines of these limits. And Wittgenstein carries this ontological-linguistic principle to its logically consistent conclusion. Hence those remarks by which he explains that the range of possible questions cannot transcend the range of meaningful answers. But the conception of thought and language as reflective of the ontology of the world does not mean that the world is all. It only means that the world is all we can think or speak about. Neither does it mean that it is impossible for man to confront whatever transcends the world. It only means that it is ineffable. It can show itself—but not in the world. This coincides completely with Thomas's statement that to be in a state of rapture means to be "separated from that which naturally belongs" to man. The Wittgensteinian analogue to this statement is 6.432, "God does not reveal himself *in* the world." The emphasis, indicated by the italicized word "in," seems to imply that God, insofar as he reveals himself, reveals himself beyond this world.

Thus, both contentions are in Wittgenstein, and with logical propriety, namely that "there is, indeed, the ineffable," and that it *is* ineffable, i.e., not in this world and thus not something about which one can think or speak. There is, therefore, no absurdity or equivocation here. The difficulty comes when we ask how Wittgenstein knows all that he proclaims in an almost oracular manner. When he, with a further show of consistency, states

> 6.54: My sentences explicate in this way: that whoever understands me in the end recognizes them nonsensical when, by means of them—upon them—, he has stepped beyond them.

we are left to wonder how seriously to take the implied alternative 'either the intellect or mysticism'. Surely he has spoken about that of which one cannot speak, and he has not been silent about it.[65] But this is philosophy, i.e., more than intellectual thought, less than mystical insight. No doubt one of the things which Wittgenstein attempts to express is that matters which transcend the range of the intellect, particularly in its empirical employment, cannot have the same literal and theoretically determinate truth value as scientific discourse, and are, therefore, 'riddles' or 'mysteries'. But the sense of mystery which the scientific consciousness engenders does not necessarily lead to the absolutization of the intellect as in positivism, or to the alternative 'either the intellect or mysticism' as in the Wittgenstein of the *Tractatus*. Quite rightly, therefore, Stegmüller says that

> Wittgenstein's remarks about the mystical surely show that his philosophy *could have* taken a turn which it actually did *not* take. It would have been conceivable if he had subordinated 'philosophizing as activity' to the securing of a mystic vision or at least to a non-theoretical purpose, as in the case in Jaspers's illumination of Existenz.[66]

That there are points of departure for such a development, in Wittgenstein, is clear. This is evidenced by his concern over values, the 'problem' and the 'riddle' of life, and above all his marvelling over existence.

There are also some striking parallels between Wittgenstein at the time of the *Tractatus* and certain other authors writing at the same time, namely Buber, Marcel, Jaspers and Barth. We find in them an intense consciousness of the 'riddle' or 'mystery' of ultimate questions. With the exception of Karl Barth, this intensity more or less reflects the conclusion to be drawn from the development of modern science, i.e., that man's knowledge is limited to the empirical world but what is of man's greatest concern in this world transcends these limits. Thus Wittgenstein says

> 6.53: The right method of philosophy would really be the following: to say nothing except what can be said, i.e., propositions of natural science,

i.e., strictly speaking, science is the only literally cognitive kind of discourse. But,

> 6.52: We feel even when *all possible* scientific questions have been answered, the problems of life remain completely untouched.

Buber, in *I and Thou* (1923), distinguishes the experiencing and cognitive relation of the 'I' to the 'it' from the immediate meeting, presence and acceptance of 'I and Thou' in their whole being. Both relations are "primary," both in the world, but the latter exceeds the former in being and in comprehensibility and most particularly in the case of the relation of I and eternal Thou.

Marcel, in the *Metaphysical Journal* entries of January 1919, on the one hand, locates the 'mysterious' beyond the known and, on the other hand, contributes an important distinction between the unknown and the mysterious. To the first: "By its very essence the objective order excludes all mystery. The object can only be thought as indifferent to the act by which I think it."[67] And, four years later: "In the objective order there is no more place for revelation than there is for mystery: the two notions are complementary."[68] We are reminded of similar statements in the *Tractatus*, i.e., "The riddle does not exist"; "God does not reveal himself *in* the world." To the second: Marcel points out that an unknown is mysterious only if it is thought as knowing, as not wishing to be known, and as being of interest to man.[69]

In *Psychologie der Weltanschauungen* (1919), the earliest work in which he deals with these matters, Jaspers points to the many meanings of 'mystical' but characterizes the term generally as designating the "secret . . . incomprehensible, enigmatic."[70]

Karl Barth's *The Epistle to the Romans* (1920) naturally reflects the consciousness of mystery traditional in Christian theology, and it is analogous to that of the other cited authors who wrote at about the same time.[71]

The cited references show how Wittgenstein's *Tractatus* and writings by contemporaneous authors coincide in displaying awareness of mystery, i.e., an awareness of questions which escape the cognitive pursuit of the intellect. However, there is also a decisive difference between Wittgenstein and the others. In order to articulate this difference we must make the crucial distinction between an *awareness of mystery* and *mysticism*. In the present context mysticism may be characterized as follows. The failure of the intellect with respect to riddles or mysteries means the failure of human thought altogether when it comes to such questions. For there is no other mode of human thought beside the intellect;

moreover, the world is the only object of human thought, and entities such as values are not worldly objects. Man cannot preoccupy himself with mysteries by power of his thought; he can partake of them only insofar as the otherworldly shows itself to him. The question now is whether awareness of mystery necessarily implies mysticism in this sense. Buber, Marcel, Jaspers and Barth deny this; Wittgenstein does not. Moreover the former authors uphold a counter-mystical fideism, each in his way maintaining a mode of thought which, rather than being the expression of a vision of ultimates, is an expression of faith. They also uphold a concomitant pluralistic conception of the world. According to this view, the world as known is indifferent to value; in this they agree with Wittgenstein. But, contrary to him, they also maintain that we can bring invoked values to bear on it; it is the arena in which man realizes himself in his value-directedness, and, in this sense, the world can itself be of value. The difference between them and Wittgenstein can be indicated in the case of each author.

Thus, from a theological viewpoint, Barth considers it "a grave misunderstanding" to "think of silence before God as the final leap of human piety—as, for example, when we read the mystical sayings of Angelus Silesius."[72] However, in Wittgenstein we read, "whereof one cannot speak one must be silent." "Grace," Barth says, "breaks through both mysticism and morality, transforms the indicative into an imperative."[73]

And, as if in response to Wittgenstein's saying

6.41: The sense of the world must lie outside the world. In the world everything is as it is, and everything happens as it does happen; *in* it no value exists—and if it did exist, it would have no value,

we read in Marcel,

Our world is certainly not a world from which the mysterious is excluded, a world in which all that has the power of communicating itself communicates itself directly and spontaneously. Hence there is an intimate relationship between the idea of mystery and the idea of value. Only that which is capable of interesting me and presenting a value for me is mysterious.[74]

We note particularly in Buber, whose *I and Thou* has been more prone to a mystical interpretation than the notions of any other existential thinker, that mysticism is rejected. Even in the relation with the 'eternal Thou' the 'I' which the mystic gives up in the mystic union is, for Buber, "as indispensable to this, the supreme, as to every relation, since relation is only possible between I and Thou."[75]

The issue, however, goes beyond whether or not we can distinguish a sense of mystery from mystic vision. When we juxtapose the statements of these authors we note a disagreement which we can attribute to a divergence of outlook on the nature and scope of thought and of conceptions of the 'world'. A theoretical arbitration of these disagreements would hardly be conclusive. But they work themselves out in practice and in the consequent struggle between outlooks. Jaspers, as we have seen, contraposes mysticism and positivism, and upholds philosophical faith as the third possibility. And in his interpretation of Thomas vis-à-vis Anselm we found that the denial of philosophy is concomitant with the alternative 'either the intellect or mysticism'. If the denial of philosophy and the upholding of mysticism as the alternative to intellectual thought do not stand in the service of a church and a revelation, as they do in the case of Thomas, the question arises as to what media remain to carry on the business of public communication about matters of human concern which transcend the publicly verifiable.

In Wittgenstein we are offered the alternative 'either the propositions of natural science or the translingual, transmundane revelation of the mystical'. It has often been said that Wittgenstein was not a positivist. And his statements about the mystical have been invoked to bear this out. If positivism is any theory by which the physical world and knowledge of it are absolutized, then Wittgenstein's position is that of a positivism modified to escape one of the basic difficulties of positivism, namely that that absolutization precludes any proposition of the positivistic position. In this respect he says,

> 6.45: To view the world *sub specie aeterni* is to view it as a whole—a limited whole. The feeling of the world as a limited whole—that is the mystical.[76]

One always has to be more than a positivist in order to maintain a positivistic position. In principle, Wittgenstein can be said to be a mundane positivist and transmundane mystic. This does not mean that he was a mystic in practice. If he was, there is no report of it. Even 6.522 only says that "there is the ineffable," that "it shows itself." These statements are in the indicative and therefore cannot be said to signify mere possibility. But they are indeterminate; we are not told what fulfills them or that the ineffable has shown itself to Wittgenstein or to anyone. It seems devoid of content. This philosophy revolves around a sharply dualistic conception of man's position, particularly with respect to the world, a conception which is diametrically opposed to one which affirms man's historicity. The obverse of a mundane positivism which is accompanied by an absolutely transmundane mysticism is a nihilism with respect to the world accompanied by a worldlessness with respect to values. If we cannot speak of what is of value or if our speaking of value is vacuous, and if our concern over value is a matter of private revelation which, even if granted, has no bearing on the world, then the crude result in the realm of action is the law of the jungle. *In* the world of human agency there would be no mystery—everyone would be right; and there would be no mediative communication about what we do not know but invoke in faith—only either the assertion of our right, if need be, with might, or else the role of the uncomprehending bystander who is in the end overwhelmed by a world for which he is not at all responsible.

In the earliest of Jaspers's philosophical writings (1919) we can already find his contraposition of positivism and mysticism with philosophy as the way of mediation. At the center of his treatment stands the awareness of mystery. The positivist is characterized as "amystical" and therefore, "necessarily uncreative," a success under circumstances which are intellectually commensurable, a failure when his humanity is taxed to an extent where he has to tap unknown resources.[77] Admired in the person of Lao Tsu or Plotinus, abhorred in the form of "stupid Indian asceticism or dense Mount Athos monasticism," mysticism is for the young Jaspers already essentially a "vacuous anticipation of that which stands at the end of an infinite path." He sees its positive significance, however, in its function as guardian against finite objectification into which synthetic thought tends to slip.[78] The idea of faith, philosophically considered, is not yet strongly articulated in this early work. However, it is clearly adumbrated.[79] He speaks of the mystical as postulated and as being realizable only at the completion of an endless process of bringing "presuppositions" to bear on the concreteness of the experienced world, presuppositions which are articulations of "ideas." Characteristically Jaspers presents this view of philosophy vis-à-vis positivism and mysticism in connection with an interpretation of Kant, contraposing him to Plotinus as the representative of mysticism. Thus, for example,

> Plotinus is in immediate union with the absolute; Kant is ever removed from the unreachable absolute to which he is related as direction, as task and as meaning, but with which he is never united.[80]

As if to underscore his relationship to Kant from the earliest time, Jaspers appended to this work (epoch-making in being the first of a group of works which, together with those of Barth,

Rosenzweig, Buber, Marcel and Heidegger, inaugurated modern existential philosophy) a seminar paper which he wrote while still a student on the topic of Kant's Doctrine of Ideas. The relationship to Kant which Jaspers expresses in this early work persists in his more mature and in his later works. It issues, as we have seen, in a conception of philosophical thought as critical explication of faith. As such it stands in critical conflict not only with positivism and mysticism, particularly in the form of revealed religion, but also with traditional metaphysics.

Chapter Three

The Actuality of Faith

The different distinctions which we find in Jaspers's writings show us where faith cannot be found, where it is possible, and indicate where it is actual. Faith cannot be found where thinking is naive, where all objects of thought are of equal value, where the distinction is not made between the empirically real and transcendentally problematical, the intellectually determinable and indeterminable, the world and the extramundane. But even where such critical distinctions are made, faith is not possible where, by some absolutization of the intellectually determinable, any possible concern over questions transcending the mundane understanding is gainsaid. We also cannot speak of faith where thought, directed beyond the understanding of the intellect, is fulfilled in mystic union, or is misguided in superstitious or gnostic concretion of the transcendent. But faith is also not simply given to man together with a possible concern over truth trancending the understanding of the intellect. It all depends how this possibility is actualized. Thought directed toward such concern but fulfilled in mystic union is not faith.

Art, according to Jaspers, is a step removed from mysticism, but is not faith. Art and its contemplation is not mysticism because its perfection is not fulfillment but the fanciful creation of possibilities of transcendental visions; the work of art is interposed between self and the transcendent object. But art is also not the actuality of faith. For in the contemplation of art, man is removed from the concreteness of his temporality, confronted with possibilities of transcendent truths which as such are not responsive to the vicissitudes of his situation and which therefore neither guide him, nor oblige him, nor incite him to decision.

Faith is an actuality only for the person singularly existing in his mundane situation. Man as *Dasein*, as merely mundane being, does not ask "why" and "whither." Only where the world as "being as it is" (Wittgenstein) is insufficient can there be faith. As intellect or "consciousness-as-such" one man is like another, representing what is objective and conditionally certain for anyone. Only insofar as man is more than can be known of him, only where man can risk his being for certainties which are not verifiable can we speak of faith. In mystic union with transcendence man is devoid of self and of the concreteness of his mundane existence. Only where man does not anticipate the end of time but grasps time as the condition of his existence can we speak of faith. In contemplation of art, man is removed from the earnestness of situation, choice, risk and action. Only where possibilities are anchored in existence can one speak of faith. Accordingly, Jaspers speaks of the actuality of faith in terms of existential certainty of being, unconditionality, historicity and agency.

Faith is the *fundamental certainty of being* on the part of the self existing in its situation and time. It is manifest in thought. All thought requires for its fulfillment in truth something other than thought. Empirical thought gains its truth in its reference to sensuous perception. Also, the certainty of empirical thought and of all determinate thought is founded on conditions. Thought which is the expression of faith is different. It also requires an other for its truth, namely the existing self, which illumines its faith by means of thought. But such thought is 'objectively' unfounded; it expresses the existential awareness of unconditioned truth intimated at the limits of determinate knowledge. Such *unconditioned truth* is the condition for all conditional truth, and the unconditional certainty of faith is the condition for all other certainty, for cognitive and ethical certainty. Faith, then, is the original certainty of being which is the indeterminate source of certainty concerning all other beings and modes of being. Thus faith is also the motive force and task master of thought. That the self turns toward being and how being appears to it accords with its faith. For this reason Jaspers ascribes to Existenz the proposition "faith is being."[1]

The certainty of being is an expression of one's irreducible selfhood, independent of other beings. Imbued with this certainty, one is also provided with the freedom to risk being with other beings. One cannot will such certainty; all willing springs from it.

Faith, viewed as fundamental certainty of being, is expressed in the form of *convictions*. We have already seen that for Jaspers conviction is a form of certainty which is distinct from but correlative with that of cogency. The truth which is cogent can be "proven and elicited." The truth of conviction cannot; it is "lived and shared." No one is singularly responsible for cogent truth. Convictions, on the other hand, are true by risking one's being for them. Hence we can say that a person's actuality is identical with his convictions. A person is what he believes, what he stands for. "If someone did not have any convictions, he would, as it were, not be there."[2] The correspondences which serve as criteria of cogency are not available as tests of the truth of conviction. We may speak of the correspondence between the expression of conviction in "speech, deed and life" with "Existenz . . . ideas . . . transcendence." But this cannot be taken literally or objectively ascertained, because the latter terms of the putative correspondence are, in principle, indeterminate. The ascertainment of the truth or untruth of convictions is a matter of inwardness; but inwardly it is inescapable.[3] The correlativity of cogency and conviction manifests itself and can be characterized in many ways, as we have seen on several occasions. Fundamentally, the relentless pursuit of cogent, scientific truth has its origin in a faith; and it is, in turn, the condition for the illumination of the truth of faith. Only in distinction from objective knowledge can the unconditional and historic character of the conviction of faith become clear.

The unconditionality of faith signifies the freedom of the self in its relation to the world. The self, insofar as it realizes itself as being more than its worldly being, is independent of the world. And insofar as it realizes its essential selfhood in the world, it is a free agent. The vicissitudes of his situation have certain claims on man which impose conditions on his cognitive and ethical agency. But not all demands are conditional. Beyond acceding to the mundane being as I find myself to be, psychologically, culturally, biologically, beyond yielding to the demands of my mundane situation, I am as I choose myself to be, I shape the world as it ought to be, I am guided by the demands which intimate themselves beyond all conditions and considerations of purposes and desires, and participate in the indeterminate ground of being whence springs the demand to be myself. Thus the unconditionality of faith is also the source of steadfastness, of fidelity, and of loyalty. For whatever is conditional can change, and whoever changes conditionally is in bondage, or fickle. In this way, Jaspers says,

> unconditionality consists of the resolution of an Existenz which has passed through reflection. This means that unconditionality does not arise from reality as it happens to be but from freedom, a freedom which cannot do otherwise—not because of natural law but by virtue of its transcendent ground.[4]

In the actuality of faith the freely invoked guidance by the transcendent ground is historic. According to Jaspers, if we may alter a Wittgensteinian sentence, God reveals himself only *in* the world. I am independent vis-à-vis the world only in the world. And this independence is concrete in my active involvement in the world. We are not surprised to find such paradoxical characterizations of the *historicity* of faith in Jaspers. In Jaspers, as in Kierkegaard's

The Sickness Unto Death, historicity is the indication of the paradoxical character of human existence as self. In the actuality of
faith the self participates in eternity—but only if he attains it ever
anew in time.[5]
   In faith the self attains a fundamental certainty from which
spring all other certainties—but only if this certainty is cognitively
questionable and without the guarantee of authority. Faith is absolute for the self—but only if relativised by the actuality of faiths
of other selves. In faith the self is imbued with fundamental
truth—but only if it vouches for this truth with its own being, in
deed and at the risk of failure. In faith absolute truth intimates
itself in answer to the questions which arise at the limits of knowledge—but only if the self formulates these answers and is the carrier of their truth. Thus, for Jaspers, the truth of faith is both giv-
en and created.[6] The certainty of faith is not constituted by possession or conclusion but by the search and risk which it makes
possible.
   But, above all, the historicity of faith is expressed when in and
against the world the openness for possibilities is maintained in
situations whose realities speak against all possibilities. Consider,
for example, the situation of the young Jews in the Warsaw
Ghetto in 1941 and 1942. They were an "assimilated" generation,
not more, if at all, devoted to the faith of their fathers than to
partaking, with vigor, ability and ambition, of the possibilities
offered by modern, secular life. This effort was increasingly frus-
trated by the anti-Semitic excesses of the new Polish state. Then
came Hitler's armies and executioners. They were herded together
in the Ghetto in conditions designed to kill the human being—who
lives, in the face of threatening actuality, by grasping at possibility—before exterminating him biologically. There, in the depth of
despair, never before imagined, for which none could be prepared,
in a moment when the world was in need of redemption if ever it
had been and where no redeemer came, there this young generation of assimilated Jews in the face of death escaped their assassins
by singing a song. For its text they harked back to the Jewish lit-
urgy and, ultimately, to Maimonides: "I believe with firm faith in
the coming of the messiah, and though he tarry, yet I believe."
Thus in defiance of grimmest realities they gave most powerful
testimony to the possibilities of man and his dignity when mundane forces would deny them. The historicity of faith in such ultimate situations, which challenge selfhood as they test faith, can
also be characterized in paradoxical phrases. It is tragic consciousness without despair; it is the power to endure and the power of

patience in the face of forces and prospects of destruction; it is hope without illusion. In Jaspers's words,

> While the consequences of knowledge would have to make living impossible, faith is the ability to live in knowledge.[7] As mundane beings we seek surety; we despair of impossibility. Faith is able to forego surety in the realm of appearances. In all danger it keeps a fast hold on possibility; in the world it knows neither surety nor impossibility.[8]

Jaspers's characterization of faith as radically historic is a reverberation of ancient insights into an apparently fundamental existential actuality. We recognize in it Job's response to the message of calamity and the rebuke of his wife. We see reflected in it the test of Abraham and of Socrates, Abraham of the episode of Isaac's sacrifice and Socrates of the *Crito*. We hear in it the words of the hermit about Confucius: Is that not the man who knows that it won't work and yet goes on?[9]

The actuality of faith, as the risk of being in time, means *being active*. We have already mentioned that, in Jaspers's analysis, the truth of faith as expressed in convictions can be ascertained only by the inner sincerity of conscience. This, however, must not be understood to mean that one can assent in the manner of a proposition to what one has faith in. For Jaspers this is amiss for many reasons. For one thing, the content of a statement of faith cannot be ascertained by the methods of discursive reasoning. The formulation of faith is never appropriately literal and always tenuous. Thus, for example, formulations in the manner of articles of faith, or assent in the manner of confession to a creed are specious. Thought-formulations, in their transtemporality, require evidence for their truth. But the evidence of the truth of faith rests on the self in its temporality. The truth of its faith is not confirmed with finality until the end of time. But to be a being in time does not mean passively passing through time or lazily loitering in time, and in this way to remain possible and to miss being actual Existenz. The actuality of faith demands actual Existenz. The faith of a possible self is, at worst, lip-service or, at best, readiness. To exist as being in time means that, with respect to the sincerity of one's faith, one is constantly in the court of one's conscience. For how one has lived and acted out of one's faith is, indeed, a question of conscience. But the judgment is inconclusive for two reasons. On the one hand actual existence is existence in the present moment. One's past loyalty does not detract from the ever new, ever original moment; nor does it mitigate the earnestness of the decision by which one's selfhood and the truth of its faith hang in the balance. Essentially, the proof of one's faith is now and yet to come. Hence, Jaspers maintains that "if one is sincere, one does not know *whether* one believes."[10] On the other hand, for this reason and for others already mentioned, one does not know *what* one believes. To know this would be an anticipation of the end of time. Hence, though in time one is the instance of judgment concerning one's own sincerity, one is not an absolute instance. Sincerity impels the test and proof of faith in activity as constitutive of temporal being. For the actuality of faith and for faithful activity, Jaspers holds,

> the inner test, the last instance is itself still on the way, and incompletable. Believing and acting I must decide in every essential moment and yet keep myself on trial into infinity.[11]

"I have run my race, I have preserved the faith," writes Paul to Timothy. Happy the man who with pious pride can say this! But from a philosophical clarification of faith, such as Jaspers's, this passage must be taken as the yearning for fulfillment and the extinction of time, as is suggested by the next verse.[12] In time and only there can faith be an actuality. And no one existing in time has run his race. Hence no one who carries the burden of time can pride himself in having kept the faith. The race goes on; to preserve the faith the effort must go on unabated. Plato uses the image of the shadowy existence in the cave. If there are any who have seen the light which is the source of the play of shadows, their duty is to return and to bring what they have seen to bear on the task of promoting order and well-being.

Certain concepts are usually associated with faith, namely love, hope, despair and private legality. Let us look at Jaspers's treatment of these associations. Treatises on the many aspects of love occur in all major works of Jaspers. In ever new variations he circumscribes what, according to him, defies definition or demonstration except in its sexual and erotic phase and its matrimonial manifestation. For our present purpose it signifies an aspect of the fundamental certainty of being. To love means to affirm being—the being of an other, to affirm it unconditionally, i.e., as being, and to affirm it without reservation as issuing—like oneself—from the ground of all being.[13] Faith and love are two aspects of the certainty of being. But faith is explicit in its consciousness and activity.[14] Love, on the other hand, is the well-spring and confirmation of faith.[15] Love, we must conclude, is, for Jaspers, more basic. And there is ample evidence for this. For example, in *Von der Wahrheit* he shows that where faith fails, sexuality, as the minimum of love, can remain as the last vehicle of a modicum of affirmation. For Jaspers, as for Plato, there is no love in any larger sense without sexuality. In sexuality, he says, there can be "a remnant, satisfying actuality in the blood-hot nearness of a human being to another,"[16] words akin to those Odysseus speaks to the gentle Negro fisherboy in Kazantzakis's *Sequel* to the Odyssey:

> but I love man's sad flesh, his mind, his stench,
>   his teeth,
>   the mud-soaked loam I tread upon, the sweat I spout.[17]

The underlying faithlessness becomes fully explicit upon "weariness and despair of sexuality."[18]

Another example can be found in one of the lectures of Jaspers's television series of 1964 in which he discusses Paul's discourse on love and the famous words, "So faith, hope and love endure. These are the great three, and the greatest of them is love."[19] Without claiming that his understanding of this passage is theologically orthodox he interprets it as follows:

> A faith in the manner of a credo becomes doubtful. Hope reaches boundaries in this world against which it shatters. Love alone sustains us. In our love we experience the singular certainty that fills us and suffices. Only for love does the full truth dawn. It will not be dimmed by objective credos and by hope of another world.[20]

However we must be cautious. Love, though a more fundamental manifestation of certainty of being, is blind without the consciousness of faith. Only faith can translate the affirmation of being from dark passion to ordering activity.[21]

Faith ought not to be confused with what Jaspers calls "private legality" (*Eigengesetzlichkeit*). In both cases we can speak of autonomy. But with regard to faith, it is the autonomy of a self in its singularity which freely chooses its being. With regard to private legality, it is the autonomy of a realm of human enterprise whose characteristic and rules are educed from its posited self-value. Jaspers gives some examples of realms of private legality: science, morality, religion, art, politics, the economy, the erotic.[22] The difference, however, is not sufficiently clarified by this distinction between personal singularity and suprapersonal, communal enterprise because these spheres, by virtue of their private legality, are deemed to have claims upon the person. But the suppositional self-value of these spheres is supported by their precipitation as institutions, cultural goods and traditions which seem to be self-perpetuating actualities sweeping the individual along, or leaving him by the wayside, as the case may be. Moreover, each sphere is, from its own position, absolute, and the other, therefore, relative to and subsumed under it. Or else we may arrange a hierarchy amongst privately legal spheres. These characterizations indicate the difference between private legality and faith. The claims which the self-legality of those spheres have upon us we can accept or reject. Thus, private legality, absolute in itself, is relative to us; it does not become absolute by our commitment to it. Also, the absoluteness of the private legality of a realm can be intellectually grasped, studied and ordered; it is subject to conditional cognition. On both counts private legality is conditional in its absoluteness. The absoluteness of faith is unconditional. Faith is original for this singular person. Unlike the private legality of a realm of human enterprise, it cannot be subsumed, arranged, played off against another, purposefully used, or left to fade away for lack of commitment or participation. All these things can happen to privately legal realms because they are animated by the commitment and participation which, if they are genuine, are engendered by faith. Faith, in turn, gains content, and with it actuality, by its precipitation in the form of a privately legal realm and its requirements. We have already seen that, for Jaspers, the clash between realms, each with its own laws and 'oughts' is, in the end, the foreground of a more profound struggle between faiths. Hence he can say that

no existential force springs from the autonomy of private legalities. [But] they are capable of becoming instruments of any faith. In the case of genuine combat it is not private legality which is aligned against faith, but faith against faith.[23]

Chapter Four

Faith versus Faith

i. One Truth or Many Truths?

A conception of faith which stresses the historicity of faith leads
to the problem of the oneness of truth. Jaspers, as we shall see,
comes to terms with this problem by conceiving the human concern with truth as a struggle whose most eminent form is communication.

The actuality of the problem of the oneness of ultimate truth
can be indicated in many ways. First of all, in perusing the history
of thought, we can see the multiplicity and conflict of ultimate
positions. It is as if the diversity of visions of the one truth belies
the oneness of truth. Let us consider the following consequence of
the distinction between evidential knowledge and faith which we
discussed in chapter 1: cognitive evidence is universally valid. In
practice this means that it is valid for all; its certainty is compelling. But where objective validity and cogency are absent, we can
speak of truth only as being subjectively valid, validated at the risk
of self, and privately certain. While evidentially justified agreement
is the essence of evidential knowledge, the truth of faith cannot
claim recourse to such means of agreement. It seems to follow that
there are as many truths as there are selves. And this is borne out
finally by the perennial collisions of faiths in everyday disagreements and in the larger confrontations of a political, religious and
spiritual nature.

The thought might insinuate itself that truth is not one truth but
many truths. Opposing this suggestion, Jaspers maintains the
meaningfulness and asserts the inevitability of the notion of the
oneness of Being and of the truth of Being. The mind, in grasping
truths and in distinguishing modes of truth, finds their indifferent
juxtaposition repugnant. It will search for their relations, for the
unity behind their apparent irreconcilabilities, for the order among
them.[1] The most informed awareness of the fragmented character
of reality will not quash the concern over the oneness of Being. As
Jaspers sees it, the choice is not between unity and disunity but
between different ways of grasping unity.

All depends now on two things which, in Jaspers's treatment, are
closely connected. First, there is the question of whether true unity is upheld or whether a mode of being is, by a process of absolutization, taken as Being in its oneness. Secondly, there is the question of whether or not the historicity of the seeker of unity is duly
regarded, and, if it is, what consequence is drawn from it. We disregard historicity, for example, if we consider that man's insight
into Being can be completed. But no truth, however extensive, is
completable if disclosed within the confines of time. Any mode of
Being transcends and encompasses the truth disclosed with respect
to it. And the unity of Being encompassing all modes of Being is
absolutely transcendent. To posit anything man has thought or
realized as the ultimate unity of truth is an anticipation in time of
what transcends time, and thereby a loss of the looked-for unity.
Thus the distinction of meanings of truth and of modes of Being,
and the resultant realization of the fragmentation of Being as it
confronts man is, for Jaspers, a necessary function of what, without doubt, is the main task of the second of his two main works,
i.e., the immense *Von der Wahrheit (Of Truth)*, namely the re-
opening of the question of Being and the oneness of truth in consideration of the historicity of man.

This question is not to be taken as purely theoretical. As such it
would lose its significance. For then either the question of the
oneness of truth would soon be seen to be insoluble, and thus
meaningless. Positivistic philosophies have run on this tack. Or else
the one truth is many. But this is contradictory and the end of all
truth. Or else a comprehensive synthesis might be envisaged or
even attempted. But this is utopian, unrealizable for a mind thinking in time and, hence, indifferent, i.e., merely 'theoretical'. Philosophy will disregard Kierkegaard's cutting comment on the 'system' at the peril of critical thought:

> A thinker erects an immense building, a system, a system
> which embraces the whole of existence and world-history,
> etc.—and if we contemplate his personal life, we discover to
> our astonishment this terrible and ludicrous fact, that he him-
> self personally does not live in this immense high-vaulted pal-
> ace, but in a dog kennel, or at the most in the porter's lodge. If
> one were to take the liberty of calling his attention to this by a
> single word, he would be offended. For he has no fear of being
> under a delusion, if only he can get the system completed . . .
> by means of the delusion.[2]

As is suggested by this passage, the theoretical question of the oneness of truth, posed with due regard for the historicity of man, requires the ground of selfhood. For, in the end, it is only the existing self which can be said to be historic. The existing self's concern over oneness provides the exigency for the theoretical question and, in this way, animates it. The theoretical question is the articulation and the vehicle of this concern.

In Jaspers's view, whether man's selfhood is actualized or remains a mere possibility depends on whether or nor he directs himself toward oneness. Let us suppose that the multiplicity of man's pursuits, of modes of truth which are disclosed to him, and of claims upon him, were not founded on an ultimate, though transcendent, oneness. Then all would be relative and nothing absolute. All would be conditional and nothing unconditional.

If there were no absolute, there would be no source of meaningfulness by which to educe ideas of completeness to measure the worth of things. Decisions would be tenuous or made according to whim, and actions would be of a merely transient significance. The cogency of obligation and of the deliberate choice of one's destiny would be absent. In Jaspers's words:

> If all might have been different, then I am not myself. If I want everything, I want nothing; if I experience everything, I dissipate in the endless without reaching Being.[3]

If beings, in their multiplicity, did not participate in an unconditioned ground of being—conceivable only as one, then, insofar as beings stand in mutual relationship, all would be conditioned. Since this includes human actions and choice, there would be no freedom. Absolute conditionality means absolute dependence. We can speak of the mutual independence of limited beings only if they partake of a source of being which is one and unconditioned. Without this oneness, all independence would be relative. For the self, as limited being, cannot be conceived as the absolute source of its own being. The conception of its freedom vis-à-vis other limited beings requires that its being be not exclusively thought of as conditional upon other limited beings but that, by virtue of its conscious participation in the one, unconditioned source of being, it be a factor in deciding its own being.[4] Only rootedness in the unconditioned ground of all that is conditional breaks the limitation upon possibility which is the essence of conditionality. In this way, direction toward oneness is the presupposition of freedom. And, since for Jaspers freedom, as its main mark, is synonymous with selfhood, we can say: no oneness, no selfhood. Again, in his words,

> Unconditionality of action becomes perceivable through the
> identity of selfhood with the One which it grasps in empirical
> existence (*Dasein*).[5]

We see that for Jaspers the question of the oneness of truth,
insoluble or indifferent as a merely theoretical concern, obtains its
urgency and significance as an existential concern. With this in
mind, Jaspers comes to terms with the difficulty contained in the
seemingly inevitable conclusion that if the oneness of truth is a
matter of historicity, it is likely that there are as many 'one'
truths as there are selves. This difficulty is obviated if we draw the
full consequence from the distinction between facing a question
such as that of oneness in a purely theoretical manner, or facing it
as an existential problem which is articulated theoretically. In this
connection Jaspers relies on a presupposition which pervades all of
his thinking, namely, the age-old distinction between being and its
appearance, particularly as clarified by Kant. Accordingly we can
speak of the multiplicity of oneness only in its appearance—but
not for the existing self. This self, obtaining its existence by its
truth, testifying to its truth by its very being, is identical with its
truth. The 'theoretical' objectification of its truth is mere appearance—but not the existing reality of this truth.

It serves many purposes. By means of this objectification, the
self articulates its truth, communicates with other similarly articulating selves, clarifies it by exposing it to challenge, and confesses
either to the truth, or to its own failings with the truth as its measure, or even to its own failure to soundly grasp the truth at all.
The objectification of its truth is more than mere appearance if
the self identifies with it by being responsible for it, or if, in the
challenge of its objectified truth, it recognizes a threat to its own
existence, or in the acknowledgement of its objectified truth, a
confirmation of its own being.

Only apart from the identification of selves with their truth can
we speak of the multiplicity of truth. Stated succinctly: for the
radical reality of existing selfhood there is but one truth; only in
the objectification which is abstracted from it do there appear to
be many truths. The self can be itself, i.e., the truth with which it
is identical can be its only truth, only if the truth is one. The self
therefore can speak of there being many truths only if its truth is
one amongst the many. But it can be one amongst many truths
only in its appearance. Its truth can appear to the self, i.e., it can
be mere appearance only if the self does not identify itself with
this truth, that is, if it steps outside of the truth by virtue of which
it is itself. But such a self would not just be beside itself; it would

be a disembodied, non-existent self. Hence, while theoretically it is indeed possible to say there are many truths, existentially it is impossible to say this.[6]

Can we then say that there is only one truth? Yes, if we mean the truth in its encompassing transcendence by which we gain our freedom and become ourselves in directing ourselves towards it. No, if we mean the realization of this truth by the historic self. For the truth in its encompassing oneness transcends time; but in its realization by the self it is, like the self, historic, that is, bounded by time. Therefore, if we view the problem of the oneness of truth from the historicity of an existential concern, we can neither say that there are many truths nor that there is one truth. This seems to be contradictory, but it is not. It means that no historic realization of the one truth can take the place of the truth in its transhistoric comprehensiveness. If there were many truths, then, as we have seen, the self would be nothing. If the self's truth were the only truth, then the self would be everything, and man would be God.

But "ich bin nicht alles," "I am not all," is a constant refrain in Jaspers's work. Where Being is actualized in time and in mundane existence, it must appear restricted. To be in time means for the self to partake of Being and not to be all of Being. The decision to be a self in time means to be determined by one's faith, to formulate it in ideas, to express it in convictions, and to testify to it by one's acts.[7] The form which a self's directedness toward oneness takes and whereby it exists as self is absolute for that self. It has no choice between alternative truths; if there is a choice at all, it is one between being oneself and not being oneself.[8] But what is absolute for a historic self as the ground of its selfhood is not universally absolute. Faith, as we have seen, does not have recourse to the methods of universal agreement.

ii. The Struggle of Communication

What, then, is the relationship between men with respect to transcognitive matters, i.e., matters of faith? Fundamentally, according to Jaspers, they are locked in a struggle of faith versus faith. The question now is whether it is a loving struggle or one fought out of hate, whether or not the transcendent unity is upheld toward which all ought to be directed and in which all may partake; and, if so, whether unity is maintained by authority or upheld by the reign of reason. The ideal of the former is catholicity, the ideal of the latter is communication.

The struggle of faith against faith differs from other forms of struggle, particularly from that for mundane existence. Some prominent features of the latter follow.[9] The motivation is to secure and increase material benefits and to maintain life. The associations in it are partisan. Its outcome is victory for an individual or a party, which means defeat, or subjection, or destruction for another individual, party, or state. Possession and gain are possible only by depriving others. Subtle or brute force is the pervasive characteristic of this form of struggle, power its most eminent means. Abstention from the struggle means self-destruction.

A form of struggle which dispenses with force but still is distinct from the existential struggle which we wish to characterize is the spiritual contest. Its means are "creation and achievement," its outcome "rank and influence." While the spiritual life can civilize and bring order to the struggle for mundane life, it would be a perversion of the spiritual contest if its achievement were to be measured by the material gain of the spiritual creator or the deprivation of others to which his material gain inevitably leads.[10] The appropriate benefit which may accrue from success in a spiritual contest is recognition.

The struggle of faith against faith is neither the struggle for mundane survival and success, nor the vying for spiritual excellence. Rather, it is the struggle to realize oneself by existing in accordance with the truth upon which one grounds oneself; hence, it is a struggle for the truth itself. For, in time, the truth does not reveal itself immediately and as it is in itself. In time, the patency of truth requires that it be freely and actively disclosed by man and that it appear in man's words and deeds. The process of self-realization mediates the appearance of truth in time. Accordingly, this process, which Jaspers views as a struggle for self and truth, is as much a struggle with oneself as with other selves. In one's struggle with oneself one "quashes possibilities, prevails over impulses, shapes one's capacities, and questions what one has become"; above all, one remains "aware that one's being is not a possession" but a continuous task.[11]

The struggle for existing selfhood and truth reaches its appropriate profundity in the confrontation of self and self, of faith and faith. The characteristics appropriate to this struggle must reflect the following three factors. First, the appearance of truth in time depends on the decision on the part of a self what form this appearance takes. Secondly, the self gains its being by that decision insofar as it is an unconditionally free decision. Thirdly, the truth in its absolute unity transcends its appearance for each historic self. Accordingly, the two salient features of this struggle are, on the one hand, the combatants' equality of level vis-à-vis the truth which, in its encompassing unity, transcends both; and on the other hand, the absence of reserve on the part of each in confrontation with the other. The struggle ensues when man shows his mettle, when the self, and thus the truth as envisaged by it, appear in the concreteness of its actions and its spoken thought, and, having appeared, are challenged by other selves similarly appearing and by the truth which they thereby decide. But the struggle reaches its highest pitch when it is carried out deliberately and with clarity and within the limited sphere of one person with another. Force is absent and so is spiritual ascendancy; instead there is unreserved exposure of self to the unrelenting challenge of the other, the relentless questioning of the other, and the unwavering response to the other's questioning. The aim is not victory or defeat but a more profound realization of the truth through the realization of a self which grounds itself in this truth and which, in its temporal limitation, exists together with other selves similarly grounded and similarly limited. In Jaspers's words,

> The struggle is directed toward the ultimate unrevealed meaning in its origin and goal, yet in such a manner that it takes place in situations and tasks of the moment; thus the concrete present is its arena, and the least concern is not too insignificant for it.[12]

Such absence of reserve is, of course, possible only under the mutual presupposition that the other is a possible self, i.e., that he is grounded in truth, that he seeks to realize a vision of truth which, though it be different from one's own vision of truth, partakes, like one's own vision of truth, of the transcendent, encompassing truth in its unity. It is possible only if it results in a "solidarity" of seekers of truth.

The struggle for self and truth can, for Jaspers, only be a "loving struggle," even if carried out between combatants of diametrically opposed visions of truth. One recognizes, according to Jaspers, a spark of truth in the other as long as his vision is recognized as questioning one's own. A man who fails to recognize a minimum of truth in another fails to acknowledge his selfhood. The struggle for truth in time then ceases, for the struggle is for one's own selfhood together with that of the other. Where the struggle for truth and selfhood ceases or is absent, the relation between men is either an unconcerned, mutually indifferent and fruitless coexistence, or a struggle whose outcome is advantage, domination or annihilation.

The genuine struggle, for Jaspers, is a struggle of faith against faith. All other struggles are conditional and relative.[13] Faith is the certainty of Being and a vision of truth upon which one grounds one's selfhood unconditionally. But the proper expression of faith is not the formal confession; rather it is the concrete action which this faith makes possible. And this action of word and deed forms the content of communication between selves.

iii. Tolerance and Historicity

'Communication' is Jaspers's well-known conception of the 'loving struggle' between selves, of their meeting ground, of the arena of their appearance, and of the different modes of their relation. The notion of communication lies at the heart of Jaspers's conception of the concern over truth and of the philosophical enterprise. It is one of Jaspers's particularly attractive notions and has gained wide currency. This has resulted in some misunderstandings which prove to be instructive. Bultmann, for example, commences his "reply" in the famous demythologising controversy with the accusation that Jaspers's critique of his efforts hardly displayed the spirit of genuine communication.[14] It is not surprising to find a reply to the accusation in Jaspers's "rejoinder" which borders on lamentation: "You know very well that this judgment is a blow at the very heart of my philosophy."[15] More to the point, he indicates that communication can take many forms and use many methods. These include "radical characterization" of the opponent's standpoint, "energetic judgments," and certainly also sharp critique. For, as we have seen, only by taking the other seriously as self grounded in his truth can I provoke critical examination and thereby critical self-reexamination. If the concern over truth in time is a struggle, then it is a betrayal of truth not to join in the battle when the occasion arises, to miss the moment of truth, to make it easy for myself or the other, or to expect it to be made easy for me. All this, of course, with the proviso that the battle is a genuine battle, is a genuine struggle for the truth, and not a covert process of denying the other and his truth.

Intolerance, indifference, refusal to join in battle, silent tolerance are all perversions of the combative character of man's way to truth. *Intolerance* rests primarily on the confusion of faith and cognitive objectivity. If I deny the truth in the faith of another, while considering mine to be valid for all, I deny at the same time the historicity of faith. I thereby confess to the weakness of my faith. I require for its truth general agreement, the absence of challenge by other faiths, and dare not testify to it with my own being.[16] *Indifference* may be confused with genuine tolerance until it reaches its limit. It turns into intolerance and forceful opposition when the other seems troublesome or disturbing. In no case is the other taken seriously or as a challenge to my being.[17] *Refusal* to join in battle may be based upon my putative communication with God.[18] Fritz Kaufmann, in his elaborate and in many ways profound contribution to the Schilpp volume on Jaspers, seeks to extend Jaspers's notion of communication in this as well as in some other directions. However, in response Jaspers maintains that "because real communication takes place only between men and in its ultimate meaning rests upon faith . . . we can speak of all other kinds of communication only allegorically, inasmuch as they are carried on by us onesidedly."[19] The refusal to join in battle, and *silent tolerance*—which may be a fruitful expedient in political life—fail to affirm the historicity of truth which is the mark of true tolerance.

For Jaspers, true *tolerance* necessarily means abstaining from identifying the one truth which is absolute for me with the one truth which is absolutely absolute, and hence, it is an abstention from requiring that what is true for me be binding on all. It expresses the restriction on the part of the self in time to its historic vision of the truth by which it gains its selfhood, and to its communicative solidarity with other selves who are similarly restricted to historic visions of truth which may be other than one's own. *A fortiori*, tolerance presupposes the transcendence of truth in its unity of which we may partake, each according to his unique historic restriction. Encomia of tolerance occur often in Jaspers's works, particularly in politically relevant ways.[20] Thus he responds sharply to Karl Barth's mockery of his notion of transcendence and its consequent requirement of tolerance. Barth says with implied reference to Jaspers:

> "Transcendence" can indeed mean nothing else, nothing more definite, than that . . . ahead of the human act lies something open, some abyss which man . . . is destined to tumble into. And the somewhat arid commandment of tolerance, i.e., of . . . refraining from all positive statements on its possible contents or directives, seems to be the one comparatively sure thing to be derived from a contemplation of this spectre.[21]

Jaspers responds as follows:

> On the soil of faith in revelation, it would appear, no under-
> standing of the "somewhat arid commandment of tolerance"
> can grow. It is truly not arid.
>   In politics it is the basis of rights and duties that we, today,
> are infinitely grateful to live by. It is the most magnificent
> human victory over the inhuman faith in ecclesiastic dogmas
> which marked the time of the religious wars. It still inspires us
> to think historically of the period of the Reformation and its
> consequences, that witches' sabbath into which the struggle in
> the realm of ciphers had turned, and to hear the men whose
> valour and whose sacrifices blazed the trail of tolerance in
> those days. . . .
>   Inwardly, however, tolerance is the essential expression of
> the will to communicate. There, mere toleration—which is
> meaningful and is attainable in politics—would be an insult;
> the essence of this tolerance lies in receptiveness, in concern,
> in acknowledgement. It could be "arid" only on the premise
> that the theologically interpreted faith in revelation alone is
> not arid. Tolerance does not spring from the contemplation of
> a spectre. . . .
>   But why this talk about a "spectre"? . . . Where do we end
> up if on the crucial existential issue we berate each other as
> spiritualists?[22]

Tolerance, like the faith from which it issues, is active or else it
is not at all. Our historic visions of the truth are proximate and
many. But these proximate visions must not block the view of the
one truth which remains distant. For Jaspers it is precisely the
most intensive realization of the one truth as transcendent which
makes possible the realization of truth in time by and through the
self with other selves. "True Existenz," Jaspers says,

> cannot lose sight of the far God above the near one. Even in
> opposition it is willing to see the God-relatedness of the other.
> God is my God as well as that of the enemy. Tolerance be-
> comes positive in the unrestricted will to communication.[23]

In this connection it is instructive to take note of another criticism which is offered by the theologian and philosopher Paul
Ricoeur. The book *Karl Jaspers et la philosophie de l'existence*
which he and his co-author Mikel Dufrenne brought out shortly
after the second World War, having written it during their German
imprisonment, established Jaspers's reputation in France. It is primarily a conscientious account of Jaspers's three-volume work

Philosophie, followed by about seventy pages of astute and interesting criticisms. Among these, in a chapter dealing with the question of religious conciliation, we find the following:

> The believer can share the atheist's suspicion that Jaspers, in
> spite of himself, subverted the idea of transcendence together
> with that of God. The philosopher who both unmasks myths
> and courts them is altogether nothing other than a Don Juan
> of religion who, having wanted to embrace "the world of
> ciphers"--from the myths of Karma, to the paintings of van
> Gogh, in passing also the trinitarian theology, has lost the con-
> fines of existence as well as the intensity of faith. . . . He [the
> believer] thinks that an integral philosophy of existence in the
> world and under God is not possible except under the aspect
> of a particular conciliation which is the essence of religion.[24]

The accusation of Don Juanism of faith is reiterated five years
later. This time it is presented solely under Ricoeur's name and is
based on a study of both main works of Jaspers, the *Philosophie* as
before, and *Von der Wahrheit*, which had been published in the
meantime. However, this second time the accusation is mitigated
somewhat by being presented as a strong possibility of Jaspers's
thinking rather than an actuality as heretofore:

> And how can the myth, once unmasked as myth, remain for
> the philosopher the "unique universal" (*das Einzigallgemeine*)
> in which is expressed the hidden divinity, if one of these
> myths does not, in the form of revelation, take them out of
> their discordant relationships and re-order them through a
> pronouncement to the philosopher which would simulta-
> neously heal him of his very vanity? Does not the philosopher
> run the risk of losing the "narrowness" and the "commit-
> ment" of Existenz when he embraces the *totality* of myths—
> those of Greece, those of India, those of Christianity—like a
> Don Juan courting all the gods?[25]

We shall have occasion to speak of the concept of 'cipher'. At
present we are concerned with Jaspers's conception of the historicity of faith. In this regard Ricoeur's accusation of Don Juanism is
of clarifying relevance. What is the meaning of this accusation? It
means that according to Ricoeur, Jaspers's conception of the historicity of faith precludes the earnest commitment of a faith
above all other possible faiths, a commitment which, in the end,
would have to render all the other faiths impossible. In a manner
reminiscent of the hero of the legend of sensuality, the man of
faith, according to Jaspers's putative conception of it, loves all vi-

sions of truth so much that he does not wish to part with any of them, woos all that come his way, stays with them—for a day, but neither loves nor is captivated by any of them enough to risk his life for it. However, it seems to us, that this neither coincides with nor follows from Jaspers's conception of faith, as can be seen from what has already been said. Indeed, statements contradictory to Ricoeur's interpretation can be found in the very work against which the first version of Ricoeur's criticism is directed. For example:

> It takes faith to understand faith. And to understand it does not here mean to make it my own, or to understand just the contents; it means that at the bounds of intelligibility the unintelligible is experienced as akin to myself yet alien to me by virtue of the otherness of the originality of faith.[26]

Clearly Ricoeur's accusation cannot be a matter of mere misunderstanding; as such it would be gross. What is involved here is an implicit difference in the conception of historicity and, concomitantly, of the predicament of freedom and the objectivity of matters of faith. There has been much talk about historicity in recent theology. And no wonder, for the concept of historicity is, in fact, not new but is rooted in the biblical conception that the eternal one makes his will known in time. Theologically oriented conceptions of historicity either culminate in or are restricted to the concept of revelation, i.e., the notion that an objectively ascertainable historical event determines for man the saving eternal truth, and that an objective doctrine and institution and cult testifies to it in time. No doubt this is reflected in Ricoeur in questioning Jaspers's separation of the realms of freedom and of objectivity, which emphasizes the tension between authority and conscience; in questioning Jaspers's distinction of Being and its appearance, which drives a wedge between known historical facts and the risk of historic faith, i.e., between history and story, between bodily existence and indication by myth and symbol; and, in particular, in questioning Jaspers's conception of freedom and guilt. For Ricoeur the conception of freedom is primarily a consciousness of its vanity. And again and again he indicates that "the believer cannot understand . . . a doctrine of guilt loosed from a doctrine of forgiveness."[27] In other words, Ricoeur's very conception of faith is tied to the specific orthodoxy of the Christian doctrine of salvation. It would seem that Ricoeur views the problem as an alternative: either *this* faith based on the highest authority of revelation, or many faiths; and if many faiths, then a Don Juanism of faith.

For Jaspers, the problem of historicity, of the coincidence of
time and eternity, extends beyond the range of the orthodox theologian. For Jaspers, the problem becomes acute when the self
with its faith is confronted with another self with its other faith;
for the theologian, in the last analysis, such a confrontation does
not exist. The reason is twofold. First, he lacks the means of pre-
supposing a diversity of faiths. Secondly, he lacks a conception of
freedom whereby the self, in such a confrontation, is no less responsible for the authority it follows as is the authority for the
truth of his faith.

iv. Dialogue and Communication—Buber and Jaspers

a. Affinities and Differences

The confrontation of Jaspers with three of his critics (Bultmann,
Barth, Ricoeur) focused our attention on a certain feature of the
communicative mode of man's search for truth. It is the feature to
which a radical conception of faith leads when viewed under the
aspect of historicity: the conception of communication as a struggle. The further significance of this distinct feature of Jaspers's
philosophy of faith and communication comes to light in a juxtaposition of Jaspers with Martin Buber as the other of "the two
great dialogists of our day."[28] No doubt the affinities of Jaspers's
idea of communication and Buber's idea of dialogue are very
strong. Both conceive the being of the participants in communication and dialogue as radical, i.e., transcending determinacy and
mediation. Both conceive the existential concretion of these beings, particularly in their communicative and dialogical relation, as
requiring, occuring in, and infecting the realm of determinate immanence, the world. Both consider the eminent realization of this
relation as a relation between two. And in both the realization of
the communicative and dialogical relation is seen as man's way of
realizing his relation to transcendence. Thus we read in Jaspers,

> The most penetrating communication is possible only in lim-
> ited spheres. Only here transcendence reveals its depth in his-
> toric form.[29]

And in Buber:

> The extended lines of relations meet in the *eternal Thou*.
> Every particular *Thou* is a glimpse through to the external

Thou; by means of every particular *Thou* the primary word addresses the eternal *Thou.*[30]

Exemplifications, such as this one, of the remarkable congruence of Jaspers's and Buber's understanding of the foundation of dialogue in the God-relatedness of the participants also points to their divergence. For Jaspers's conception of the radical historicity of the revelation of transcendence, communication is essentially active, searching penetration. For Buber's ontology of the God-relatedness of I and Thou, the gift of meeting the particular Thou is a manifestation of the grace of the eternal Thou.

This difference—of activity and manifestation—which prima facie is one of emphasis, bespeaks a difference of principle. Jaspers's communication is essentially a struggle for truth in time. Buber's dialogue is essentially the recognition of God through communion with his creatures. Thus, in Jaspers the mutual immediacy of the participants in communication consists in mutual challenge and response without reserve, a challenge and response which is the more genuine and no less a struggle the more loving it is. The participants' presence is constituted by their risk of their being for the realization of truth in this encounter. It is a struggle between men for the becoming of the being of truth. On the other hand, the immediacy of one participant to the other in Buber's conception of dialogue consists in fervid hearkening, in prayerful response, and in loving responsibility for those who cannot hear. Their presence is constituted by their dialogical "action of the whole being . . . suspension of all partial actions."[31] Dialogue is a meeting of man with fellow creature—not necessarily fellow man, and through this meeting a meeting with God, a meeting which is the fulfillment of Being in the fleeting of the moment.

The distinction in principle between 'communication' and 'dialogue' points to larger issues on which Jaspers and Buber are divided, which, in turn, shed light on it. Let us look at the respective sources of their ideas of communication and dialogue, at their conception of man's relation to God and at their mutual criticism.

The relation which Buber's conception of dialogue bears to its source describes an hermeneutic circle. Man's meeting the fellow creature as Thou in the unifying presence of the Eternal Thou is that mode of being human whereby he is wholly what he is. The dialogical situation is not a program or enterprise but, as Buber says, "something ontic."[32] And his dialogical principle is a theory of man insofar as he is man and viewed in his primal being. This is what Buber means when he maintains that "the dialogical situation is sufficiently grasped only ontologically."[33] Buber derives the ontology of man as dialogical being, in the main, from the teachings of Judaism. And, going in the other direction, the articulation of the dialogical principle and its emphasis determined the development of his views of the esoteric and the exoteric significance of Jewish actuality, particularly the Jewish faith and ethos. Thus, on the one hand, the hasidic experience, and such themes of Jewish religion as the redemptive *yihud*, (i.e., the unification of worldly disparateness in the presence of its divine source),[34] or the Jewish "remembrance and the expectation of a concrete situation: the encounter of God and man"[35] blossom, in Buber, into the dialogical principle. On the other hand, its recognition as the heart of Jewish teaching enables Buber to reinterpret the Jewish essence and to enact a shift in its emphases. He places some prominent themes of Jewish religion into perspective, such as the law, the rabbincal tradition of its interpretation, and the rituals of purity. But he also finds a foundation for a renewal of Jewish activism, be it political as in Zionism, or social as in the development of the land of Israel, or spiritual, i.e., an activism of Jewish consciousness vis-à-vis philosophy, other religions, other theologies. "Ontic" man is dialogical, and dialogue is the essence of Judaism. Accordingly we read in Buber,

> I am far from wishing to contend that the conception and experience of the dialogical situation are confined to Judaism. But I am certain that no other community of human beings has entered with such strength and fervor into this experience as have the Jews.[36]

And concerning his conception of the "primacy of the dialogical" as "ontological" he says:

> This thought . . . is rightly called religious. But it may not—this too must be reiterated here—be regarded as a thought based on a religion.
>
> Mordechai Kaplan unjustly ascribes to me the view that the religious tradition of Judaism is self-sufficient, from which it follows that I am concerned with a theological anthropology that is grounded on a religious tradition. I have on different occasions . . . pointed out that this is not so. As to the tradition of Judaism, some of its great expressions, beginning with the biblical one and ending with the hasidic, together form the strongest testimony of the primacy of the dialogical known to me. No doubt this testimony has been the divining rod which led me to the source; but this source could be nothing other than the experience of faith which I was granted.[37]

We shall see how this relation of the dialogical principle to its Jewish testimony affects Buber's evaluation of Jaspers's conception of communication.

We must now mention that Jaspers's 'communication' is, like its Buberian cognate, related to its sources in the manner of an hermeneutic circle. What are these sources? Among them we must count the "dialogic principle" as an implicit and explicit constituent of Western thought. Jaspers acknowledges this, moreover in its eminent connection with ancient Judaism:

> In the cipher of the personal God transcendence—supersensory, beyond reason, above Being—becomes the Thou . . . that man can talk to, pray to, appeal to for comprehension when incomprehensible calamity drives him to despair. Nowhere in the world has this powerful urge to find the embodied reality of the Thou in God's overwhelming omnipotence been more powerful than among the Jews. Through them it became determinative for the West.[38]

The recent history of the dialogic principle, about which Buber wrote a paper which will soon be of particular interest to us, includes, of course, Buber himself. However, as we have just seen, Jaspers does not relate the notion of God as personality, addressed as 'Thou', in particular to Buber.

Of even greater weight, for the development of Jaspers's conception of 'communication', than the dialogical principle is the fundamental fact of multiplicity of human awareness of truth. This fact pervades all areas of human activity, including politics and law, custom and morality. In particular we have to mention, first, the confrontation of diverse religions, a confrontation which can take the form of a collision with grim results if one or both claim exclusive authority for its teachings and, in the exercise of its authority, have recourse to temporal power. Secondly, there is the great philosophical debate throughout the ages on particular and ultimate questions in which minds of diverse persuasions have joined, taking up the testimony of those who came before, and, fired or repelled by it, renewing, modifying, sharpening, criticizing, and creating views on these questions, and, thereby, adding to the testimony. Recent generations of concerned philosophers have been taking stock of this heritage. The array of paradoxes and the diversity of opinion have suggested—to theologians no less than to positivists—that philosophy is, at worst, a vacuous enterprise or, at best, an aporetic one.

The one thing which must be regarded here above all others is that it is truth which is at stake in such confrontations and debates. It is this fact, no doubt, which suggested to Jaspers that man's partaking of truth consists in the struggle for rather than the possession of truth. And it also led to the suppositions by which truth under these circumstances can be deemed possible: Man's realization of truth and his being himself are inseparable. Man realizes truth, and thereby himself, under the conditions of his temporality and his temporal limitation. Becoming in time is equivalent to being with and, thus, for others, and being for others is tied to *what* one is for others as a being that becomes itself in the realization of one's truth. Hence being oneself and the human realization of truth are essentially communicative.[39] Moreover, as long as truth is tied to becoming in time it can only be communicative and not dogmatic.[40] Since the finality of truth as such is not available to man, truth is for man in its appearance, i.e., in communicative objectification. Hence truth is not the aim of communication but is in communication. Since truth is incomplete for man, communication as the way of truth is never without untruth.[41] Because untruth is the inevitable fellow traveller of incomplete truth, the motive of overcoming it can impel the unrelenting movement of communication. In this way, untruth can be a vehicle of truth.[42] Communication is, therefore, not an activity of transmission of the truth by those who supposedly possess it to those who do not. Rather, it is the loving struggle of bringing each other forth, of mutually impelling the other's becoming himself and his truth.[43]

Untruth as a goad to overcoming itself and as the inevitable fellow traveller of one's limited vision of truth never lies less within oneself than within the partner in communication. Blindness for the untruth within oneself, particularly when sensitive to that within the other, betrays communication and, insofar as it is man's way of truth, betrays truth itself. The lack of openness for the other's truth, at least as truth for the other and as challenge to one's own, particularly if understood as following from the perfection of one's own truth, is similarly perfidious, even if one's truth is tied to a consciousness of a divine revelation or address. If the equality, vis-à-vis the transcendence of the one truth, of those struggling for the truth in communication is less than radical, the struggle is not communicative of truth and self. Hence Jaspers says:

> If the technical arsenal of the combatants differ, if one is more knowledgeable or more intelligent than the other, has a better memory or is less prone to fatigue, both will equalize the level by handicapping themselves. . . . Where the stronger psycho-

logical equipment carries the day, not to mention the possibility of sophistry, communication also ceases. In existentially embattled communication each will put everything at the other's disposal.[44]

Yet love alone is not communication; it is a struggle that must be loving if truth is to be brought to its realization in time:

> Equalization requires each to be existentially as tough as possible on himself, and on the other. Chivalry and all kinds of disembarrassment have a place here . . . only as transient safeguards. . . . If they last, communication is at an end. On the other hand, the need for toughness applies only to the most essential grounds of substantial decision.[45]

It is precisely the earnestness of communication that confirms for the truth the significance of the search for truth, and upholds the dignity of the searcher and of the confession and testament of his partaking of truth in time.

Let us state the circular relation which Jaspers's conception of 'communication' bears to its sources in summary form. The one truth is the motive of self and reason. The consummation of this motive is then understood as resulting in the warring plurality of the realizations of truth. At the same time only this motive can invest this plurality with earnestness, with the import of being the vehicle and appearance in time of the one truth. On the realization of this import rest the chances of upholding the motive of the one truth for man, who is directed to it within the bounds of time. And this realization is achieved precisely to the extent that the struggle between visions of truth is neither eschewed, nor joined with the conviction of the ultimate insignificance of the truth of the other, but is joined with communicative generosity.

b. Buber's Criticism of Jaspers

These explications of Buber's and Jaspers's philosphical intentions in their respective conceptions of 'dialogue' and 'communication' enable us to proceed to a consideration of how the position of each actually has been or can possibly be regarded from that of the other. Let us cite in its entirety the passage in which Buber criticizes Jaspers's conception of 'communication' before turning in the directions to which this criticism leads:

> Jaspers belongs here most eminently by virtue of the section on communication . . . and that on the reading of the cipher script. . . . Both form the paradigmatic conclusion of a phase of development in which "free" philosophy seized the new

discoveries in a reductive manner. Reductive, I say, because the connection between transcendence and concretion, which is peculiar to this discovery, is treated as arbitrary, and the advance to the limitlessness of the Thou is, in effect, annulled. This philosophy, not fastened any more to a root-ground of an experience of faith, thinks it can move in the new territory without restraint if only it guards the the basis of existentiality of the philosophizing person; and, in its way, it succeeds.

We have recognized that the same Thou which goes from man to man is precisely the same which descends to us from the Divine and ascends from us to it. At issue was and is this equality within extreme inequality. That biblical interlacing of God's love and man's in the dual commandment, directs our attention to the transparency of the finite Thou, yet also to the infinite Thou's grace to appear where and how it will. And now saying "Thou" to the Divinity is to be banished as illegitimate. No doubt the philosopher is inviolably warranted to declare that "philosophical Existenz" can bear "not to approach the hidden God." But he is not warranted to designate prayer, which thus is strange to his experience, as "questionable."[46]

Here Buber adds a footnote:

In the book "Philosophical Faith"[47] (1948) Jaspers, to be sure, expresses himself noticeably more positively about prayer in order to bring the two realms closer together. Yet he obscures the most vital distinction by understanding "speculative assurance," "wherever it became genuine contemplation," as the eminent form of prayer.[48]

The footnote shows that Buber is not only acquainted with the *Philosophie* but also with Jaspers's later work. The latter, particularly the cited *Der Philosophische Glaube*, does not present views on our topic which are different from those in the earlier work. However the understanding of philosophy as faith is now the main theme, and its relevance for an earnest dialogue with any thinking inspired by doctrinal theology becomes explicit enough for all to see who did not see it before. Buber's suggestion that Jaspers's purpose in the cited work was "to bring the two realms together" would be acceptable if we could be sure that he means by it that the living struggle of communication between theology and philosophy, in which each regards the other as a repository for historic realization of truth, can now begin. But Buber hardly encourages our understanding the suggestion in this way since the mark of what he is prepared to acknowledge as a rapprochement is what he regards as a concession on Jaspers's part, the putative concession being Jaspers's "noticeably more positive" expression about prayer. However, speaking of a concession here presupposes two things, neither of which can be attributed to Jaspers. First, everything speaks against there being any intention on Jaspers's part to make a concession here and to regard concessions as preconditions of joining any communicative struggle and this one in particular. Secondly, there is no change in Jaspers's expressions about prayer; in fact, what he says in the little work of 1948 previously cited is a summary of his several treatments of prayer in the *Philosophie* (1932), particularly that in the section on "religious action."[49] If anything, what Buber would welcome as "positive" expressions about prayer are more positively expressed in the *Philosophie*. Moreover it is hard to believe that Buber would hesitate to extend this welcome even with respect to passages in which Jaspers recognizes in prayer a consciousness distinct from but approaching philosophical contemplation, a comparison to which Buber objects. For example:

> Prayer, to start with, is the individual soul's intercourse with God. It must not be confused with the philosophical contemplation that actively aims at transcendence. The mark of prayer is the real relation to God, who is conceived as personal, as listening, as effectively present. Even in its purest forms, in thanksgiving and praise, I am praying only insofar as I am conscious of being heard by God and having my prayer accepted. . . . The objectivity is reduced to a minimum; God appears in the inwardness of the soul. . . . The borderline between this and the active contemplation in which Existenz concerns itself with the hidden God is vitually imperceptible and yet clearly drawn.
>
> Pure prayer is a late and rare result of man's historic self-becoming. Almost always, prayer is impure, a plea for earthly purposes and thus connected with magic, which ruins its import. . . . Magic has spread universally, and in veiled forms it still remains an element of the world's great religions. It was completely eliminated only once in history: in the old prophetic Judaism and on the basis of that Judaism—in parts of the Protestant world. The elimination resulted from an unconditional religious faith, but magic itself no longer has an inherent unconditionality.[50]

We said that it is hard to believe that Buber would not look with favor on this appreciation of prayer; the kinship is too great for that. Yet believe it we must lest we reach the somewhat lame conclusion that Buber did not absorb the works he cites. An additional basis for believing that is the fact that the number of other decisive parallels in Jaspers's thinking which Buber disregards are striking. Let us take a closer look, therefore, at the offence which Buber finds in Jaspers that causes him to pass over the many marks of kinship.

Buber, as we have read, regards Jaspers as the eminent example of "free philosophy's" "seizure" of "the new discoveries" in "a reductive manner." Buber is justly and duly honored for distilling the dialogical way of the consciousness of faith from the essence of Jewish experience, and for opening up, by virtue of his persuasive and irreplaceable articulation, a realm of possibilities of human relation and realization whose scope and effects exceed our vision. But it was neither honor nor credit that Buber claimed in his proprietary expressions regarding the discovery of the dialogical principle ("we have recognized . . ."; "the new discovery"), in contesting a comparable degree of originality in cognate conceptions (philosophy "seized," Barth "appropriated"), in rejecting the legitimacy of the distinctness of these conceptions and of the concerns over truth which form the basis of such distinctness ("a reductive manner"). Rather, what Buber means to guard, what "was and is" "at issue" for Buber is his own distinct conception of the dialogical principle. His first basis of criticism is the question whether cognate conceptions incorporate the feature peculiar to the principle, i.e., "the connection of transcendence with concretion." Formally, of course, this can be said about Jaspers's conception of communication as the breakthrough of truth in its transcendence into the historicity of man's realization. Clearly then this is not enough for Buber. Hence the rejection of Jaspers's "reduction" of the dialogical principle in his conception of communication, on the ground that the latter renders the connection of transcendence with concretion "arbitrary," requires a further basis. This is indicated in designating Jaspers as prime example of the misappropriation of the principle on the part of "free" philosophy.

What is "free" philosophy? Introducing the section of his brief history of the dialogical principle which deals not only with Jaspers but also with Löwith, Litt and Griesebach, Buber says that he means to designate thereby any philosophy

> which is not any more existentially rooted in the actuality of a religion, as were, for example, Descartes and Leibniz, and

which therefore excludes the concern of the connection between intercourse with the conditioned Thou and intercourse
with the unconditioned Thou.[51]

We already know that with regard to Jaspers Buber reiterates these
points in somewhat different words. Jaspers, Buber says, is "not
fastened any more to a root-ground of an experience of faith."
But the "root-ground of an experience of faith," we now find, is
"the actuality of a religion." Without obligation to such a "root-
ground" Jaspers is now regarded as enabled to move "without
restraint" in the "new territory" if only he "guards the basis of
existentiality of the philosophizing person." Since the rootedness
("in the actuality of a religion") sanctioned by Buber is itself "existential," the emphasis in this expression of reprobation is not on
guarding the *existentiality* of a person but on the *philosophical*
persuasion of the person. We see, therefore, that for Buber philosophy which is not beholden to a religious actuality, to "an experience of faith," is an absurdity and leads a bastard existence.

This explains Buber's use of certain expressions which occur in
this connection. Thus, first, regarding Jaspers's "banishing" of
"saying Thou to the divinity" as "illegitimate," he raises the question of the source of legitimation. It is evident that under the aegis
of the immediately preceding reminder of the "infinite Thou's
grace to appear where and how it will" this question is decided
before it is articulated. And the "free" philosopher's suggestion
that truth for man in time means not only harking to the address
of the infinite Thou in the "transparency" of the finite Thou, but
articulating it by virute of the challenge of the finite Thou in communicative combat, must seem to be at worst effrontery, at best
incomprehensible. For the "discovery" that the dialogical relation
of I and finite Thou is in its transparency the address of the eternal Thou to the harking I is itself the result of such harking.

Thus, secondly, the legitimation denied the "free" philosopher is
not denied the philosopher who is not "free" in this sense. Indeed
this "freedom" is a restriction, the absence of which enables Buber
to delineate what the "free" philosopher "is inviolably warranted
to declare" and what not. He is "warranted" to declare that "philosophical Existenz can bear not to approach the hidden God."
That this is ironical is quite clear if we consider that the philosopher is deemed "free" precisely because "not any more fastened
to a root-ground of an experience of faith," God remains hidden
to him. He is warranted to declare anything within the realm of
subject matter which does not fall under the designation of a fas-
tening to the actuality of a religion. And precisely such indebted-

ness warrants Buber to deny Jaspers's warrant to question prayer as "strange to his experience."

Thus, thirdly, Buber speaks of the dialogical relation of I and finite Thou in the presence of the infinite Thou as a "principle," as something that "we have recognized," 'recognized' in the sense of 'cognition' (German: *erkannt*), as a "discovery," as perhaps "postulative" in its formulation, but at "its core . . . ontological."[52] And speaking of the "primacy of the dialogical" he says "this is, in fact, the theme to which, since I laid hold of it, or rather since it laid hold of me, my work . . . has been dedicated."[53] He both laid hold of it and it laid hold of him. We see an aura of authoritative certainty about the "primacy of the dialogical" which raises with considerable urgency the question of the nature of the realization of and discourse about this "theme." Can one speak here of "cognition" and "discovery" in a literal sense? No doubt in an exegetical sense we can, insofar as one can interpretively comprehend (*verstehen*) that what we formulate as the experience of the infinite Thou's address in the relation of I and Thou lies at the basis of the prophets' faith and the hasidic way of life. But exegetical grasp of the theme is one thing, being grasped by it another. It is possible to grasp that the dialogical has been or is actual for some person or persons whose testimony I perceive; but this does not imply its actuality to me. To "recognize" its being truth for another is "cognition" and "discovery" in a literal sense. To "recognize" its being truth for oneself—whether presupposed for or occasioned by exegetical "discovery" does not matter—is not. It is, rather, "experience of faith." As such the dialogical can indeed be "ontic" but not in any "ontological" sense but "existentially." And that this accords with Buber's own intentions seems evident. We recall, for example, the following passage, referred to earlier from his "Reply" to his critics:

> The tradition of Judaism . . . forms the strongest testimony of the primacy of the dialogical. . . . This testimony has been the divining rod which led me to the source; but this source could be nothing other than the experience of faith.[54]

Neither is there any question about the primacy of the dialogical being an expression of faith which is the "faith of the prophets," i.e., that one of the "two types of faith" which is trust in the truth which has made itself heard rather than that which is belief and cognition of the truth which has been made evident. And yet Buber chooses the idiom of cognitive objectivity to express the actuality of faith which is the primacy of the dialogical: "ontologi-

cal," "discovery," "we have recognized." We may endorse Emil
Brunner's somewhat obvious observation that it is Buber's concern
"to differentiate the relationship with God as one of the I-Thou
relation from every abstract, material It-relationship."[55] On the
other hand it may well be that 'cognition' reflects for Buber the
biblical meaning-connection of 'to know' and 'to be familiar with';
in *Two Types of Faith* he says:

> The relation to the future . . . becomes for the early Israelite
> assurance, because he trusts in the God with whom he is inti-
> mate (for this is the Old Testament meaning of the word 'to
> know' when it is used of the relationship between God and
> man).[56]

However we cannot disregard the fact that the context, presently
under consideration, for the use of "we have recognized" is the
debate with "free" philosophy for which "cognition" is distinct
from the truth of faith. Moreover, that the dialogical is a "principle" and has the status of "primacy" surely is also meant as indicative of assertions which—though expressions of faith—also express
a claim to validity which is universal.

c. Limitations of Buber's Dialogue

As we follow Buber's directing his attention, from the vantage
point of the dialogical principle, to Jaspers, and in the same little
essay to Barth, not to speak of his grand examination of Christianity in contraposition to Judaism in *Two Types of Faith* and of his
responses to critics, we come to realize that these dialogical efforts
on his part are to probe for the primacy of the dialogical in the
efforts of others. The 'dialogical principle' in the sense in which it
has been widely accepted is more vague and broad than what
Buber meant. It is not only the meeting of man and man, it is not
only the warmth of speaking together, searching together, being
together, it is not only the whole presence of one to the other—
heart, hand and head, that Buber meant. Rather, "at issue," we
remember, "was and is this equality within extreme inequality."
By virtue of attending to "the transparency of the finite Thou" we
attend "to the infinite Thou's grace to appear where and how it
will."
   That Buber's engagement in dialogue is impelled by the motive
of realizing the primacy of the dialogical as thus conceived and
with the Jewish realization of it as standard, is a conclusion which
is hard to avoid. And that, in consequence, the validity of the
other's faith is restricted should be equally clear; for if it were not

thus restricted it would have to restrict the primacy of the dialogical as here conceived. The primacy of the dialogical denies the other a basis for dialogue if he does not enter it with the concession of recognizing God's address in the meeting with the fellow creature. This explains Buber's repudiation of Jaspers. But it also raises a difficulty, that of accounting for the vigor with which Buber recognizes and meets challenge. For this recognition presupposes that Buber takes actualities of faith which challenge his "type of faith" (distilled into the dialogical principle) as valid enough to defend his type of faith against them. To explicate this point let us look at some relevant texts. In the foreword of *Two Types of Faith* Buber says,

> There is scarcely any need to say that every apologetic tendency is far from my purpose.[57]

And:

> There is something in the history of Israel's faith which can be recognized only from Israel, just as there is something in Christianity which can be recognized only from Christianity. I have touched on the latter only with the ingenuous reverence of one harking the word.[58]

Yet who would question the justification of this observation of Brunner, who is a Christian theologian sympathetic to Buber:

> Although Buber, in the preface to the book, declares that both apologetics as well as polemics are entirely foreign to his intentions—and anyone who knows him will not question his word—his presentation of Pauline theology is so convincing that, without or even against the author's will, the book turns out to be a major attack on Christinaity.[59]

With the sovereignty of scholarship Buber probes Christian faith for its realization of the dialogical and finds it to be another mode of faith. With equal sovereignty, albeit the sovereignty of orthodoxy, Barth, developing the foundation—in the Christian conception of grace and love—of man's relation of I and Thou, notes in passing that similar notions were entertained by non-Christians, by the "wisest among the wise," "for example by the heathen Confucius, the atheist L. Feuerbach, the Jew M. Buber."[60] One of Barth's concerns in this explication is—far from crediting these non-Christians for their initiative—to explain how his notion might have occurred outside of the Christian consciousness by virtue of which the actuality which the notion refers to is seen in its foundation. For example, Barth says:

Since we ourselves have arrived at the assertion that precisely
in this conception of humanity is to be found the nature of
man . . . we shall surely not take umbrage at the fact, rather
shall we accept it . . . as an indirect proof of our assertions that
a certain knowledge of this conception has been possible for
man as such and in general, also for the heathen, the atheist,
the Jew, and that, as this shows, it has actually also been represented outside of Christian theology. Natural man is, after
all, . . . in the realm of divine grace, i.e., in the realm in which
Jesus was also man. How could it then be otherwise than that
besides much worse knowledge he also be capable here and
there within certain limits, of a good amount of better knowledge. The theological doctrine of man has and retains even
with respect to such better knowledge of natural man the advantage of possessing a criterion—its *cognition* of divine grace,
its *cognition* of the man Jesus.[61]

This example may suffice for the display of what one person
might call just righteousness of true belief, another the pride of
faith, a third a Protestant version of triumphalism. With the economy of irony Buber gives as good as he gets. First of all he reminds
the author of *Church Dogmatics* that he is "notwithstanding the
amplitude and his own power of theological thought"—"appropri-
ating"

the specific gain of a movement of thought initiated in the
eighteenth century by a believing idealist outside of the church
and in the nineteenth by an unbelieving sensualist and which
found a somewhat adequate expression in the twentieth century by virtue of the not inconsiderable participation of some
believing Jews.[62]

A Jewish reverberation of triumphalism? This is impossible in Judaism; hence we dispel this spectre as vigorously as it insinuates
itself wherever we read its rhetoric in Buber. To be sure the articulation of the dialogical through the participation of "some believing Jews"—Buber means Rosenzweig and himself, perhaps also
Hermann Cohen—is not mentioned here as being a coincidence.
But ungrudging credit for the initiative of the "believing idealist"
Jacobi and the "sensualist" Feuerbach is, in confrontation with
the pre-emption of the dialogical in the name of Church Dogmatics, important because it shows that the primacy of the dialogical can be rooted in ground other than the faith of the Christian
Church. Not only the idealist's faith "outside the Church" can
testify to a "presentiment" (*Ahnung*) of this primacy but also the

materialist, the "sensualist," precisely the one who in Barth's reference is presented as without faith, as an "atheist."

It would seem that Buber's point is to remind Barth that there is actuality of faith outside of what Barth would acknowledge as faith. This is the more urgent particularly since it cannot have escaped Buber that he is being put off by Barth as one of the "wisest of the wise" among "natural" men, i.e., not just a "wisest among wise" who happens to be Jewish, but as a "Jew" who as such is of a breed of "natural" men, as one not graced and justified by faith in Christ. Precisely because of this relegation of the "Jew" to mere "natural" mankind, living in the realm of grace, to be sure, but a grace no different from that of the "heathen" and the "atheist," the reminder of there being faith outside of the Church is not enough. Buber endorses Barth's recognition of the dialogical as grounded in a religious faith. But it is precisely as thus grounded that Buber presents himself to and demands to be recognized by Barth, moreover, as a believing Jew who as such has shown the primacy of the dialogical. Hence Buber says,

> It would certainly be awkward to be dependent on opposing the doubts which come from outside with one's own certitudes.[63]

The reason is that Buber regards his "own certitudes" as reflective of something wider. His role in the present confrontation need be no other than that of a spokesman. But Barth's position is, then, nothing more and nothing less than that as well:

> As it happens, we need not speak here of my personal world of ideas nor of Barth's; rather here the Protestant world of faith as he understands it is confronting the hasidic one as I understand it.[64]

Barth's derivation of the dialogical in the Christian Church's dogma of grace presents a challenge to Buber's—not exclusive but fundamental—identification of the primacy of the dialogical with the hasidic faith. And with this faith he meets the challenge. The confrontation Barth-Buber is not a dialogue; it is about dialogue. It ends as follows:

> Among Hasidim—in a world of faith whose most important doctrines are commentary on a lived life . . . openness of heart is . . . inner presupposition, the ground of ground. Hark what is said there: "Cleverness without heart is nothing. Piety is false." For "true love of God begins with love of man."[65]

Here Buber indicates the direction the debate would have to take
for it to turn into a dialogue. And he does so by tapping resources
of his faith. He does not say such resources are available to his
opponent but he also does not deny it. Buber challenges him to
tap them—if they are there. That and only that will decide whether the dialogical is actual and where it is grounded. But then Buber's "discovery" of the dialogical principle would not be an
"indirect proof" for a point in Barth's theory of grace but an existential, untheoretical supposition of the ground in faith of the
other's recognition of the dialogical principle. The articulations of
this grounding would occur precisely in this recognition, in accepting the other as presenting a challenge, in responding to it by vying
for the realization of dialogue, in letting the "love of God begin
with love of man." For to love man means to recognize and affirm
him wholly as man not merely as "natural" man and what makes
man wholly man is the faith which is his ground. Then, if Buber
had this last word, it would not have to be the last word.

Or would it? There is another side to this issue which really was
the issue in the first place. Himself a literary warrior, Barth would,
no doubt, appreciate Buber's gambit of reprimanding him for failing in the love of man by tapping the resources of the hasidic faith
with which Buber confronts him. But as a believing proponent of
Church dogma he would be astonished, for it is nothing less than
the Christian's love to proclaim the message of Christ's grace and
love as basis of the dialogical. And if the "love of God" did not
begin with the "cleverness" of the Church dogmatist's theory of
grace but with the "love of man," i.e. not with the consciousness
of God's grace and love as Christ but with hearkening to God's
address immediately and wholly in any encounter of man and
man, then Buber would indeed have the last word, and not for
himself but for the sake of the faith which had "grasped" him.
Seen in this light the confrontation Barth-Buber appears as the
self-assertion of each faith versus the other, where in the absoluteness of each the claims to universal validity are made for it, denying the absoluteness of the other faith for the other. We cannot
and must not forget that the idiom of the claims to universal validity appears equally in both: Buber: "We have recognized [*erkannt*] . . . "; Barth: The theological doctrine's "cognition
[*Erkenntnis*] of divine grace. . . ."

With respect to either case—Buber struggling to open the possibilities of loving dialogue or Buber embattled to assert the self-
consciousness of hasidic faith in confrontation with that of
Church dogma—there are noteworthy discrepancies between his
position in this confrontation and his treatment of Jaspers's 'com-

munication'. Reflecting on our explorations we can now summarize them. Buber recognizes an actuality of faith, challenging his own, in Barth but not in Jaspers. Buber rejects the repudiation of the validity of his faith by Barth but in turn repudiates the actuality of faith in Jaspers. Buber questions the universality of the Christian's faith, upholding the validity of his own as another "type of faith," but activates the idiom of universality in branding what he takes to be Jaspers's appropriation of the main tenet of his faith as "reductive." Thereby he must regard Jaspers's understanding of his faith as one amongst others locked in a communicative struggle as trivializing his faith, as rendering it "arbitrary."

But let us turn to that aspect of the distinction between 'dialogue' and 'communication' which is fundamental. There is talk about love. Love is actual for Buber to the extent that there is a mutuality where an I is responsible for a Thou, meets the Thou in its wholeness, in its limitlessness, as the transparency of God's presence. Can love be actual, i.e., can dialogue take place, only where the difference in different faiths has been dispelled, and only where mutuality is deliberate? This seems implied in Buber's reprimand of Barth's forgetting, for the love of God, the love of man. But then what is the status of a struggle, such as Buber's, to disclose the conditions under which a genuine dialogue can take place, a struggle which he carries out with considerable vigor? Is it merely prolegomenal to dialogue? If the truth of faith is at stake, then would it not have to prove itself in this very struggle, and would its proof not be precisely in the actuality of *love within the struggle?* We see the chances for such a loving struggle of communication, and some of its marks, in the confrontation between Buber and Barth, in their debate about the ground of the primacy of the dialogical. But we see no evidence that, in his conception or practice of dialogue, Buber ever seriously located man's partaking of the infinite in the actuality of struggle, of a struggle for what has not been vouchsafed man, and a struggle which, precisely by virtue of what it is directed toward, is loving. There is the point of departure for this in Buber. Toward the end of his life he says,

The "complete," the legitimately religious existence of man, does not stand in a continuity but in the genuine acceptance and mastery of a discontinuity. It is the discontinuity of essentiality and inessentiality that I understand as that of the I-Thou relation and the I-It relation to all being. To deny this discontinuity means to deny the decisive character of existing as man, which means incontestably: being able to stand in the face of Being without subsisting—and that means persevering—

in the face of it. This discontinuity cannot be abrogated. . . .
That a continuity of the I-Thou relation is not attainable in
this our life, that it is impossible, indeed, even *to attempt* to
attain it, this everyone knows who knows from his own experience what is in question here.[66]

And forty years earlier, at the beginning of Buber's sequence of
dialogical writings, in *I and Thou*, we read:

But this is the exalted melancholy of our fate, that every Thou
in our world must become an It. It does not matter how exclusively present the Thou was in the direct relation . . . the Thou
becomes an object among objects. . . . And love itself cannot
persist in direct relation. It endures, but in interchange of
actual and potential being.[67]

In vain do we look in Buber for any attempt to grapple with
the fact of "discontinuity" sufficiently to educe possibilities of
its being the vehicle of "what is at stake." The reason for this is,
no doubt, to be found in the entanglement of Buber's conception of the dialogical with the actuality of his faith. What we are
referring to is not the fact that the primacy of the dialogical is at
the same time the content of Buber's faith. In this respect Buber's and Jaspers's positions are comparable. 'Communication' is
not merely the consequence of a systematic reflection on the
possibility of truth for man in time, particularly in consideration
of the historic multiplicity of man's realization of the one truth.
It is, analogous to Buber's dialogical principle, also a faith, the
faith in the possibility of truth in its oneness in the face of historic multiplicity. Buber, we have most likely noticed, deliberately and significantly fails to recognize such actuality of faith
in Jaspers, and in fact denies Jaspers's debt to a "root-ground of
an experience of faith."

What is at play, rather, is the way in which Buber understands
the content of his faith, particularly, as testimony of God's
address and response. This is the reason why, in his consideration of Jaspers, he emphasizes the question of the conception of
God as personality and that of the significance of prayer, rather
than the question of the possibility of dialogue between men of
different faiths, even between one for whom God's being as person is of the essence with one to whom it is questionable. The
former emphasis need not exclude the latter, though in Buber it
does. Openness for dialogue with an other actuality of faith—not
by restricting one's own faith but by virtue of regarding it as
historic for oneself and tested in the concerned acceptance of
the other's challenge—seems irreconcilable with Buber's concep-

tion of testimony even though its significance is, as with Jaspers, existential. With reference to the import of the notion of God's personality, Buber says,

> The existence of mutuality between God and man cannot be proved, just as God's existence cannot be proved. Yet he who dares to speak of it, bears witness, and calls to witness him to whom he speaks—whether that witness is now or in the future.[68]

d. Jaspers's Position

Here we can most naturally insert a brief appendix dealing with Jaspers's criticism of Buber. No explicit published criticism is known to me. Jaspers and Buber met a number of times about the time of the First World War. At that time, Jaspers formed an unfavorable opinion of what Buber spiritually represented. This opinion seems to have determined his later relation to Buber and his own philosophical thinking. Buber appeared to Jaspers to bear himself like a prophet.[69] Not only the possibility of prophetic thought became clear to Jaspers through this encounter but also the realization of the impertinence of this possibility for the modern situation characterized by the restriction of universal validity to science, and the failure of metaphysics and the authority of religion with respect to the transcendent ground of man's freedom. At the time of their acquaintance Jaspers was working on his *Psychologie der Weltanschauungen*. Characterizing this work thirty-five years later, in the foreword to its fourth edition, as his groping toward philosophy, Jaspers says,

> I did not desire a prophetic philosophy but had no notion as yet of the other, secretly looked for philosophy.[70]

The first and decisive fruition of this search was Jaspers's *Philosophie*. There the separation of Jaspers's conception of philosophy from prophetic philosophy is briefly touched upon twice. With respect to the self-distinction of philosophy vis-à-vis science, Jaspers characterizes philosophy as "awakening" possibilities of the self's free realization of what is and what ought to be rather than as "prophetic" proclamation which aims, in the end, at "subjection and imitation."[71] The other result of this search was Jaspers's consideration of the methods of metaphysics. He rejects the possibility of metaphysics as quasi-scientific research into Being, and also "prophetic metaphysics." He opens the possibility of a critical incorporation of historic metaphysical realization; this was not explored in that work—but later became the task of his "world-history of philosophy." And he presents the methods of transcending developed in the *Philosophie:* formal transcending, existential relations to transcendence, and reading of the cipher-script. Concerning prophetic metaphysics he says:

> Prophetic metaphysics is able to proclaim its contents on the basis of original certitude. It believes itself to have advanced to knowledge of what really is. This could be done in truth only at the dawn of philosophical thought; but [under the condition] of reflective clarity, knowledge of the world and assurance of freedom this can work only at the price of a blindness which is able to suggest community devoid of communication but not to speak as self to self. . . . It lacks a faculty of irony with respect to its own thought-formulations. . . . In other historical situations prophetic metaphysics creatively produced and expressed experience of transcendence. Today it can only reiterate, without truth, the outer form of proclamation without original substance in the service of spiritual rape through superstition.[72]

Any doubt that such criticisms are aimed at Buber's conception and consequent mode of presentation of the primacy of the dialogical might be dispelled by another passage from a different context. We have to precede its quotation with the observation that we could not find any evidence that Jaspers had read any of Buber's dialogical writings prior to the publication of his *Philosophie* from which it is taken. The only philosophical writings of Buber which can be found in Jaspers's library are two copies of *Daniel* (1913) and the German version of *Between Man and Man* (*Das Problem des Menschen*, 1948). The fundamental book of Buber's conception of the dialogical which was published prior to Jaspers's *Philosophie*, i.e., *I and Thou*, is not to be found there. One of the copies of *Daniel* is marked, but much more infrequently and sporadically than Jaspers was wont to mark books which interested him. Moreover, on the first inside leaf of the book he wrote a devastating comment about Buber the "prophet" which was characteristic of the decisive judgments Jaspers made in his youth. While it is not impossible that Jaspers may have had a copy of *I and Thou* which has now disappeared there is no good reason to assume that this is the case. Jaspers was an avid buyer of books in any field which might have been of interest to him. And from the period under consideration there are to be found Buber's two main works on Hasidism, both in editions of 1916, i.e., *Die Geschichten des Rabbi Nachman* and *Die Legende des Baalschem*. Also I remember how, during a conversation with Jaspers, Jaspers's high praise of Buber's work in behalf of bringing the hasidic world to public attention was in marked contrast to his rejection of Buber as a philosopher.

I conclude that Jaspers's experience with Buber prior to 1920 and with the reading of *Daniel* was decisive for his later lack of interest in his philosophical work. Yet he must have known about *I and Thou*, presumably from periodicals, from his friends and students. Only this can explain why passages such as these epitomize what from Jaspers's viewpoint is the danger contained in Buber's conception of the dialogical as if it were written with direct reference to it. This section on the distinction between the voice of conscience and the voice of God appears in an exploration of conscience as a mode of absolute consciousness:

> Although in conscience I am in view of transcendence, I can neither hear it nor heed it like a voice from another world. The voice of conscience is not God's voice. It is precisely when conscience speaks that the deity is silent, that it remains hidden, here as everywhere. My conscience points me toward transcendence but leaves me on my own. The deity has not deprived me of my freedom, and thus relieved me of my responsibility, by showing itself.
>
> An identification of the voice of conscience with God's voice confuses me about myself *and* the deity if it puts me into the position of being addressed by God, confronted by him as by a 'thou'. The self-communication of conscience is put into objective form, then, as a supposedly direct communication with God.
>
> The first consequence would be to void the factual communication between Existenz and Existenz. If I consort with God directly, how can another individual be of absolute import to me? God as a 'thou' I consort with is a means of self-seclusion, of intolerantly closing my mind to the other conscience. The truth of a relation to God can lie only in existential communication, and any that falls short of prompt communicative realization is not only questionable in itself but a betrayal of Existenz.[73]

This can serve as the last word in our explication of Jaspers's account of the combative character of the way to truth on the part of man in time and in freedom, and of his hope of civilizing man's combat in behalf of truth by means of realizing it, together with love, as characteristic of the very conception of truth for man.

Chapter Five

Authority and Tradition

i. Force and Power

The certainty of being which is the fruit of the concern over ultimate truth is, for man, who thinks in time, an expression of faith.
According to Jaspers, faith in its appropriate realization is historic
and engaged in a struggle with other faiths. This means two things.
First, a person is responsible for his faith and, by risking his being
for it, bears witness to its truth by virtue of his freedom. On the
other hand it means the self-restriction of the being in time vis-à-
vis the source of truth in its transcendent absoluteness. In both
meanings the realization of faith in its historic and combative conception raises the problem of authority. For where the person
stands absolutely on his freedom, the role and scope of authority
are questioned. And where man conceives of his limitation and
seeks sources of guidance beyond himself, authority is invoked as
the concrete form of guidance. It is, therefore, not surprising that
in the development of Jaspers's philosophy of freedom, the question of authority merits frequent and major consideration.

First of all, we find in his works a concern to indicate the precise
location of genuine authority. The outward phenomena of authority are power and the deference to power which is both claimed
and received.[1] Deference can take many forms such as influence,
succession, the prevalence of norms, or precedents. The power of
authority is exercised either by virtue of the confidence it inspires
or by virtue of the force it wields.

On the problem of force hangs the fundamental distinction between authority which is genuine and that which is not. It would
seem that historically no authority exercises its power without
force which appears in many forms and is justified in many ways.
The exercises of power may be based on a conception of man
which derives from certain psychological insights. Man, for example, has some fundamental needs and the will to live; there are
limits to his ability to exercise his freedom and stand on his own
responsibility; "everyone has his price" is a well-known American
adage. The form of force by which such power is exercised is to

find man in appropriately dire straits and to remind him of the limits of his endurance, and thus to secure or maintain his submission either with or without catering to his needs. Of course this is extreme. Force based on a purely psychological image of man can take on broader forms of paternalism which render to the masses of men the tutelage they naturally desire, and maintain a satisfying order for their lives whose achievement by their own choice and labor would be impossible. In the relevant explanations Jaspers quotes Dostoevski's *Grand Inquisitor* in justifying the arrest of Jesus for his disturbing reappearance:

> Dost Thou care only for the tens of thousands of the great and strong, while the millions, numerous as the sands of the sea, who are weak but love Thee, must exist only for the sake of the great and strong? No, we care for the weak, too. They are sinful and rebellious, but in the end they too will become obedient. They will marvel at us and look on us as gods, because we are ready to endure the freedom which they have found so dreadful and to rule over them—so awful it will seem to them to be free. But we shall tell them that we are Thy servants and rule them in Thy name. We shall deceive them again, for we will not let Thee come to us again. The deception will be our suffering, for we shall be forced to lie. [2]

Different from the exercise of power which uses force based on such psychological and sociological means and considerations, and from that which uses brute, physical force, is the power of intellectual force. [3] The power of the intellectually superior to secure obedience without conviction instead of giving the other the tools of insight and agreement, is notorious. Even more acute is the problem of the authority of the specialist and expert. This is a typically modern phenomenon engendered by the development of the more or less autonomous fields of science and their technological application. It is one thing if the beneficiary of the expert's knowledge or service is free to ask questions, and, sharing the insight, makes his decision. It is another thing if the expert demands confidence simply because, vis-à-vis the beneficiary, he is the expert. For two things can never be certain: that the beneficiary is incapable of sufficiently understanding what the expert understands, and that the demand for unquestioned deference is not merely a front for a measure of incompetence. Jaspers says,

> Only those who are really knowledgeable and competent, and therefore capable of unrestricted justification and response [to questioning] have the right to authority as experts. On the

175847

other hand, only those who are capable of knowing, of distinguishing the meaning and the possibilities of what can be known, have a right to know as beneficiaries.[4]

An acute and particularly vexing form of intellectual force is the case where, for reasons of state, information, on the basis of which decisions are made which affect great multitudes, is kept secret. That this may—upon occasion and temporarily—be necessary, may be conceded. However, it must also be conceded that such necessity engenders a way of life which may reach ominous proportions.

A final example of power through insight is that exercised over the believer in the transcendent source of salvation by the temporal representative of this source: "There is force in the representation of physical tortures in hell and the exclusion from the sacraments, as long as the reality of these effects remain undoubted."[5]

In the case of each one of these examples, power is exercised through force precisely because man is conceived as subject to conditions which can be known and, hence, manipulated. In the one case these are the psychophysical needs, drives, desires, and weakness of man; in another, the social-psychological proneness to dependence and peace; in another, the ignorance of and need for knowledge which he is unable to gain or to use; and in another, his fear for his salvation which is tied to a superstitious version of a faith, a version which appeals to his common experience. But insofar as man is conceived as conditioned and knowable we cannot speak of genuine authority. As we shall see, genuine authority is, for Jaspers, intimately tied to man's freedom. In his freedom man is unconditioned. It is not a factor which can be observed, explained and, hence, maneuvered. It cannot be known but only appealed to and aroused—if it is there. Therefore, what remains of an authority which fails to appeal to man's freedom or discounts the possibility of freedom is the exercise of force.

This is not to say that authority can be actual without being a power in the world. It means, rather, that a strong distinction must be made between power and force. Whether this distinction can be translated into concrete life is, of course, problematical. Presumably Jaspers considers this to be a task assigned both to those who, by exercising the power of authority, appeal to man's freedom, and those who, by virtue of their freedom, defer to authority. He therefore speaks of authority as a tension between the poles of concrete power and the truth content which the authority represents: "Mere mundane power would turn to empty force. And truth which would claim validity without power would not be authoritative."[6] The ideal resolution of this tension and the negative relation of force to authority Jaspers expresses as follows:

> In its pure ideal, authority would be powerful but free of force, firm but without compulsion. The more compulsion, the less authority. The measure of the use of force is a measure of the loss of authority. The ideal of authority without force is opposed to terror without authority.[7]

ii. The Tension Between Freedom and Authority

The first result, therefore, of Jaspers's concern to find the locale of authority is that while it prevails only as mundane power, it is not merely mundane power. Something is represented in authority which is the concern of freedom. Jaspers's conception of this can be formulated as follows: it is the concern to realize truth in human awareness and to will its realization in human deed. The respective positions of authority and of the free self with regard to this realization differ but are of mutual concern; therefore there is a tension between authority and freedom, which is a mark of both.[8] The oneness of truth which reason seeks and of which the self means to partake by virtue of its historic faith and its unique and particular realization is highly restricted by virtue of the limitations attending this historicity and uniqueness. Vis-à-vis the temporal restriction of the self and its faith, authority may make claims which tend to reduce the insistence on one's own freedom of conscience to a show of pride and a loss of truth. The authority—of the social order and its institutions, of the cultural goods, of the heritage of a civilization or of a religion—may claim to represent the bursting forth into human actuality and history of the oneness of truth in the form of a comprehensive universality. For such a universality, the labor of the concern over truth on the part of selves in their singular freedom looks like an "arbitrary multiplicity of opinion and desire."[9] The claims of authority on the self are indeed overwhelming. Jaspers's examination of these claims is animated by three considerations. First, the free, thinking self is the inevitable and indispensable carrier of human realization. Secondly, authority, in its expression and with respect to those who exercise it, is itself as human as the one who defers to it. Finally, authority is only one way in which truth breaks upon the human scene; another way, and incompatible with authority, is the exception. Hence, in considering the tension between authority and freedom, the primary question is that of the significance of authority for freedom. The correlative question of the importance of freedom for authority is secondary.

The actuality of authority is grounded on an exigency of free selfhood, which may be characterized as follows. In the conception of freedom, Jaspers follows paths trodden by many men of the philosophical tradition; men, for example, as different as Spinoza, Kant and Kierkegaard. For him, freedom is not incompatible with necessity. On the contrary, according to Jaspers, arbitrariness (*Willkür*), i.e., choice out of unlimited possibilities and, hence, without rhyme or reason, is not identical with freedom, though easily and often confused with it. Freedom is more than that; it is the narrowing of possibilities to that one which is the expression of truth in time. It is the resolution to act in accordance with truth. It is, thus, the self-determination of the self as carrier of truth. It is, speaking in terms of historicity and in the language of Kierkegaard, the choice, made in time, of eternal validity. The need for authority does not arise from the self-creating self-restriction to what the truth demands. This need arises, rather, from man's limitation with respect to his knowledge of the truth. He does not always grasp what his situation and the required decision entail. Or else he is not always able to make use of his resources to hit upon the decisive possibility. Man realizes himself by realizing the truth which he believes. But concrete reality is the arena of this realization. Hence much depends on the extent of man's grasp of concrete reality. Also, actions are based on the judgment of the consequences of the truth which man believes. Furthermore, the resources which man has to tap and the situations for realizing truth in time vary and change. The grasp of reality, the judgment of consequences, and the availability of resources and situations are seldom so comprehensive that a person can take the decision of the course of events upon himself without recourse to some form of authority. And, of course, all this is predicated on the supposition that the person has mastered the distinction between, on the one hand, freedom through the restraint of insight and concern over truth, and, on the other hand, the freedom of arbitrary choice between a multiplicity of compossibles. There are, indeed, times when such a multiplicity offers itself; but then there is at stake neither the risk of self nor the prevailing of truth.

Genuine authority springs, then, from the limitation of the self in knowing what one must know in order to do what one ought to do. The ideal way of deferring to authority is to affirm *within* what is offered by the authority *without*. But to think for oneself, to be fully responsible, means, ultimately, to dispense with authority. Moreover, for the one who thinks for himself, particularly as regards his concern to realize truth in its oneness in his singular selfhood, authority seems to interfere with truth. For "genuine authority urges man not to depend on himself alone."[10] Hence, the tension between freedom and authority.

Indeed, no man can dispense with authority. In childhood, before we awaken to ourselves and to our relation to authority, it nurtures our selfhood, guides us toward realizing truth and provides us with the first certainty of being, particularly in the form of tradition, ethical norms, knowledge and religious faith, and by means of education.[11] If we deny such authority and turn against it, we deny ourselves. And even those rare persons who, in due time, can succeed in responding to the high demands of thinking and speaking for themselves, will affirm authority in two ways. They will use authority where they fail or reach their limitations. Or else they will measure their independent achievement against the standards upheld by authority. Hence, Jaspers states that

> the contents of one's own freedom impel toward the approval by authority or toward the opposition to authority; to prove oneself in this opposition is a sign of the possible truth of those contents without which they cannot be distinguished from random impulses. Authority either provides confirming strength, or, by opposition to it, it provides form and guidance and prevents unreasoned choice (*Beliebigkeit*). Precisely the one who can stand on his own feet wills that there be authority in the world.[12]

Just as no freedom seems possible without genuine authority, so no authority is possible without freedom. Authority solicits the consent and agreement of its followers, and is sustained by the free faith that in it and through it truth prevails. The ideal statesman is an educator. Authority which does not appeal to freedom is a sham; it will subsist on fear and force, and collapse if it should fail in its total enforcement. It would not be authority over men because that would discount the freedom by which man becomes human. Absolutely stated, the difference between sham and genuine authority is contained in the alternative: either appeal to force or appeal to freedom. Either preside over a humanity which is constituted by whatever remains of it when freedom is denied, or exemplify the power of truth through mundane impotence. We find a characterization of the former alternative in Jaspers's writings on the potentials and dangers of totalitarianism and in this passage from *Von der Wahrheit:*

> We cannot reject the conception that a future potentate would force the whole planet into a single house of labor which is dominated by his authority. This would not succeed but only lead to tremendous catastrophes simply because, first, the ruler would deceive himself, at a decisive point, about the real relations of events, the disregard of which would result in the collapse of the whole scheme. Secondly, man would, unconsciously and explosively, break through all orders so as to gain renewed chances at being human.[13]

And apropos the other extreme we find the following exemplification in Jaspers:

> Perfectly true authority means the rejection of all force. Our Western symbol is the crucified Jesus, the man prepared for total impotence, suffering, failure, and death, prepared to renounce all power that is not love.[14]

iii. The Transcendent Ground of Authority

However, the dependence of authority on freedom is fraught with difficulty. It is as possible for the totalitarian or nihilistic potentate or the charlatan to demand freely chosen deference as it is for genuine authority. This phenomenon is quite familiar. The reader of Orwell's *1984* will no doubt be haunted by the vision of Winston who, at the end of the story, is moved to tears as he experiences for the first time his own grateful deference to the implacable, inescapable omnipresence of "Big Brother." This vision is not merely the product of an imagination gifted with dismal prophecy. It is apposite to the recent actualities and the present real possibilities of totalitariansim whose nature was subjected to acute analysis by Hannah Arendt. Among the points of her book which are relevant for us is the observation that it lies in the nature of a totalitarian regime to require its victims to be instruments of their own destruction. Of the innumerable additional examples, the public is well aware of the instances of show trials with their confessions and "brainwashing."

Precisely in considering this difficulty can we fully understand Jaspers's contention that the transcendent grounding is an indispensable feature of genuine authority.[15] This means several things.

First of all, all authority issues from man, either a person or a group, an institution, or a product of human endeavor. Yet it is not man as man who is the authority but the one truth which is intimated in and through man and which in its absoluteness always transcends human realization. Genuine authority does not prevail by virtue of its "say-so" but by virtue of its appeal to the truth which can bind all men by transcending man and human testimony. It is not the mundane power but the truth speaking through it which constitutes genuine authority.

Secondly, conditional and evidential truth or a realm thereof or an absolutization thereof cannot be the basis for man's guidance and cannot be the basis of authority. Such absolutization can, to be sure, provide the unity of truth over which man is concerned and which authority represents. Examples have been provided by referring to authority based on a purely empirical conception of man. In this category also belongs an authority which bases itself upon the foundation of a putatively scientifically derived conception of the inevitable course of history, as in dialectical materialism. Genuine authority does not make man entirely conditional upon an immanent necessity. In appealing to freedom it appeals to a dimension of man whereby he transcends mundane conditionality. It leaves man the recourse to a source of his and of all being, to a source of possibilities in whose realization he himself participates. It is the role of authority to facilitate this participation.

Third, it means that no actual authority is absolute. The human situation is fluid, aspirations and their realization grow and lessen, knowledge and its use never stand still, and cause a constant change of conditions. There are ever new challenges and the man and humanity facing them are ever new, and the determination to face them becomes stronger and weaker. Thus man's directedness toward the unity of truth is attuned to the range and content of realized truths. Authority is the proponent of unity in consideration of the limitation of the single person. The cogency of the unity it proposes is a function of the human labor and experience which it reflects, and of the actual humanity to which it speaks and whose deference it demands. A mundane authority which is absolute would have to comprise possibilities of the human realization of truth which have not as yet occurred. Or else it would have to arrest the temporal movement of mankind. The persistence of authority and of man's deference to it presupposes the transcendent grounding as source of its being and its renewal.

Authority, like the personal concern over truth in its unity, must reflect the "fundamental discrepancy" of human existence, a notion which underlies all of Jaspers's philosophy of truth and without which it cannot be understood. The discrepancy is that thought and the human concern over truth are directed toward unity; but this unity must constantly be sought; we are constantly on the way to it.[16] In time there is no rest, no finality, no completion of truth—but also no meaning without the search for it.

Hence authority is, like the personal directedness and realization of truth, historic.[17] No authority is absolute. No authority is timeless. No authority is universal. No authority is the only authority; rather, there are many authorities, engaged in mutual struggle.[18] And no authority cancels out personal autonomy and conscience.

iv. Philosophical Critique of Authority

Jaspers's characterization of authority vis-à-vis the distinction of force and power, with respect to the relation of freedom and authority, and as transcendently grounded, culminates in the assertion of its historic nature. In consideration of its historicity, Jaspers subjects authority to philosophical evaluation. Of the many issues which he raises, three are of particular interest to us. First, how do authorities tend to actually function and how ought they to function? Second, what is the relation of authority to the exception? Third, what is the relation of the philosophically independent person to authority?

Two facts, which Jaspers considers basic and which we have already mentioned, underlie his various descriptions and critiques of the function of authorities: the fact that authority is grounded in and ultimately concerned over truth which, in its absolute oneness, transcends human realization and the fact that the power by which authority becomes effective in the world tends to resort to force. As to the first fact, the claim of truth by an authority challenges other authorities or persons who question it or follow other truths vouchsafed by other sources. In mutual confrontation, genuine authorities are fundamentally

antagonistic to that which makes them genuine, i.e. their relation to transcendent truth. This circumstance points to what, in
Jaspers's view, is an inevitable and fateful constituent of genuine
authority, namely, its claim to exclusiveness. This claim, he says,

> indeed belongs to authority. It seems that it has to deny all
> authority other than its own. . . . It has the One, the true God.
> It pre-empts the exclusive relation to transcendence. It has
> entered a covenant with transcendence. Everything else be-
> comes, before it is known, material for transcendence, i.e., in
> the world, for one's own authority.[19]

This claim is present no matter what the relation between contending authorities. Even where there is accommodation, each
party reserves for itself the right to decision if there is a conflict of
interest.[20] Jaspers's treatment of the problems of exclusiveness is
a touchstone of his philosophy of truth and freedom and of his
critique of politics and religion. This severe criticism and rejection
of the claims to exclusiveness in the biblical religions and of totalitarianism, which he regards as its political descendent, does not
mean that he absolutely rejects this sort of claim as a human possibility, i.e., a claim which would fulfill reason's natural penchant
for unity, which would tend to unite mankind and comprise man's
various pursuits by virtue of an all-embracing faith, a single vision
of truth. Thus, the startled reader of Jaspers stumbles over the
following manifestation of nostalgia which he expresses in an evaluation of the results of the revolts against the *"una sancta ca-
tholica"*:

> Profound mourning overwhelms us as we regard the breaking
> up of the one occidental church. How precious was this unity!
> What untold forces, particular and ruinous in kind, were un-
> leashed! How much more stringent has oppression and dog-
> matization become, how much more abysmal the chaotic arbi-
> trariness! The possibility of the lofty polarity of authority and
> freedom in vital motion is extinct.[21]

Hence Jaspers rejects the claim of exclusiveness only in a specific
sense. He does not suggest that authorities can abrogate all claims
to the exclusiveness of their truths—for this claim is unavoidable:
any genuine authority must be prepared to make it in some form.
Neither does he reject the object of the claim of exclusiveness, i.e.,
the realization of the oneness of truth, unifying disparateness, as
the aim of reason and as the basis of the meaningfulness of human
existence. All authority, if it is genuine, must in some way mediate

this oneness for man. Jaspers rejects the claim of exclusiveness if this means that the aim of realizing the one truth mediated by an authority is deemed to have been reached, if this means that the form of the truth represented by an authority congeals into dogmatic rigidity, if this means that the human formulation of the truth transmitted by a human—and therefore limited—authority is mistaken for the authority of truth in its transcendent oneness, and if this means that the claims to truth on the part of an authority need not be and are not exposed to the challenge of communication. This type of claim to exclusiveness obtains when the second of the two relevant facts concerning authority comes to fruition, namely, when the power of an authority has recourse to force.

In Jaspers's view the possibility of an all-embracing human authority, with recourse to temporal power, though it cannot be rejected in principle, is remote, and unrealizable as long as it can revert to the exercise of "sheer force or arbitrariness,"[22] and the tendency toward it must be considered an error and a danger for freedom and truth, and must therefore be curbed. He says,

> Whatever appears in the world is, as such, made, done and lived by man. A human authority—so also every church—can never be the highest for all and for ever but only for some people and for some time. Wherever a human authority[23] is believed to be the highest authority, then, in a tortuous crisis which cries out for truth, the most terrible disappointment gives proof of this error by the neglect of its representatives and the failure of its institutions.[24]

What, then, of the future of authority which for Jaspers, as we have seen, is indispensable for man's potentiality of freedom and truth? For him the solution to this problem lies in two directions.

First of all, there ought to be a distinct separation of authorities, whose truths are matters of faith, from force as a means of exercising their power. This, of course, accords with the previously mentioned "pure ideal" of authority which is "powerful but free of force."[25] It is the concern over ultimate truth and the free pursuit thereof that makes man into man. But, though the truth, which is the object of this concern and pursuit, is one, its realization is historic and hence not one for all men. If, however, the claim to the exclusiveness of one's truth for oneself is allied to temporal force, then the validity of this claim can be extended to others and all. And this, in the end, destroys the freedom with respect to ultimate truth which is the *conditio sine qua non* of man's realization of truth. For Jaspers this holds true not only for the relation of religious faith to the resources of enforcement of the temporal powers but also for the relation of *Weltanschauungen* to politics. None of his apothegms, which he formulates with singular facility, is as earnestly documented as it is passionately proposed than the one stating that "one cannot talk with fighters for a faith" (*mit Glaubenskämpfern lässt sich nicht reden*). For Jaspers, the separation of force on the one hand, and matters of faith and the authorities concerned over such matters on the other hand, is not only a historical mark of the development of the Western idea of democratic, political freedom,[26] but the key to the joining of personal freedom with the perpetuation and revitalization of the truths of faith by which human life gains its meaningfulness.

Freedom of conscience with respect to matters of faith and ultimate truth require the abolition of the use of force by authorities which are concerned with such matters. If the historicity of faith and authority is duly regarded, then the openness and loving struggle of communication is, for authorities no less than for the singular person, the alternative to enforced exclusiveness. This abolition restricts the use of force to the less lofty realm of matters which men clearly have in common, matters rooted in natural necessity. Men are alike in their struggle for mundane existence. They have a claim to the goods and opportunities which make such existence possible. The natural state, in this regard, is *bellum omnium contra omnes*. The greatest chance for equitable distribution of goods and the opportunity of attaining or partaking of them lies in deliberation, agreement, specific legislation, and administration. This is, of course, the realm of politics and voluntarily accepted enforcement, and, for Jaspers, the only proper realm of politics and enforcement. If politics steps beyond this realm, it infringes on freedom; if it remains within it, it provides the opportunity for personal freedom. Of course, political freedom can only promote, it cannot guarantee personal freedom. Jaspers summarizes his restriction of law and politics to an authority of a lower order as follows:

> Politics that spring from man's will to liberty, however, effect a self-conquest that leads to moderation. Their aim is confined to the interests of existence, in which they seek to give scope to all human potentialities that are not inimical to that which is indispensably common to all. They are tolerant toward all who do not strive after force through intolerance. They follow the path of a continual diminution of force.[27]

For Jaspers, the restriction of enforcing authority to the concerns of mundane existence is suspect if it is not accompanied by the recognition of this authority as being of a lower order. For then the determinable immanence of the world is all, what man can demonstrably know is the sole guide, and the man who is in the seat of power is the only authority.[28] The result of the conflation of mere mundane authority and genuine authority is subjection and submission, discontinuity and upheaval, the sealing off of the sources of freedom and selfhood.

We have, so far, shown one aspect of Jaspers's critique of authority, namely that concerning the need to divorce the power of genuine authority from the means of enforcement. Another important aspect is his discussion of the relevance of opposition to authority. The concept he employs to designate this opposition is that of indignation. This concept has a much wider significance for Jaspers, being one of two extreme existential positions vis-à-vis the experienced fundamental disruption of Being, the other being tranquillity.[29] The position of tranquillity with respect to the transcendent authority—or its human mediation—of the oneness of Being which has been experienced as disrupted and awry, is obedience. The opposite position is revolt. For Jaspers, the former is exemplified by Jeremiah ending his days in Egypt, the latter by Ivan Karamazov.[30] Since human authorities, despite the fact that they are historically the most comprehensive forms of human representation of Being in its unity, are only approximations thereof and historic, human realization of Being which defies established authorities is a constant possibility. Indeed, according to Jaspers, "authority which is vital contains the tension which makes indignation against authority possible."[31] Within the realm of human realization, where authority prevails and is accepted, such indignation can be either extrinsic to or intrinsic to a given authority. The former is the struggle to supplant one authority with a truer one; the latter is the struggle from within to raise an authority to a higher realization.[32] Outside the realm of authority stands, on the one hand, the one whose indignation turns against all authority whatever. However, since freedom reqires authority, the destruction of the latter destroys the former. On the other hand there is the exception.

v. The Exception and the Philosopher

In considering, even if only briefly, Jaspers's treatment of the exception,[33] it is helpful to keep three things in mind. First, nowhere else is Jaspers's kinship to Kierkegaard manifested with such constant reference to, dependence on and interpretation of him. Second, Jaspers conceives of the exception in polar relationship to authority. Third, both his conception of authority and that of the exception are essential parts of his theory of truth.

Exception and authority are mutually incompatible: the mark of authority is universality which, in its intention and potentially, comprises and concerns all men. The mark of the exception is singularity defying universality. The exception is neither comprehensible nor justifiable, particularly from the viewpoint of authority, because comprehension and justification require subsumption under universality. The exception is, therefore, disturbing when it is noted and, when it is taken seriously, a potential danger. On the other hand, it is, potentially, the inception of a new universality, a new authority. In both respects Kierkegaard, the person, serves as a case in point, first as a gadfly of the established church, particularly in Denmark, then, in this century, as a rallying point for a new orthodoxy.

Since the exception is, from the viewpoint of authority, incommensurable, it might be an instance of irrationality, destruction and chaos. This judgment would be correct only if authority were the only signal of encompassing truth for man. But it is not. The exception as well as authority, its polar opposite, is a form of the "break-through" of the encompassing, transcendent unity of truth. What does this mean? Man aims at the unity of truth; nothing less than the realization of this unity will fulfill this aim. Yet man's search and research, his thought and experience confirm the fragmentation of being and disruption of truth. The pieces do not fall into place to form a unified whole. Absolute oneness remains transcendent. But it can be regarded as intimating itself, as approximated in, and mediated by both—authority and that which does not fit the authority: the exception. Neither of them can be deduced or justified; they can both only be believed by virtue of faith. In the case of both, the one truth "breaks through" the haze of fragmentation and man's limitation. But both are, in turn, incomplete and historic.[34] Hence, for the sake of truth, authority requires the challenge of the exception which breaks the limitation of human universality. And, for the sake of human realization of the transcendent universality of truth glimpsed by it, the exception requires the communicability of the human universality, whose instrument is authority. In fact, authority, as historic universality, is less than the transcendent universality of truth in its unity, and hence itself an exception.[35] Irrationality in whatever form, such as non-dialectical contradictoriness or the plunge into unmitigated vitality or sensuality, does not seek the communicability which is the mark of authority and the problematical aim and requirement of the exception. Irrationality is, therefore, opposed to both, authority and exception. It is less than authority. The exception, as the breaking forth of transcendent truth into human historicity, is not less but, perhaps, more than authority.[36]

Because of its very concept, no general, positive characteristics of the exception can be given, aside from what it shares with authority, i.e., they are grounded in transcendence, they are historic, and hence unique and incomplete intimations of the one truth, and their truth is a matter of faith, not of knowledge.[37] Only negative characterizations of the exception can be given. And because of these it is impossible to desire to be an exception. For to be an exception means, first of all, to be excepted, to experience a call to which one then subjects oneself.[38] Whether one has been truly chosen, however, remains problematical for, by being an exception, one swims against the stream and one does not have recourse to the universality which is embodied in authority. (*Vide* Kierkegaard's interpretation of the temptation of Abraham.) Authority is a shelter and the condition of self-realization as mundane being. The exception must affirm the reign of universality and authority as the sound, normal and desirable condition for human realization, yet deny for itself what it acknowledges to be universally incumbent on man. The negative phenomena of the exception are, therefore, its problematical nature vis-à-vis the others, its negative decisions with respect to one's mundane realization (*vide* Kierkegaard and Socrates), and, ultimately, its essentially sacrificial character.[39] Exception is a sacrifice by which new visions of truth burst through the dams of authority, or by which old visions may be received and lifted to new heights of realization, or by which an age or mankind might measure its veracity.

We have, so far, spoken of the radical exception which, for Jaspers, is exemplified by men such as Socrates, Kierkegaard and Nietzsche. However, basically every man is potentially an exception if he is historic in his self-realization as the temporal witness of eternal truth. Hence Jaspers says,

> We ourselves and everyone are what in its extreme form was designated as . . . exception, insofar as we are historically actual and reflective; and no one is [an exception], insofar as every genuine exception relates to the universal which it illuminates.[40]

We are exceptions if we, though temporal creatures, are imbued with the one transcendent truth whether by benefit of authoritative mediation or by being graced with imbibing it at its sources. In either case truth, ultimately, lies outside of authority. But in either case, also, we must uphold authority as the inevitable vehicle of truth for man. If we are able—and graced—we must work, for the sake of the truth, within authority against what it is for what it ought to be. The radical exception, on the other hand, storms the bastion of authority—albeit as a tragic offering, i.e., as instrument of the truth against its will. Yet even it is fated to be the soil on which authority grows.

The question of truth causes the treatment of authority and exception to be pervaded by a certain dialectic. They are opposed to one another. Yet as the breakthrough of truth into human limitation they stand together against narrowness and irrationality. However, authority is the truer the more it confirms its historicity, i.e., its exceptedness. And the exception, in the primary affirmation of truth, affirms authority as a way thereto. Only the radical exception is destined to break with authority—only to be the potential foundation for a new one. This dialectic raises the question of the position of philosophical independence vis-à-vis authority.

Jaspers illuminates the nature of philosophy and philosophizing with many rays and from many vantage points. The following is not a comprehensive account of Jaspers's conception of philosophizing but one which will serve our present purpose. It is the risk, freely undertaken by a singular self in search of fulfillment, to reflectively realize the one truth in time. Authority and exception are forms in which the one truth breaks into time. Is, then, the philosophizing person in a third position vis-à-vis authority and exception, and does he gain his independence by virtue of this position? In Jaspers's sense this has to be denied. For the polarity 'authority-exception' exhausts the possibilities; there is no position outside of it. The position of philosophy is, therefore, to be found within this polarity. Strictly speaking, to philosophize means to be an exception. Jaspers states this explicitly, in the apparent particular reference to the rare great philosophers.[41] However, such exceptedness through reflective thought is an achievement, partial and in stages, and a task, recurrent and continuous, of freedom. Sovereign independence is not attained by the mere desire for it or the resolution to attain it. And sovereignty such as it is, even at the highest level, must maintain itself communicatively with respect to other sovereign minds and measure itself against authority and universality. Authority nourishes the reflective person and even if, with sovereign independence, one rises above it, it is a piece of oneself. This is the way we understand passages in Jaspers such as the following:

The person who is awakening philosophically . . . entrusts himself to tradition as long as no self-vitiating contradiction arises;
he obeys authority wherever examination and decision are not,
as yet, possible or not necessary. . . . He meets the heritage
with awe, and the persons, through whom it is transmitted,
with piety. Deciding for oneself is never questioned when the
position of independence is attained, but one resorts to it only
if the concrete situation requires it because of one's responsibility toward oneself. . . . He does not throw off claims with a
light heart, for, in accepting, he wishes to be loyal and not to
forget. Whoever has become aware of his full independence,
risks it in quiet resolution and does not grasp it in blind joy.
He has a decisive sense of heritage and tradition.[42]

In this passage we see a significant implied distinction between
two kinds of authority, i.e., between heritage and the institutional
authority. The latter, unlike the former, has an objective palpabil-
ity and a tendency toward recourse to the means of enforcement.
Hence there may be found, in Jaspers's writings, a difference in his
characterization of the position of philosophical independence
according to whether it is vis-à-vis the former or the latter. One's
relation to one's heritage can be as free of reserve as it is free of
force.[43] Man's heritage bestows its benefits of selfhood and truth
according to the intensity of self-realization and profoundity of
truth-seeking with which one approaches, penetrates, and incorporates it. And the incorporation need not only mean accepting as
true what was valid before and for others. It also means rejecting
for oneself what, in confrontation with transmitted testimony, is
found to have been an actualized possibility of humanity for another. One becomes oneself as much in recognizing oneself in the
truth of another as in delimiting one's own truth from what is true
for another but not for oneself. In either case one is liable to miss
becoming what one can be by not searching out and comprehending the heritage of transmitted testimony of vision and realization,
of folly and failure. For Jaspers, the incorporation of the broad
range of historic possibilities can only bring forth and promote,
and cannot destroy, one's own historicity. Opposition to the human heritage does not consist in one's rejection of it but in one's
indifference or blindness to it. Genuine realization of truth and
self is then still possible, but it will be meager, primitive, uncritical. For this reason the significance of the heritage for man's realization of truth in time looms large.

Jaspers's characterization of the position of philosophical independence vis-à-vis institutional authority is quite different. Almost

all that we have said about his dialectic of authority pertains primarily to it and only secondarily to the authority of the heritage and tradition. One of his autobiographical anecdotes is as revealing as any theoretical account:

> In my last year in the *Gymnasium* . . . I came upon the idea that, for the sake of veracity, I would have to leave the church. When I disclosed my intention to my father, he said something like this: My boy, you may, of course, do as you please. But in your own mind you are not yet clear about what you mean to do. You are not alone in the world. Co-responsibility requires that the individual should not simply go his way. We can only live together with our fellow-men, if we conform to the regulations. Religion is one of the regulative forces. If we destroy it, unforeseeable evil will break through. That much lying is connected with the church as, indeed, with all human institutions, in this I agree with you. The situation will be different, perhaps, once you are seventy years of age. Before death, when we are no longer active in the world, we may clear the deck by leaving the church.[44]

As it happens, Jaspers's father did, indeed, leave the church at seventy, and as we have seen, this action accords with Jaspers's conception of the single self's relation to authority. Yet this conception also accords with the fact that, to the best of our knowledge, Jaspers himself did not, even past his seventieth year, officially leave the church. For we read in his *Philosophie:*

> As one who philosophizes I do not aim at nothingness but, perhaps, venture to be—in the idiom of former times—a heretic in the church, or essentially, a protestant. I need not break off entirely; for my own person I can let my own real relation to the ecclasiastical actuality shrink to sociological minimum. I do not wish to deprive the new generation of that which was for me foundation, nor to lose my reverence for tradition.[45]

Jaspers's critique of religion and church is a special topic. What is of immediate interest in this passage is that the possibility of being "a heretic in the church" would, in Jaspers's view, far from weakening authority, raise it to the realization of its ideal. For in its ideal form, genuine authority, acknowledging its own historicity, avoids the enforcement of its claim to truth, promotes and is engaged in communication and, preferring truth to itself, provides for the possibility of indignation against itself. In the end, so Jaspers might say, the profundity of truth an authority upholds is proportionate to the range of historic possibilities for which it provides communicative solidarity, and not to the number of people it unites in like-mindedness.

Jaspers discloses a notion of self-realization through realization of truth as grounded in transmitted heritage which does away with the alternative: either to live one's life in one's time and let the other do likewise as he sees fit, or be molded by and perpetuate tradition. If, as Jaspers thinks, the chance of truth for man lies in communication, then the idiom in which each communicant presents himself for this loving struggle can only be enriched by the nourishment of tradition. Since, moreover, the realization of truth through communication can only be historic, life lived for the mere perpetuation of tradition infects no reasoned action, and both are lost: the possibilities of truth resident in the tradition as well as the chance of selfhood through the realization of such possibilities. For man, there is no truth in the heritage as such; and man's truth is impoverished without heritage. And the heritage's nourishment of the communicative way to truth depends as much on not imposing it on the other as on permitting it to promote one's own realization of truth. This notion of truth for man finds truth embedded in the active mode of man's existence, and thereby considers the logical and abstract criteriology of truth to be not a central but an aspectual, though essential, position. It will not have escaped the reader that this provides for the inevitable political import of philosophical thought and for a radical philosophical foundation of the political encounter of men and peoples of diverse views. The promise for peace and integrity contained in the prospect of a community of communicants is incalculable. The effectiveness of Jaspers's notion will lie in philosophy and in politics together, and the key to it is the incorporation of his characterization of authority and heritage. Perhaps no one has realized this as consistently as Hannah Arendt, who says,

> Just as the prerequisite for world government in Jaspers' opinion is the renunciation of sovereignty for the sake of a worldwide federated political structure, so the prerequisite for this mutual understanding would be renunciation, not of one's own tradition and national past, but of the binding authority and universal validity which tradition and past have always claimed. It is by such *a break, not with the authority of tradition* that Jaspers entered philosophy.[46]

Chapter Six

The Idea of Philosophical Faith

i. The Ambience of Philosophical Faith

The stream of Jaspers's thought can be regarded as the conflu-
ence of the conception of reason, which has its main source in
Kant, and that of Existenz, which has its main source in Kierkegaard; it is fed by the experience of the different modes of
Being, channelled by the rockbed of modern science, and issues
into the open sea of philosophical faith.

For Jaspers, faith is thought which seeks to master the disparateness of what can be known. Such thought consists, first of
all, of unities regarding but transcending the actually known
manifold; it is therefore other than, and not to be confused
with, cognitive thought. Faith which assumes the posture of
knowledge—be it in the form of a religious dogma to which the
experience and tradition of revelation (as in Christianity) supposedly testify, or in the form of a political ideology supposedly
inferred from an analysis of pertinent actuality (as in Nazi racism or dialectical materialism)—is relative to exchangeable presuppositions and procedures and subject to the falsifiability
criterion; hence it is not worthy of the risk of self which is of
the essence of faith. However, philosophical faith not only
means mastery of the diversity of knowledge by means of transcognitive unities; it also means mastery of what is known. Without such decisive mastery man remains dispersed over and
subject to what may be known but which, by merely being
known, is not yet evaluated and controlled, as, for example, our
own and other people's drives, desires and aversions, acts and
impositions, things and ideas which please or displease, interest
us or leave us indifferent. Faith lifts us above such helter-skelter,
not to deny cognizable actuality but to give it structure, value,
wholeness.

Philosophical faith is, therefore, not indifferent to the concreteness of knowledge and what is known; it is not otherworldly. Neither does it reach its fulfillment in its verbal formulation or a verbal confession. It is fulfilled in the concreteness of

life and activity, which it invests with meaning and which it animates. As such it is the wellspring of decisiveness and loyalty to
the self and the truth one seeks to realize, no matter what trials
of misfortune or joy the vicissitudes of life provide. It is on the
idea of philosophical faith that the distinctions are based between selfhood and despair, loyalty and fickleness or oppor-
tunism, personality and its dissipation, strength and weakness,
service and lip-service. Philosophical faith is concrete action or,
at least, readiness to act; otherwise it is nothing at all. There is
no actuality in confession without deeds.

The conception of faith as a way of thought beyond evidential
knowledge is an important feature of Jaspers's idea of philosophical faith. But what marks the distinctiveness of this idea,
particularly as the culmination of the impulse of reason toward
unity in time, is its radical recognition of the historicity of faith.
This means, first of all, that nothing objective guarantees the
truth of faith—no evidence, no authority, no particular revelation. The truth of faith is absolute and unconditional—but only
for the believer, whether or not others believe as he does. One
adheres to one's faith at one's own risk and testifies to its truth
with one's own being. Others, especially authorities such as one's
parents, or heritage, or culture, or religion, can nurture or
awaken one's faith; but they cannot confirm its truth. They can
only confirm it for their own faith. And even then the confirmation is a continuous task of the testimony of deeds. When all is
said, testimony of word and deed means no more than that this
vision of truth has animated this person or this people. It is,
therefore, not incumbent on the recipient of a tradition to adopt
its truth as his own, but merely to measure his own vision
against it. In this sense it is, of course, possible that the reception of transmitted truth may awaken a person to his own truth and
that this may have the appearance of adoption. But it is appearance only, even if the recipient testifies to this traditional truth
with his own being. Such testimony is authentic existence by
virtue of an original realization of truth which the reception of
tradition occasioned. There is an obligation which goes along
with the reception of transmitted heritage, namely the obligation to the truth which intimates itself mediately in this heritage. Since the transcendent truth is not identical with its historic transmission, the obligation does not exist, with respect to
the limitation of its mediation, in the same primary sense as with
respect to the truth per se. Hence the historic intimation of the
truth for the historic person in his singularity can occur immediately, or in confrontations other than those with authority and

heritage. Confrontation with man's past failures to realize the truth which animated him, with his folly in missing the truth and thereby missing to realize himself, with his suppression as genuine or abortive exception, or as victim of an authority which was able to prevail by virtue of its recourse to the means of enforcement, can be no less an occasion to hear one's truth than the acceptance of an authority. And, above all, it is the confrontation with fellow man which occasions clarification and assurance of one's foundation in truth.

At bottom, then, the relation of man to man, where the historicity of the human realization of truth and the indispensability of freedom for it is valued, is that of communication no matter whether 'man' in that relationship be a fellow human being or a human actuality such as an authority, an institution, or one's heritage. Jaspers's idea of philosophical faith is founded on the conception of the "unreserved," "unrelenting," "boundless" "loving struggle" of communication as the historic and the free man's way to truth. The more intense the awareness of the historicity of truth for man, the more intense the appreciation of the multiplicity of this truth. The consequence of this awareness is a person's affirmation of another person's truth for that other person, even as one's own truth is absolute for one's own historicity. The submission to or even the flirtation with another's historicity is as truly the death of communication as is the imposition of what is absolute for oneself upon the other. The search for the one truth by virtue of philosophical faith does not imply a community of believers in one faith but a communicative solidarity of believers, each with his own historic vision of truth upon which he freely risks grounding his life, without confusing this vision with the one truth transcending all historicity.

It is precisely for the sake of enhancing the possibility of man's historic realization of truth that Jaspers finds it useful to engage in the task of formulating a general fundamental knowledge. This would be merely formal, and would not anticipate the content of faith. It would merely disclose the dimensions of man's realization of Being and not proceed, as the person in his singularity will and must, to determine the historic realization within these dimensions. Moreover, this task is continuous and fluid and not fixed for all time. Jaspers, as we already know, offers his periechontology—his philosophy of the 'encompassing'—as a body of general fundamental knowledge which reflects the experience of human realization, which is adequate to the historic situation, and which is amenable to the requirements of world-wide communication between a diversity of philosophical,

political, spiritual, and religious historicities. Quite rightly he
anticipates the main objection which can be raised against this
idea of a general fundamental knowledge:

> Each fundamental knowledge is in fact one statement of faith
> among others. The one sought here is not the only one either.
> But as each source of faith regards itself as the only true one,
> so does the source of this fundamental knowledge. It is self-
> delusion to believe that a general fundamental knowledge
> might be gained, so to speak, before and beyond all faith; this
> philosophical attempt that claims to be neither faith nor sci-
> ence, that purports to throw off the bonds of faith in order to
> pretend to a general, uniting truth, merely hides an abstract
> faith—as is shown also by the lack of general acceptability of
> any such fundamental knowledge.[1]

This putative objection is not contrived by Jaspers but reflects
his experience of the opposition he encountered from philosophers who pursue ontological or scientific aims in their philosophizing, or by Marxists, or by theologians. Apropos the latter, a
prominent Protestant theologian who strongly favors Jaspers and
his thought told me that from a theological position Jaspers's proposed general fundamental knowledge must be regarded as a Tro-
jan horse. Jaspers's response to the projected objection is as follows:

> This argument itself is abstract, for it does not deal with our
> concrete attempt to draft a fundamental knowledge. But the
> argument is not unfounded—for this is not a matter of com-
> pelling science. Only the conclusion is unfounded: that be-
> cause it is not a matter of science, it must, as all philosophy,
> be a matter of faith.
> At bottom it is indeed a matter of faith. But this faith has no
> religious content that would exclude others; it is solely the
> faith in the possibility of unlimited mutual understanding. It is
> the faith that says: Truth is what unites us.[2]

Philosophical faith as the historic fulfillment of the oneness of
truth towards which reason impels is, formally, a paradox:

> We do not possess the one truth and we shall not posess it—
> yet the truth can only be one.[3]

This paradox bespeaks, first of all, the impossibility of the realization of the unity of truth in time. However, attempts and claims
of such realization have always been and are being made. Thus a
mode of Being, or a correlative theory or method of apprehending

Being, might be isolated and absolutized, and all there is might be reduced to this mode. Our tradition and culture are fraught with a plethora of 'isms' corresponding to such absolutization, e.g., naturalism, existentialism, idealism, et al. In the end, specific approaches to the apprehension of reality, usually culminating in a system, are pitted against one another: rationalism versus empiricism, realism versus subjectivism, positivism versus idealism; what is inadequately regarded in one is absolutized in the other. Another kind of putative realization of unity of truth in time is the ontological system. The different modes of Being are held to be different pieces of a picture which fall into place to form a composite, orderly whole by virtue of a set of principles or a schedule of categories. Yet no system is all-inclusive; it would seem that what it gains in consistency it loses in its grasp and breadth of reality. And even if a congeries of fundamental problems is solved in a certain way in a given system, this does not mean that a solution at variance with it is impossible in another system which is also internally consistent, though based on different presuppositions. One sees systems next to other systems, each grasping aspects of reality which others, on the basis of their presuppositions, cannot grasp, or whose understanding of reality is at variance with the former ones. The array of systems can become a chaos of dogma, and in the end the unity of accomplished systems is shattered against man's continual unfolding and grasp of reality.

For Jaspers, such attempts at determining the unity of truth are not devoid of significance. But their significance lies not in what they accomplish but in what they fail to accomplish, in their foundering against the unchartable rocks in the unfathomable depths of Being. By means of the experience of such shipwreck—a characteristic and important concept in Jaspers's thinking[4]—in carrying out the task of realizing truth in time, man can be reminded of the transcendence of the one truth, can prevent its substitution by a limited human realization of it, and uphold it as the ground of the freedom of and communication between men. Human realization of ultimate truth can only be the active testimony of faith, not a knowledge which proceeds by way of an operation with evidential concepts.

Hence the paradox which was cited from Jaspers's writings has the further significance that truth in its unity does not as such appear in time, is not known, cannot be constructed or derived, but can be intimated only by bursting through the limitations of palpable human realization. Since nothing that is palpable leads to this break-through, it presupposes a radical change in the direction of human concern over Being and truth. This change in direction is

not merely one from transient temporal reality to the realm of
eternal verity and value, but the investiture of immanence with
transcendent truth and value whereby the merely temporal becomes historic. It is a matter of seeing the here and now in a new
light. In the form of thought such redirection consists in turning
from determinacy to indeterminacy, i.e., from the methods of
determination to the transcendental method. This, for Jaspers, is
the "fundamental operation" of philosophy and philosophical
faith. In his conception of this radical shift in thought and human
concern, which belongs primarily to his later thinking, Jaspers
deliberately refers to corresponding conceptions in the history of
thought. For example, he cites Kierkegaard's call to a "leap into
faith" which, for him, means the Christian's readiness to suffer in
the face of the claims which the world raises against him.[5] But
Jaspers rejects this for philosophical faith, as he rejects Marx's
version of redirection which is the call to promote the transition
from capitalism to communism, a call justified by man's insight
into the historical necessity of this transition.[6] Closer to Jaspers's
own conception of redirection is that of philosophizing as continuous learning to die, which is Plato's simile for the constant task of
"rebirth to a true life."[7] And in connection with his interpretation
of Plato's Allegory of the Cave and its explicit simile of turning
about, Jaspers says,

> Human insight is tied to a turning around (*metastrophe, peri-
> agoge*). It is not given from outside as though eyes had been
> set in one's head (they are already there) or a seed had been
> implanted. But as in the cave the turning of the eyes involves
> the whole body, so knowledge, together with the whole soul,
> must turn from the realm of becoming to Being. Accordingly,
> education (*paideia*) is the art of bringing about such a turn.
> Because of its divine origin, the faculty of rational insight is
> always present as a hidden power. But it becomes a wholesome
> power only through the turning; otherwise it is harmful.[8]

Few of his philosophical conceptions play as important a role in
Jaspers's political thinking as that of redirection. It makes itself
felt in his call to purification in the Post-World-War-II discussion
of German guilt;[9] it becomes explicit in his exploration of the role
of reason and of the individual in the political situation engendered by the dual threat of atomic annihilation and totalitarianism;[10] and again in his warning against the political lethargy of the
German people with respect to past transgressions and renewed
threats to political freedom.[11]

In all this Jaspers points out that self-renewal is not merely a matter of redirection, and moreover one which is accomplished once and for all time. Rather, redirection is a continuous task and a readiness to recognize and realize possibilities to which man remains blind if in his concerns he is tied to the palpable as such and in his thinking to the determinate. For this reason he says,

> We can do nothing to plan the future realities of faith. We can only be ready to receive it, and live in such a manner that this readiness increases. We cannot make our own transformation the goal of our wills; it must, rather, be bestowed upon us, if we live in such a fashion that we can experience the gift.[12]

This caution is reflected in his treatment of the two forms which the breakthrough of the oneness of truth can take, i.e., authority and exception.[13] The faith of authority becomes the shrunken, atrophied caricature of truth unless it is, in turn, breached by the exception. And man, in the exception of his faith, intensifies his limitation unless nourished and challenged by authority.

Absolutization and ontology are, in Jaspers's view, perversions of thought, which is concerned over the ultimate unity of truth. Differing from this is thought according to which ultimate truth, its unity and ground are denied. This is the unfaith of nihilism which is a frequent topic in Jaspers's writings. Yet, as was indicated in our discussion of unfaith, even nihilism can be a function, and hence a moment, of the clarification of faith as a fundamental certainty of being and in its character of thought beyond knowledge and of being verified by personal testimony. To exist as self in time means to risk what cannot be known; Jaspers holds that

> Existenz is faith and is despair. In contrast to both there is the yearning for the tranquillity of eternity where despair has become impossible and faith vision, i.e., complete presence of complete actuality.[14]

Reason and its efficacy in the form of philosophical faith can thus maintain some kind of dialectical relation to absolutization and nihilism whereby they become moments of man's rise to a sounder realization of the historicity of his quest for truth. However, for Jaspers, the quest of reason for the unity of truth cannot be regarded as being fulfilled in time, and cannot lead to the manifestation to man of truth in its oneness. Even though reason is the impulse of the quest for oneness, the putative fulfillment in time of this quest is absolutely at variance with reason because, in Jaspers's view, reason is essentially also the affirmation of the historicity of the quest. The position of the fulfillment of truth in time is, for Jaspers, therefore, the final and, in a way, the only contender against the rule of communicative reason. He calls it, wherever in human affairs it may appear, whether in culture, politics or religion, the position of catholicity.

Reason, according to Jaspers, is time-bound man's impulse toward the unity of truth against and in spite of the historic diversity, disparateness and dismemberment of experienced and cognized being. Philosophical reason, as we have seen, is not at odds with authority but affirms it as a fact and condition of man's concern over and realization of the unity of truth, provided that authority is not at odds with the historicity of that concern. Genuine authority stands in polar relation to the exception, does not preclude indignation and rebellion against itself, nurtures and promotes the exceptedness of self-actualization through independent realization of truth. In alliance with or under the aegis of authority it is possible to realize self and truth in freedom, and at one's own risk to envisage in time by virtue of faith what, in its encompassing unity, eludes time; indeed, authority is indispensable for this. Jaspers's idea of philosophical faith is the faith of reason and freedom in affirmation of genuine authority, particularly that of the heritage of the great philosophers.

Opposed to reason is the perversion of reason, i.e., the supposition that the oneness of truth in time towards which reason impels has been essentially realized in time, and hence for all men. What is opposed to reason, in Jaspers's view is, then, not authority or even its apparently indispensable claim to exclusiveness, but that position of some authority by which it deems its vision of truth to be valid for all and binding on all, and thereby reduces the significance of other and denies the historicity of its own and all human realizations. This is the position of catholicity. Let us now give a more detailed account of Jaspers's conception of reason, with which he equates the idea of philosophical faith, and that of catholicity from which he distinguishes it.

ii. For Reason

The concept of reason does not become an explicit topic in Jaspers's writings up to and including his *Philosophie*, first published in 1932. Reason reveals itself as the central concept in his thinking beginning with the lectures *Vernunft und Existenz*, delivered and

first published in 1936. In reply to an observation made by Fritz
Kaufmann, Jaspers denies that the absence of a discussion of reason in his writings prior to 1936 constitutes a shift in accent in his
thinking.[15] Rather, so Jaspers maintains, the underlying pervasive-
ness of reason is there before as well as after. What had happened
was that what was implicitly pervasive became an explicit topic.
The concern over the development of anti-rational tendencies,
especially National Socialism, was the stimulus which motivated
Jaspers, as he himself indicates,[16] to consider the topic of reason.
This is one of many examples of a distinctive phenomeonon in
Jaspers's philosophizing, namely the development of an aspect of
his thinking which has its roots in a political concern. The discussion of reason also made explicit Jaspers's conception of his own
thinking in distinction from 'existentialism', a movement which he
at that time only envisaged as an undesirable possibility, and
which was soon to become an actuality.[17]

Jaspers's characterization of reason is closely tied to his characterization of the phenomenon against which reason turns, i.e., that
of the fragmentation of Being. Thought discloses Being as dismembered; at the same time this dismemberment is repugnant to
thought. Both the disclosure and the repugnance presuppose the
transcendental idea of oneness. Whence the possibility of this
idea?

Different modes of Being are, as such, indifferent to each other.
Let us demonstrate this with regard to the different modes of
being human which Jaspers distinguishes, i.e., mundane existence,
the intellect, spirit, and Existenz. We may be immersed in the vital
pursuits of mundane existence (*Dasein*), not caring for disciplined
thinking or for the guiding ideals which build civilizations. We may
pursue the clarity of formal thought, not caring for the pain-
staking gathering of facts concerning the material world and the
theorizing by way of attempted explanation of these facts. We
may seek to know, understand and create leading spiritual ideas in
their opposition and compatibility, not caring for their meaningfulness and the way in which they may be fulfilled in the historic
individual. We may resolve to stand defiantly against all in the
realization that, if nothing else remains steadfastly dependable,
there remains one's existential freedom to accept or reject one's
fate, not caring for the submission under realized universal ideals
or the rules of valid thought which transcend individuality. We
may repose in a mystic unification with the deity, considering all
earthly reality sham, all other realization picayune and insignifi-
cant.

The dismemberment of Being is also manifest within any one
mode of Being. Let us take the case of mundane existence. It consists manifestly of entities which in their particularity are mutually
indifferent, even hostile, devoid of any bond, save in the service of
self-interest. For example, if the attempt is made to base moral
conduct on what, from the standpoint of his mundane existence,
motivates man, then it must be based on an empirically relevant
search for satiation and avoidance of harm. In view of the failure
of all attempts to date, it is questionable if this can be done. However we can learn from these failures. It was fairly easy for Bradley
and others to refute Mill by pointing out how notoriously falla-
cious Mill's 'proof' for the utilitarian principle was. The refutation
is significant in that it shows that it is impossible to proceed to a
community of interests from within the miscellaneous collection
of self-interests. The fallacy itself, however, is significant, because
it indicates that in Mill's utilitarianism a mode of Being makes
itself felt which is other than mundane existence, which grasps and
sets the limits of the latter, a mode of Being which Mill tried to
understand as being no different from mundane existence. The
realm of the spirit, of leading ideas with reference to which the
business of civilization is carried out, is at times also irreconcilably
dismembered. For example, the now forgotten romantic commu-
nistic ideal that men will be free for their highest possibilities
when, through a completely planned economy, the care for their
daily bread is taken from them, conflicts with the ideal, now also
forgotten, that freedom demands that all of man's endeavors be
personally meaningful to him, including his winning of his daily
bread, that planning for him on any level is a restriction of his
freedom. By analogy, the intellect is a matter of innumerable individual consciousnesses, and Existenzen are loving or hating, or at
any rate, caring selves, as such without direction.

We may see the multiplicity of modes, be able to distinguish
them, find incompatibilities within them, encounter strangeness,
separation, hostility, polemic, and yet seek the ground of that
oneness with reference to which all that is real obtains significance
and justification in view of what is other than itself. The living
manifestation of this impulse toward oneness Jaspers calls reason.
Reason seeks to transcend what from any one aspectual standpoint is strange, adventitious, extraneous, or enigmatic. It does not
dissolve distinctions, alternatives and disjunctions by viewing them
from a supposedly Archimedean point. Rather, it is the force
whereby distinctions are recognized as such, and whereby through
such recognition realities which are mutually delimited are

brought at least into a mutual concern in view of that oneness wherein ultimately all is cradled. Reason seeks order where there is a scattering, a lack of relatedness. It acknowledges relations and achieved unifications, but transcends these in realizing their limitations and their failures, and persists in its yearning for ultimate oneness. Therefore, it does not conceive this oneness to be a oneness among onenesses; its task is the oneness of fulfilled orderliness. Yet this task is transcendent. Reason as reason in time, i.e., as carried by Existenz, seeks to transcend time, for it views temporality too restrictive for the achievement of unity, and yet it seeks to manifest itself in time, for time is the *conditio sine qua non* of Existenz. But reason considers manifestation in time to be mere symbol and not fixation, communication and not proclamation, appeal and reminder, and not dogma and information. Reason is not committed to any one view or mode of reality because it seeks to realize the significance of and the bond between all views and modes. Reason is not estranged by the novelty of a realization, is not disposed to discard whatever may oppose it; it leaves open the possibility of ultimate oneness, and will permit nothing to take its place. In its ordering of all in view of this oneness, it relativizes all that is less than that oneness. This does not mean that reason tolerates all without principle, but that it refuses to absolutize what is less than absolute, and furthermore upholds as its task the finding of the ordering principle of this relativizing.

Reason is also not sufficient unto itself. It is the motivation toward the ultimate One above all that is less than it. It would not miss realizing the justification for being of anything which is in any manner within the one Being. Reason in its search for the One has no other content save whatever is in the different modes of Being. Whatever is, is the point of departure for reason, and, in its ordering, is the concern of reason. Whatever is in any mode, can be, in its dispersion, without reason; but reason cannot be without what it seeks to order under the ultimate oneness which it seeks.

The method of reason is transcending in thought.[18] The ultimate intention of the transcendental method is the one Being which encompasses all diremption into subject and object. This Being, however, cannot be thought. As thinkable, it would again be merely an object among objects, and an object for a subject. It can be approached in thought only by means of transcending thought, only by means of determinate thought which is its symbol for what cannot be determinate. Rational thinking in its transcending is activated at the limits of what is thinkable. The realization of limits as such is not yet the origin of transcending. For some limits can be pushed back by further research. Others may be realized as unbridgeable by research, yet may not be incentives to transcending; one may acquiesce in remaining within these limits. Or limits may be disregarded even though realized. For example, the positivist knows that there is a limit to knowledge, and, insofar as this limit is not extensible by further empirical research, it is of no meaningful concern to him; the pragmatist knows that what is absolute is beyond the limit of human knowledge, but does not wonder about the nature of this knowledge about knowledge.

Transcending is possible only when limits are realized which are not simply temporary, or which are not simply acknowledged as matters of fact, or which are not obscured by facile gnostic speculation resulting in a supposed knowledge bridging such limits, but are limits which are realized as limits in principle, limits which designate the unbridgeable gaps in the continuity of determinate being, and, furthermore, where there is a directedness toward the oneness of Being which tolerates no gaps, dismemberment or miscellaneous plurality.

The movement of reason is, then, thinking to the limits, and the transcending of these limits in thought by means of ideas which seek realization in historic activity. It is empty without inner and outer experience, and therefore depends essentially on experience and the realization that neither inner nor outer being is sufficient unto itself. It robs man of the security of knowledge concerning reality transcending these realities, yet motivates him towards a realization of such reality as a task within reflective experience. By means of reason's transcending, man seeks to designate the limits of reality in its various modes, seeks their bond, their respective validities, and seeks to ground them in that totality which cannot be coordinate with what it encompasses, but without which all that appears is meaningless because incidental and unordered. Without some form of faith in the oneness of Being, the ultimate would be the experience of constant change, or the foundering of attempted systematizations, or the aimless surrender to the humdrum of whatever may come one's way. On the other hand, this faith does not provide the comfort of a supposedly finished search, for it requires the disquiet of living. The ideas by which transcending is expressed are not determinate concepts; rather, they demand to be reflected in the determinate knowledge which they are purported to order, in the actions which they are aimed to regulate, and in the communication which they are invoked to articulate.

iii. Against Catholicity

We can now give a closer account of Jaspers's characterization of catholicity and the nature of his opposition to it.[19] The way of catholicity and the way of reason share the motive of oneness as the ground of Being and the foundation of the meaningfulness of man's position therein. The parting of the ways occurs in the respective manners in which this oneness is grasped and pursued, with their ramifications and consequences.

On the way of catholicity the oneness of truth is thought as essentially realized by man. It is the task of mankind to engage in the various human pursuits in consideration of this realized truth. Since truth can only be one, and since this truth is known, it is, in the main, the same for all and, in some sense, for all time. Hence the absoluteness with which the conception of the one truth guides human Existenz is not only valid for a unique historic Existenz, but, ultimately, for all men. Catholicity views man's devotion to the oneness of truth under the aspect of universality. Where catholicity is represented in the form of an authority, universality is the mantle by means of which it is invested with its claim to all-embracing exclusiveness. Spiritual authority of this kind bases itself on a total knowledge, at least in principle, under which all that may come to man's awareness is subsumed according to its proper category. Moral authority of this kind reserves for itself the right to be the ultimate arbiter in questions of human action. Political authority of this kind potentially or actually seeks mastery over human affairs in its broad areas and in detail; catholicity in the form of political authority is, potentially and ultimately, totalitarianism. In the light of the possibility and actuality of political catholicity, intellectual and spiritual catholicity may seem harmless and trivial. Not so for Jaspers. For the unity on which claims of catholic authority are based is a unity which is thought, i.e., which is thought determinately rather than as an idea animating reason's will towards unity. And, in accordance with one of Jaspers's tenets which we already know, all thought which is not strictly scientific and which is of philosophical relevance has potential political import. Hence any thought of unity which is not merely an expression of the *"will to unity"* as a "fundamental feature of reason"[20] but represents an *insight into unity* has totalitarian implications. This holds for the most abstruse ontological system of the most obscure philosopher, for even that is a paving stone on the way to totalitarianism.[21]

Thus Jaspers's conception of catholicity is a touchstone of two features of his thinking: First, his supposition that thought has effect and, hence, political import. Second, the significance of his adherence to and development of Kant's distinction between the intellect and reason, and his rescue of Kant's theory of ideas from Neo-Kantian oblivion. In this sense we can understand catholicity in Jaspers's characterization as prevailing in opposition to reason and in alliance with the theoretical and practical methods of the intellect, albeit in areas where these methods are inappropriate. Intellectual thought proceeds in the direction of universal validity determinatively by means of factual distinction as well as discursive and systematic connection relative to criteria of evidence, inference and connection. The intellectual thought structure is a system which is limited by what it is purported to grasp and by the relativity of the suppositions which make it possible. Though fixed, as conceptions always are, such structures are not ends in themselves but, in Jaspers's view, even in science they are significant precisely only as means of research. Where they jell and stop being in flux, science, as researching world orientation, is at an end. Hence also the practical arrangement of the world in accordance with intellectual thought structures is not an end in itself, and is dependent for its meaningfulness on sources of meaning which transcend the relative universality of the intellect. Be that as it may, the systematic form of the universal validity at which intellectual thought aims is apposite to the absolute universality which catholicity claims to grasp with respect to the unity of Being and truth.[22] However, it is not the form that counts primarily but the content and the mode of certainty of Being for which this form is the ideal means of expression. Such form expresses an essentially finished view of reality which is understood as an objective knowledge of the different facets of Being insofar as they are relevant to man, his destiny, his obligation, his conduct, his aspiration and his enjoyment. Wherever an accepted catholic authority prevails there is certainty without risk. Where all can be ordered according to the objectively knowing authority, policy and action can be determined without the qualms and vicissitudes of individual decisive choice. Reference to catholic universality promotes human order and tranquillity. "Men urge toward such universality," Jaspers observes. "It affords a footing and security, gives relief through liberation from thought and choice, veils the demands of selfhood."[23]

Catholicity, on the other hand, by reducing the risk of choice between 'either' and 'or', and under the aegis of the one unquestionable absolute truth which is the source of its universality and authority, can tolerate a considerable degree of latitude of thought and action. In this connection it is instructive to read Jaspers's apt characterizations of the catholic methods in the intellectual, the practical and the political spheres:

> In *rational systems* a totality is thought in which all that is possible has its place . . . but also its . . . limit. Nothing is left out, nothing absolutely opposed, everything is admitted, yet so that, rather than breaking open the wholeness, it functions as its member. . . . In opposition to every "either/or"—the "both/and" is sought, in opposition to exclusive decisiveness— conciliation. Exclusion is practiced only against tendencies to breaking open the principle of totality, and against any radicalism which, instead of joining, becomes heretic. Truth is seen in everything—if it is rightly understood. Untruth is seen in everything—where self-will tries to prevail.[24]
>
> In *practical conduct* the following principle prevails: A proliferation . . . of disparateness, and even arbitrariness, superstition and moral laxity is permitted under the condition that the center of catholic power and decision be recognized. . . . There is always an excuse for the perpetrator or thinker, if only he obeys in principle and joins the whole. But there is always merciless repudiation where the sprouting of inner opposition becomes noticeable, even if it rises from lofty enthusiasm, devoted love, or a morally impeccable nature.[25]
>
> In the *political conduct* of leaders of catholicity there prevails an unmitigated empirical realism. Existing powers are given room to play, the only considerations being how they can serve the perpetuation and solidification of the catholic authority.[26]

The ease of life promoted by the methods of catholicity, though in its appearance psychological in nature and described in psychological categories, is of existential import, i.e., it is a matter of realizing the one truth in time. Also it intensifies the question of the relevance of authority for man living communally and concerned over meaningfulness and truth. A consideration of both of these problems is facilitated by Jaspers's treatment of the impact of catholicity on the historicity of truth.

There have been many historic forms of catholicity. Indeed, catholicity, this "enthusiasm of universality,"[27] is, historically, the rule; in comparison reason, in Jaspers's sense, seems impotent, ineffective, utopian, or at least unrealistic, and disorderly. Jaspers treats many historic actualities as manifestations of catholicity. He sees it in several features of Christianity, primarily its notion of the God-man, its basis in revelation, and its being as a Church community. The latter pertains especially, though not exclusively, to the Catholic Church; for Jaspers Catholicism is a prime historic example of, but not an exclusive pattern for, 'catholicity'.[28] He sees catholicity in historic thought structures which have been claimed to be total knowledge. Such structures have either been of a speculative metaphysical nature which reach their fulfillment in comprehensive ontological systems. Jaspers cites the systems of Aristotle, Thomas Aquinas and Hegel as the main examples of such "magnificent, historically extraordinarily effective errors"[29] in which "all that has been thought is incorporated . . . in a manner whereby the point of every original thought is blunted."[30] In his classification of philosophers by types of greatness we find these three "creative orderers" contraposed to three equally influential philosophers, namely Plato, Augustine and Kant, whom Jaspers regards as "seminal founders" of "philosophizing" because, unlike the pinnacles of the catholic way in philosophy, the latter do not bring the examination of life to a conclusion but impel it anew in each individual.[31] Or else such thought structures are purported to be the explication of fundamental insights established with scientific certainty. For Jaspers the pre-eminent historic examples of this kind of total knowledge are racism, Marxism and Freudianism.[32] The historic examples of the penchant for and the dominance of universalistic catholicity are legion, and we shall have occasion to examine Jaspers's treatment of some of them in proper context in this and in later volumes of these *Studies*. Here it is our purpose to show, by means of the array of historic examples of catholicity, Jaspers's approach to a criticism of catholicity on the basis of the historicity of man's concern over truth in its oneness.

The aim of catholicity is the realization by man in time of the truth in its unity. But the unity which catholicity attains falls short of absoluteness as long as there is time. If we designate history as the object of oneness, then this failing in its aim on the part of catholicity can be described, in Jaspers's apt phrase, as consisting in achieving a "historic unit" rather than a "unity of history."[33] No matter how much a catholicity embraces, it is in turn embraced by an all-embracing history. Speaking of catholicity in the form of authority, Jaspers observes:

> It is the defect of authority to be, though existentially historic and thus unconditional, finitely historical in its objectivity. It will continue to be one authority amongst others, even if it should happen that the whole globe obey a single authority.[34]

A unity which is realized by man is relative in its objective historicity, i.e., its absoluteness is restricted to being a confession of a historic self's risk of faith, and does not extend in its validity universally to lay claim to the assent of mankind regardless of historicity. The unity of truth transcends any human realization thereof, so also that of catholicity. If the motive is true unity, then any substitution of the unity of truth by the human realization thereof is a betrayal of the motive. The oneness of truth can guide man's search for meaning only if its pursuit is renewed beyond all intimations of unity that may have become manifest in man's realizations of action and thought which such guidance made possible. From the point of view of reason, catholicity, far from being the achievement of unity of truth for man, is its loss precisely because in assuming the form of human realization it falls short of all-embracing oneness. "Catholicity aims at oneness in forms which appear to reason as premature and effete."[35]

Animated by his consciousness of the historicity of man's concern over truth, Jaspers seeks to come to terms with the overriding tendency towards catholicity and its actuality. At one point he suggests that the pull of the motive of oneness, present in catholicity no less than in reason, is sufficiently overwhelming for man to confuse "unconditional historic validity for Existenz" and "universality for all men."[36] Several times Jaspers observes that men expect what is valid for them to be valid for all, indeed in the acceptance on the part of others they find a "guarantee" for the validity of their own beliefs.[37] Most telling is Jaspers's evaluation of the significance of order. We have seen that in his conception of reason, no less than that of others, the aim is order. In fact, the intimate relation of consciousness of truth and the prevalence of order in thought and in human affairs is a strand which runs through the complex web of his *Von der Wahrheit*; at the very beginning of this huge work he observes that the "blurring of the consciousness of truth is like an expression of the disorderliness of the age."[38] In the present context the question is, under what auspices order, as expression of truth, may prevail. Jaspers's answer is concise: "Order is not absolute."[39] This means that precisely because reason gives rise to the idea of order from its motive of oneness, it will not abide an order which as such is established in time. Hence on the way to order, reason, in the end, recognizes the shattering of any already established order against the recalcitrance of original actualities which it fails and must fail to incorporate, and promotes the bursting of the bonds of order in favor of openness for reality which cannot be anticipated. For distinct from the methods of catholicity, the method of reason is communication. And as we know, the possibility of communication is based on the supposition that one does not know what actualities of self and other will come to light in the communicative process because a being in time *becomes* what he is. What he does not know can animate him through faith; but this requires the disquiet of search, the risk of action, the pursuit of truth in its unity as a task which does not end in time.

> The philosophical notion of reason, which recurrently bursts through the claims of catholicity, stands in opposition to the one authority. . . . In reality authority assumes a definite form. It is part of the inextricable web of existence. Hence it is both true and false, true in the form of the emergence of the movement which takes hold of it and creates it, and false in the form of a fixity that demands endless duration. Its *realization carries the germ of untruth without which there is no temporal existence.* Hence it has to move toward the ever needful annulment of its untruth. However since this untruth is not incidental and not merely an extraneous opacity but is carried in the seed of its original realization, its movement is perpetual. *As long as there is movement there is truth; as soon as movement ceases, only untruth remains.*[40]

We see in this passage a difference in the relationship of reason to catholicity and authority. Reason is opposed to catholicity but not to authority. For, it will be recalled, the life of reason takes its course in the polarity and tension of authority and freedom no less than in that of 'religion and philosophy' and 'faith and knowledge'. However, the opposition of reason and catholicity, as Jaspers notes, "seems unbridgeable and not polar."[41] The word "seems" indicates that, even though the opposition is radical and fundamental for Jaspers, it remains problematical. This we must describe further. We know that reason is able to affirm authority, particularly that of heritage, as the carrier of the possibilities and contents of selfhood, and in its potentiality to restrict its function to its historic limitation. The multiplicity of authorities is a guarantee that an authority's unconditional claim to being the source of truth remains historic, and hence for reason a desirable fact.[42] Authority need not dispute reason's prerogative of critical inquiry into anything whatever. In fact it is desirable as a challenge to undertake this inquiry in responsible freedom, and moreover to bring a degree of insight into truth and of order to bear on human affairs where the power of free reason is insufficient. In the case of catholicity, however, reason cannot prevail. The unrest of search and inquiry is at an end where "subjection to the one truth, universal and universally valid for all, in a determined form regarded as unchangeable,"[43] is demanded. Such subjection is not the way of reason which critically questions all realizations lest the richness and diversity of reality as it appears in time and to which reason is particularly attuned, petrify into patterns that lull inquiry.

> The diversity of men, the difference in the nature of and the distances of rank between Existenzen, their ways of cipher-reading, their attitudes regarding death, what God is to them—all that can genuinely unfold into truth only in freedom, outside the overarching dome of unconditional catholicity.[44]

Reason's "yea" to authority—mindful of its historicity, and "nay" to catholicity—particularly in the form of authority with access to temporal power, spells out for us that for Jaspers the opposition 'reason versus catholicity' is a matter of fundamental choice. Both parties of this opposition are grounded in history; hence the choice is not of one historicity in favor of another.[45] Also, the opposition does not rest in the nature of things but in us.[46] Hence the choice between reason and catholicity is one of what we mean to be and, in consequence of the choice, to become. Reason and catholicity, each confronted with the other, can view the other only from its own standpoint. For, even though they share the motive of oneness, there is no standpoint which both have in common. For each to account for the reality of the other is to evaluate the other; and this means that each will consider the other perverse and his own standpoint perverted in the account and evaluation of the other.[47] What a grim, uncompromising concession! In this sense we can understand Jaspers's final attempt to come to terms, in the name of reason, with the actuality of catholicity in words written from the depths of the Nazi tyranny:

> Yet the opposition is of a manner where, from the viewpoint of reason, the other, catholicity, has to and ought to be preserved. It, perhaps, *has to* be preserved because among the majority of mankind the historicity of Being cannot be realized without the illusion of the universality of its concrete form. It *ought to* be preserved so that the clarity of what is true can be reestablished through reason in steady struggle with this most dangerous, because most seductive, blunder. Reason is forced to recognize that catholicity is the subterfuge for all those men who cannot carry the burden of reason in open historicity. Yes, reason is even forced to appear to parti-

cipate, particularly where catholicity is politically omnipotent, as the Church in former centuries and, perhaps, a new other, unchristian catholicity in centuries to come. The question then is only wherein lies the preference for reason in the case of conflict. Not the participation in matters of formalities, rites and speech, but one's choice in concrete collision is decisive.[48]

Paumen, in his clear and illuminating exposition of Jaspers's theme 'reason and Existenz', briefly treats the topic of catholicity with particular insight; he says:

> Nothing matters more than to know whether we are choosing the viewpoint of catholicity . . . or the viewpoint of reason. . . . It is not only the most profound opposition; it is also the most immense opposition. There is nothing, in our thought or in our action, which does not illustrate it or which it does not affect.[49]

And Paumen adds this singularly apt juxtaposition:

> Against catholicity Jaspers . . . chooses reason. In choosing reason, he chooses . . . love. Love, like reason, by rendering us open to beings and things, renders us open to ourselves. Love coincides with reason; it is the soul of reason.[50]

The juxtaposition of love and reason emphasizes that we are involved in the consideration of man's fundamental certainty of Being. Love is the actuality of this certainty, faith its articulate actuality. Truth demands that the articulation reflect the freedom in time on the part of the being who exists by virtue of this certainty. Only then is faith 'philosophical faith' and live reason. Faith is philosophical where it is historicly absolute without being universally absolute.

Chapter Seven

The Philosophy of Ciphers

i. Introduction: The Question of the Contents of Faith

We have explored some aspects of Jaspers's thought in their bearing on the nature of faith as a way of thought beyond knowledge. We have also seen how Jaspers, stressing the historicity of faith, develops the idea of philosophical faith. The nature of faith, the idea of philosophical faith are formal topics. They may shed light on but they are not the concrete actuality of faith. Directing ourselves to this actuality we might ask what its content is. We already know that in Jaspers's view faith is essentially testimonial activity which is grounded on a fundamental certainty of Being and of which the communicable thought-content is an inseparable moment of articulation. When we consider the communicable content of faith per se we speak of something which, as residue of the existing self by virtue of which it gains actuality, is mere possibility. Hence even the communicable content of faith is largely a formal topic, albeit one which, by touching upon, evoking and clarifying human possibilities, can be a way of communication. In this sense one can find discussions of many possible contents of faith in Jaspers's works. Often such content takes the form of propositions.

In the late 1940s, at the time when Jaspers presented his idea of philosophical faith, he was wont to exemplify its possible content with a discussion of such propositions. In *The Origin and Goal of History* he considers the following three "fundamental categories of faith":[1]

> Faith in God as the realization of transcendence.
> Faith in man as the possibility of freedom.
> Faith in possibilities in the world as openness beyond
> the limits of knowledge.

In a similar vein he discussed five propositions in his radio series of 1949-1950; the first three of these were also mentioned in his lectures on "Philosophical Faith" (in English: *The Perennial Scope of Philosophy*). They are:

God is.[2]
There are unconditional claims [upon man].[3]
The world has evanescent reality between God and Existenz.[4]
Man is finite and imperfectible.[5]
Man can live in God's guidance.[6]

These propositions, their discussion and the topics which are, as we can see, associated with them—particularly the idea of philosophical faith, the reflection on history and the political import of thought—are systematically articulated in an unpublished work of Jaspers. According to Dr. Saner, who described it to me, the work comprises about six hundred pages. Though complete, Jaspers did not prepare it for publication. It was written in 1942 and 1943, the most hopeless time of the Nazi period. Its title is *Principles of Philosophizing;* the cited propositions are the principles in question. The subtitle indicates that this book was meant as an "introduction to philosophical life," a topic, incidentally, which is the subject of the concluding (though not the last) chapter of his "Introduction to Philosophy," which in English appeared under the title *Way to Wisdom.* In the light of the subsequent history of these "principles" and the related topics we must regard them as propositions, formulated in a public idiom—*vide* the use of "God" rather than "transcendence," reflective of Jaspers's own fundamental concern over truth. No doubt this merits special study but exceeds the present inquiry.

In raising, in the present context, the problem of the content of faith we do not primarily mean Jaspers's discussion of specific contents of faith, or his own faith or confession thereto, but how, according to him, any such content is to be understood. This enquiry falls into two parts, one more formal, the other less so. The former is the topic of this, the latter of the next chapter.

We must note that the content of faith can take many forms beside that of propositions, namely myths, ideas, art, philosophical speculation, conceptions or awarenesses connected with objects and experiences, et al. Jaspers calls any such contents of faith, understood as the conscious certainty of one's grounding in Being, "ciphers," or "ciphers of transcendence"; he speaks of man's concern over their meaning in terms of "reading" of the "cipher-script."

There is something paradoxical about Jaspers's philosophy of ciphers. On the one hand, his conception of ciphers and his treatment of the possibility of metaphysics as culminating in this conception, belong to Jaspers's most distinct and original achievements. In particular, they are creations of the earlier phase of his philosophical work which is connected with his *Philosophie* (1932), of which the last of the three books is essentially devoted to the task of developing the conception of metaphysics as the reading of ciphers. And yet, on the other hand, basic and age-old philosophical motives impel towards and culminate in his philosophy of ciphers, and with this philosophy we seem to be on familiar grounds.* One can, as I shall try to do, give an account of this aspect of Jaspers's thinking by reference to some of these motives. One can even find uses of the word 'cipher' which bear a family resemblance to Jaspers's later use. Examples from Kant and from Hofmannsthal will illustrate this. Kant, in his third Critique says,

> It will be said that this account of aesthetical judgments, as akin to the moral feeling, seems far too studied to be regarded as the true interpretation of that cipher [*Chiffreschrift*] through which nature speaks to us figuratively in her beautiful forms.†[11]

And in Hofmannsthal's "Letter of Lord Chandos to Francis Bacon" (1902) we find this passage:

> It is as if my body consisted of ciphers which disclose everything to me, or as if we could enter a new, prescient relation to all of existence if only we begin to think with the heart.[12]

And, perhaps even more in the direction of Jaspers's use of 'cipher', is this passage from Hofmannsthal's "Das Gespräch über Gedichte" (1903):

> Seen with these eyes animals are the real hieroglyphs, are the living mysterious ciphers with which God has written into the world unspeakable things. What luck for the poet that he also

---

*Attempts to trace the historical precedents of Jaspers's conception of cipher have been made by Salmony[7] and Tilliette.[8]

†Tilliette and Richli not only point to this passage, but each in his own way shows the intimate relation between Jaspers's conception of 'cipher' and Kant's intention in the third Critique. Tilliette notes Kant's and Jaspers's agreement in denying knowledge of the supersensible; he also sees a significant parallel between the Kantian triad nature-man-God and a Jaspersian triad mundane existence (*Dasein*)-Existenz-Transcendence.[9] To Richli Jaspers's cipher is connected with Kant's third Critique insofar as both are concerned with mediation.[10]

may weave these divine ciphers into his writings. . . . They are ciphers whose solution is beyond the capability of language. . . . I would gladly grant you the word "symbol" but it has become so stale that it disgusts me. One would have to be able to converse with children, with pious people and with poets. To the child everything is a symbol, to the pious person the symbol is the only actuality, and the poet is not able to behold anything else.[13]

Jaspers, as we shall see below, is also dissatisfied with 'symbol' and develops his conception of 'cipher' to be distinct from it; and, again like Hofmannsthal, he took note of the ingenuousness of the child's "feeling, seeing and asking."[14]

Suggestive as the cited examples are, we have no basis for establishing a link between them and Jaspers's cipher-philosophy, particularly in the case of Hofmannsthal. Which other thinkers, concerned over like problems, may have been influential in Jaspers's conception of metaphysics as the reading of the cipher-script of transcendence may not be established with any finality and would be valid only within the confines of a genetic study of this aspect of Jaspers's philosophy, if it should ever prove fruitful to attempt it; in this connection the references in Jaspers's *Nachlass* to other thinkers' treatments of 'symbol' will be of interest.[15] The cited resemblances to Jaspers's use of 'cipher' bring into sharper focus the paradox that the philosophy of cipher displays the two inseparable sides of Jaspers's thought, namely the deliberate, critical as well as receptive appropriation of the philosophical heritage, and the distinct, yet plastic formulation of his own thought insofar as it is both nourished or evoked by this appropriation and provoked by his experience.

It is appropriate, therefore, that in the treatment of our topic Jaspers's distinctive achievement of clarifying the systematic conception of ciphers be juxtaposed with an account of the historical motives which are deliberately reflected in the cipher-philosophy. We shall first turn to the latter aspect of the topic in three sections in which we focus, respectively, on the transcendental method, on enlightenment and nihilism, and on negative theology and the hidden God. These sections will be followed by three others which deal with main themes of a more systematic nature, namely, first, the cipher as historicly valid symbol, second, the interpretation of ciphers, and, finally, the ultimate limits of ciphers. A brief postscript containing some notes on critics and Jaspers's relation to Tillich and Buber will bring the chapter to a close.

A. Historical Motives of the Cipher-Philosophy

ii. The Transcendental Method

The philosophy of ciphers is to be regarded as the continuation of
the traditional transcendental method. At the same time it is, by
virtue of a synthesis, a modification and amplification of this
method which gives it a career new in scope and significance. The
transcendental method as such is, for Jaspers, insufficient insofar
as more is at play than can be comprised by it. Hence Jaspers
would rather speak of "transcending," and of the transcendental
method as a kind thereof, i.e., "formal transcending." Formal
transcending is a thought-operation. Thought is essentially determinative by virtue of its categorizing activity and in what is known
by virtue of categorization. Determination displays Being in fragmentation. If thought is directed towards transcendence, it is
directed toward the unity of Being which underlies this dismemberment. The mark of fragmented Being is determinacy; the
mark of being in its oneness and fullness is indeterminacy. But,
since thought is determinative, the indeterminate is unthinkable.
Formal transcending, as a method of grounding the determinate in
the indeterminate, is an attempt to think the unthinkable. Hence
it cannot and does not lead to an awareness of the transcendent
ground except in a negative way, in the form of an intimation
which is the counterpart of the failure of thought. With reference
to the history of the transcendental method, Jaspers classifies and
explores different possibilities of transcending by means of the
pursuit of thought to its limits according to categories of objectivity in general[16] (e.g., form and matter), of concrete actuality[17]
(e.g., time and space), and of freedom[18] (e.g., personality).*

Jaspers's critical reflections on formal transcending are mainly
twofold: Being merely cogitative (i.e., formal), it is not itself a
grounding relation to transcendence, but only a possible vehicle
for such a relation. It involves no commitment to such a relation.
For commitment to be actual the existing self in search of the

*This threefold distinction of categories is the principle of the organization of
Jaspers's projected *Kategorienlehre* (Doctrine of Categories). This was to
have been the second volume of his "Philosophical Logic." I have examined
this project in Jaspers's *Nachlass*. The whole book is planned out, many sections are in a finished state. In his "Philosophical Autobiography" Jaspers
described the state of the work as "sketched in broad areas" but "far from
ready for the press."[19]

ground of its selfhood in freedom is required.[20] In Jaspers's view selfhood in freedom is unthinkable without transcendence. There are many reasons for this, the full elaboration of which exceeds the scope of our topic. Briefly, the following is to be considered: Insofar as man is free, he is independent of and transcends the determination of mundane being. At the same time, in consideration of his limitation, he is not the source of the possibilities of his existence. Consciousness of one's freedom is, for Jaspers, therefore, intimately tied to consciousness of its transcendent grounding. He says,

> Freedom and God are inseparable. Why? Of this I am certain: in my freedom I am not through myself but am given to myself; for I can miss being myself* and I cannot force my being free.[21]

This possibility of "missing to be oneself" is as decisive for Jaspers as is a cognate phenomenon for Kierkegaard. Jaspers says,

> With the realization of this freedom, however, we realize, too, that it is not self-made but granted. The false assurance of being free by virtue of freedom alone, of a baseless, absolute freedom, is shattered by the experience that it may default. The more decisive our certainty of our freedom, the greater our certainty of the transcendence we owe it to.[22]

And Kierkegaard, in the idiom of his pseudonym Anti-Climacus, writes:

> ... there can be two forms of despair properly so called. If the human self had constituted itself, there could be a question only of one form, that of not willing to be one's own self, of willing to be rid of oneself; but there would be no question of despairingly willing to be oneself. This formula is the expression for the total dependence of the relation (the self namely), the expression for the fact that the self cannot of itself attain and remain in equilibrium and rest by itself, but only by relating itself to that Power which constituted the whole relation. ... The disrelationship of despair is not a simple dis-

---

*The phrase, which is rendered by me and by Ashton, respectively, in different ways, reads in German as follows: "Ich kann mir ausbleiben." Neither translation is entirely satisfactory. It is one of the phrases which Jaspers, in his "Philosophical Autobiography," attributes to his friend and brother-in-law, Ernst Meyer.[23]

relationship but a disrelationship in a relation which relates itself to its own self and is constituted by another, so that the disrelationship in that self-relation reflects itself infinitely in the relation to the Power which constituted it.[24]

Even as Kant shifted man's God-relatedness from the theoretical pursuit of proving God's existence to the practical concern of the moral realization of reason, so Jaspers sees man's relation to transcendence as a fundamentally existential concern. This essentially historic concern fulfills and is mediated by the methodical process of essentially unhistoric formal transcending. Existential relatedness to transcendence is more immediate and concrete than formal transcending,[25] and becomes manifest in a richness of possible forms which Jaspers explores.

Secondly, however, the significance of formal transcending comes to light precisely in consideration of such existential relatedness. Different ways of existential relatedness are naturally contradictory, and therein lies the seed of upholding the unfathomable otherness of transcendence. Nevertheless there is a certain atmosphere about man's fundamental relation to the ground of things which permits it, and in which it ever tends to be a meeting with forces* which, though noumenous, are, particularly by way of man's relation to them either palpable efficacies in this world, or at least, amenable to merely human knowledge and evaluation. To be sure this does not become sufficiently explicit but is strongly intimated by Jaspers in the chapter of his *Philosophie* which deals with the existential relations to transcendence. However, we may infer that even as formal transcending is essentially empty without the concern of freedom over its grounding, so, in Jaspers's view, personal existential relatedness to transcendence is essentially uncritical without the dialectical stringency of formal thought. For example, in connection with two forms of existential relatedness to transcendence, namely defiance and surrender, Jaspers comments on the related position according to which the deity is regarded as providence:

---

*The notion of "forces" is not an explicit topic in this work at all, though it is in a contemporaneous work.[26] The topic is raised in later works, albeit inconclusively; in his published works it remains an unfinished chapter of Jaspers's thinking. In his projected "World History of Philosophy" however it is one of the six approaches to the history of philosophical thought; the sixth book was planned as an account of this history with the idea of its being a struggle between forces.

The slightest hint of the opinion that the deity will let things proceed in a certain direction because only this and nothing else would make sense; or that it is impossible that this noble life, or this good will, or this commitment of the best should fail; or that I do or do not deserve, and hence either may expect or need not fear a certain thing; all this brings about a confusing position. Either I push toward the inapproachable in order to behold the authentic Being which is the source of providence; or else—be my thoughts ever so just—I secretly desire to influence, even to force providence. There is, in this way of thinking, a kind of sublimated withchcraft which aims to direct the deity if not by means of magic, by means of man's being and action.[27]

We see that with respect to man's relatedness to the ground of things certain questions are raised when thought reaches a certain degree of critical maturity. Such questions are: towards what manner of object are we directed in this relatedness? Of what manner of truth are we certain when we assure ourselves of this ground? What is the meaning of this truth, how do we assure ourselves of this meaning, how can we and how ought we to understand it? What manner of communication is appropriate to it? Formal thinking by means of the transcendental method challenges, with these questions, the more ingenuous, and hence more naive, thinking in which the existential relatedness to transcendence is expressed. The former must largely reject the latter as unenlightened. Existential relatedness to transcendence will collapse into nihilism without regard for the formal criticism of the scope of determinative thought which is a constant potentiality inherent in thought. If such relatedness is possible at all, it will have to be responsive to and understood in the light of the transcendental method. This, then, is the possible positive significance of formal transcending, which Jaspers expresses as follows:

By making room for the language of transcendence in the form of ciphers, formal transcending prevents with means of systematic awareness the materialization of transcendence. We desire to have the deity in an image and in an objective notion, and not to have these dissolve into mere symbols. In particular, it seems almost unavoidable to consider God as personality with his will derived from perfect wisdom and benevolence, who designs and guides. But, as a symbol, even this is to be regarded as a dissolving image, and to be suspended in transcending thought.[28]

iii. Enlightenment and Nihilism

The philosophy of ciphers is developed in response to the challenge of formal thought, particularly in the form of the modern
Enlightenment engendered by the rise of modern science and
culminating in Kant. Modern science has pre-empted the field of
objectively evidential, determinate truth and certainty. And
Kant elicited from this pre-emption the nature of transcending
as proceeding from the determinately knowable to the indeter-
minably ineffable. If relatedness to transcendence would be
deemed impossible, then, for Kant as well as for Jaspers, there
would be no basis for freedom. Such relatedness may seem inevitable, or at least man's tendency thereto irrepressible. But the
problem is to conceive of its possibility in affirmation of the
demands of the Enlightenment. If the philosophy of ciphers is
seen in this light it will be understood how Jaspers regards it as a
condition of man's liberation. For to regard the expression and
assurance of man's relatedness to transcendence as ciphers means
not only to confirm, in an enlightened form, the possible ground
and source of man's freedom, but also to retrieve man's freedom
and its basis from the objectification of its expressed assurance.
The consequence of this is more far-reaching than may appear at
first sight. It means that the notions, images and experiences
which are ciphers are the human reading of a language (of transcendence) whose meaning is not known to man. There is no
finality in any reading, and mine is no less authentic than yours.
The question is rather, what deeds of freedom, what communicative challenge and responsiveness are made possible by virtue
of a reading of a cipher of transcendence?
    Enlightenment, far from blighting man's relatedness to tran-
scendence with deliberate awareness, far from reducing it to the
inchoate impulse where it might be confused with the emotive
and even the slavery of unmitigated vitality, can, in its conception as cipher intensify that moment of man's grounding in transcendence which is its mark of truth, i.e., testimony and communication. Beyond this, however, the philosophy of ciphers is a
basis for the recognition of the relatedness to the ground of their
freedom on the part of men who do not, themselves, partake of
one's own form of enlightenment. For the philosophy of ciphers
presupposes the immediacy of man's concern over truth, an
immediacy which does not require an initiation into a certain
historic conception of the truth and much less into a certain way

of reading this conception. The task is to understand the other's conception of the vision of truth of which he partakes, or at least to understand that he lives by a truth whether or not one fully understands it. The task is to speak to all, even to the child or to the primitive, about ultimates, in a manner suitable for the common understanding required for communication without the more sophisticated and enlightened assuming a position of superiority. The reason is that the enlightened assurance of one's transcendent grounding is no less a cipher, a reading of an unknown script, than the myth or the mythical world of the other. Moreover, the philosophy of myth discloses resources of language which are locked out by a merely positivistic enlightenment; myths and metaphor when used by the enlightened person, and thus seen as ciphers, preclude their literal understanding.

By virtue of such implications Jaspers's philosophy of ciphers is apposite to thoughts as ancient as Plato's treatment of myth. Plato banishes from the ideal state many of the myths which were traditionally the mainstay of Greek education and culture; he says they are "bad lies."[29] And yet he himself is, and the philosopher-statesman is expected to be, a creator of profound myths. He means to say thereby that even though the *logos* is by nature related to ideas in their purity, both the *logos* and the *mythos* are imitations thereof. At any rate, only the dialectician is capable of partaking of Being in the form of the *logos*. But partaking counts more than the form of this partaking. Hence there are myths in the ideal state, and though his own partaking transcends myth, the statesman has to create, or at least censor, myths. They are "lies," to be sure, and "God does not need lies." Yet man does, as a "medicine," which is prescribed by "physicians."[30]

However, this apposition of Jaspers to Plato must be approached with caution. Jaspers would endorse Plato in one respect and note a distance between Plato and himself in another. Plato's accomplishment is for Jaspers a high point in the development which he calls the "axial times,"[31] the breakthrough of reason into human actuality. It spelled among other things the end of the mythical consciousness and the rise of critical thought. Yet the examination of myths for their literal tenability is the half-way enlightenment of sophism. Not merely the intellect but also reason is at play where myth is "reformed" to become metaphorical, a "language" which conveys meaning other than what it literally refers to. This sensitivity to the "new manner of mythical creativity"[32] and to its import on intercourse regarding the bearing of the vision of truth on human affairs is Plato's accomplishment and Plato's requirement of the philosopher-ruler; this Jaspers endorses. Less promising for Jaspers is Plato's idea of the philosopher-ruler as one who sustains his power of sovereign, critical decision with a "freedom which is superhuman." "The greatest of men remains a man," and therefore ruling, for Jaspers, comprises communicative sharing of the responsibility of decision with those who are ruled by virtue of a reference to what transcends any one man and all men, such as the law.[33] Myth, therefore, as vehicle of communication, cannot be a translation of a literal vision of truth into a metaphorical expression to which he who did not critically penetrate the truth may be more receptive. Rather, it is the rendering of the reading of ciphers of transcendence from one idiom into another idiom.

In this connection Jaspers speaks of "three languages" in which ciphers are read. Myth is a form of the "second language,"[34] where the "language of transcendence" "reverberates" in the form of "communicable" "images and notions." Here actuality itself can be mythical, where objects and events are pervaded by meaning beyond their apparent factuality. Or else, in the form of myths proper, the "ground and nature of existence" is determined in stories of the workings of forces, usually divine, which are "actualities juxtaposed with empirical actualities," though different from these. Or else, finally, the "second language" can take the form of revelation, where meaning and value are brought into this world by a mythical world beyond and above this world which is the source and fulfillment of such meaning.

Different from these possibilities is the "third" or "speculative" language.[35] Here assurance of transcendence occurs in the language of the reflective intellect and is expressed in the form of "objectivities" in "analogy" with logical and empirical objectivities. The uses of such language are manifold. For example, it can be understood as having literal significance, as in the case of most traditional metaphysical systems. Another example is the dialectical juxtaposition of opposing metaphysical thought structures. Such dialectic can serve as language for the transcendence of the ground of Being, and thus distinctly as cipher.

To use terms concerning the ancient Greek enlightenment, the 'second' and 'third' languages are, respectively, the languages of 'mythos' and 'logos'. Yet Jaspers recognizes another, the 'first' language, the "immediate language of transcendence."[36] By its nature this 'language' can be characterized only in a circumlocutory manner. Experience functions as the first language. Experience ordinarily comprises "perception," "Erleben" (i.e., undergoing, encountering, living through), "cognition," "thought" and "empathy." But as such experience is not the 'first language'; to be that it has to be "metaphysical experience." This is not a form of experience aside from the other cited forms mentioned by Jaspers; as such it would be mystical experience which is opposed to what Jaspers means. In fact, in Jaspers's sense, there is no experience which is not experience in the ordinary sense, i.e., in the form of or directed towards actualities of existence. 'Metaphysical' experience occurs through and within ordinary experience or not at all. It is minimally present in experience of concrete actuality when it is accompanied by an experience of its insufficiency. And it is decisively present when experience of actuality is accompanied by experience of the intimation of Being in its transcendent fullness as ground of actuality; then the experience of actuality is man's way of partaking of this fullness. Only by virtue of such transparency of experienced actuality can it be the language of fulfilling transcendence.

In such a huge book as Jaspers's *Philosophie*, with its many-storied structure organized according to the dialectic of modes and methods of transcending—a dialectic culminating in the renewal of metaphysics regarded as reading ciphers of transcendence—it may seem like encumbering a rich work with a plethora of ideas to interject the account of the three languages. Yet the idea of the three languages, inaugurating the chapter on 'ciphers', has an important function. It shows, first, that the third language and the second are equally removed from the immediacy of the first. The enlightened conceptual clarity and intellectual rigor of the third language as such marks no advancement in plumbing the depths of Being over the imagery of the second. For both share the moment of communicable generalization of the historic originality of experience vouchsafed only in the first language. Demythologizing, as self-assertion of the intellect vis-à-vis the uncritical and inarticulate world of myth, is only a partial, and hence untrue, enlightenment.

True enlightenment seeks to recognize the extent and the limits of all modes of human thought and realization of the intellect as well as of myth. In this respect the significance of both the third and the second language lies in their being ciphers of transcendence, moreover ciphers which reach their measure of fulfillment in the immediacy of the active, cogitative or receptive experience which is the first language. However, the second import of the three languages is closely connected with this: the first, no less than the second and third languages, is removed from the fullness of transcendence. The immediacy of experience, though dispensing with generalization and communicability, is at best an intimation of the ground of experienced and experiencing actuality, but is not its absorbing presence. The first, like the other two, is a language of transcendence, a cipher script. It is a reflection of transcendence in experience of actuality, historicly immediate and fulfilling both mythical imagery and speculative reflection. In time only immanence of experience fulfills the motive of fulfilling transcendence:

> I am intent to reach actuality, suspending possibility. Filled with possibility, I advance to actuality, becoming singular and limited myself because I want to arrive where there is no more possibility but the decidedly actual which is only because simple Being is. This I can never encounter in time. But to read its cipher becomes the meaning of all other deeds and experience.[37]

The philosophy of cipher, the radical recognition of man's ultimate realizations as a reading of a script whose code transcends his grasp, is Jaspers's deliberate enactment of enlightenment at the highest plane. He characterizes this enlightenment as the "irresistible responsible movement of reason."[38] Enlightenment which does not rise to the plane of reason but remains on the indispensable but insufficient plane of the cognitive intellect issues in nihilism. For example, the range of significance might be restricted to what can be positively known and to what actions can be determined on the basis of such knowledge. This implies a simultaneous rejection of guidance transcending such knowledge, even guidance experienced in the form of authority and exception. And such rejection comprises, of course, a nihilism with respect to the heritage of human realization in whatever form, be it myth or *logos*. Jaspers sees a close connection between nihilism and the disregard of heritage.[39] Or else the cognitive validity of the intellect is extended over realms which are properly those of believing thought, of thoughts which are invocations of faith and are concerns transcending evidential determination.

Such an improper extension of the will to objectively valid cognition can be executed in many ways, each with its own form of nihilistic conclusion. Metaphysical speculation, carried out or understood as evidential cognition, soon collapses in the juxtaposition of mutually contradictory though equally tenable positions. And ultimate views of reality, insofar as they are taken as being more than guiding ideas promoting orientation and action in the world, namely if taken as being reflections of reality, either shatter against the palpable facts or else offend rules of research and marks of evidence. The enterprise of proving God's existence presupposes agnosticism as long as the proof fails to be evidentially cogent. And the insinuation that the state of the world might serve as evidence for the belief in the meaningfulness of man's life and of creation offends the sensibility of anyone who not only cares but respects facts. Jaspers's simple frankness in this regard is quite disarming:

> For a man of integrity something is expressed in nihilism which is inevitable. . . . One who, in the face of terrible sense-lessness and injustice, does not acknowledge them in their full reality but in almost automatic matter of course passes over them by means of talk about God, may appear more hypocritical than the nihilist. . . . It is more justified to ask how it is possible that we do not all of us become nihilists than to overlook the experiences that can lead to nihilism.[40]

Jaspers denies that nihilism is the final result of enlightenment properly understood. However, he recognizes it not only as a human possibility but as an inevitable moment in the movement toward enlightenment on a higher plane. Nihilism, for Jaspers, seems tied to the demand that certainty concerning fundamental and ultimate questions be pursued under the aspect of the intellect, of critical clarity, of doubt. Under this aspect all will be questionable, particularly the absolutizations and the systems which are also possible with the unrestricted use of the intellect. But cognitive doubt is not the particular province of nihilism unless such doubt is itself absolutized. Negative absolutization is, of course, no more tenable than positive absolutization. Nihilism, then, conceived as the truth concerning reality, is an "error of attempting to grasp truth by means of too short a reach."[41] It is based on a partial enlightenment which, as such, "confounds the methods of the understanding with the contents of humanity."[42] Cognitive doubt is the substrate of faith no less than the intellect's basis and the nihilistic outcome of the failure of its absolutization.

The possibility of faith, of the risk of critical thought concerning questions transcending cognitive determination, is the onset of the "true" enlightenment. On its level another form of nihilism is possible, that of unfaith which was discussed in an earlier chapter. The nihilism under present consideration can have an important function, but only as a moment of the "true" enlightenment. The close connection which Jaspers sees between nihilism and the relegation of transmitted heritage to oblivion is possible only if enlightenment stops with the intellectual disclosure of the cognitive failure of the heritage. The same disclosure can, however, renew regard for the "contents of humanity" in their many possibilities which are disclosed in the testimony of heritage, and which are not exhausted in the form of their communicable expression, even if this form is that of cognitive articulateness. It is in this sense that we understand Jaspers's observation that nihilism can be the vehicle of the appropriation of heritage:

> Nihilism, as a movement of thought as well as a historical experience, becomes the passage to a more profound appropriation of historical heritage. For from the beginning nihilism has not only been the way to the primal source—nihilism is as old as philosophy—but also the acid in which the gold of truth had to prove itself.
>
> From the beginning there is something insurpassable in philosophy. In all change of man's circumstances and the challenges of his lot, in all progress of the sciences, in all unfolding of categories and methods of thought, the concern is to grasp the one eternal truth under new conditions with new means, perhaps with greater possibilities of clarity.
>
> Our task today is to regain certainty of this eternal truth within the framework of extreme nihilism. This presupposes appropriation of the heritage in a manner which is not knowledge of outward appearances, not mere contemplation, but being inwardly present to it as one's own concern. The fundamental attitude, reborn through nihilism, teaches us to take a different view of the history of philosophy. . . . The task is to appropriate the philosophical accomplishments of every age by remaining in continuously renewed communication with the great who appeared in the past regarded not as surpassed but as present.[43]

Jaspers's philosophy of ciphers is to be regarded as educed from the restriction of the intellect's cognitive employment to the empirical and formal sciences; as a recovery of man's reflection on the basis of his being not only from the nihilistic pitfalls of an insufficiently consequential enlightenment but from the constant possibility of nihilism; and as responsive to man's and fellow man's grasp of truth no matter what form of communicable expression it may take or may have taken.

iv. Negative Theology and the Hidden God

It is a telling fact that the possibility of nihilism and its tendencies in recent thought can be shown to be a decisive moment in the formation of Jaspers's philosophy of cipher. For in Jaspers, the dialectic of negation is a principal function of recalling metaphysical thought from the unfitting and potentially nihilistic fixation which the indispensable expression in the idiom of intellectual thought entails. In the conception of the cipher-script and its reading, dialectical negation is raised to a principle of transcendental thought with decisive radicalism. Many powerful traditions of thought reach a culmination in this conception. Of those two closely related notions, namely 'negative theology' and the *deus absconditus*, deserve particular mention. Negative theology comes to Jaspers's mind at the inception of both his major treatments of the conception of transcendence in the form of ciphers.[44] And he bears witness a number of times to the pertinence to his own thinking of the biblical injunction "thou shalt not make unto thee any graven image or any likeness."[45] Characteristic for the apposition of the notion of God's hiddenness to his conception of the ciphers of transcendence is the following:

> Philosophical faith does not wish to lose the distant, solely real God in the proximate Gods [to be regarded] as ciphers, but wishes live experience of the distant God in the proximate ciphers.[46]

But let us consider these two notions more closely.

With the philosophy of ciphers in mind, Jaspers characterizes the function of negative theology as follows. As Existenz, i.e., as self assured of the ground of its freedom, man is related to transcendence. But this relatedness does not imply a subject-object relation where the object, transcendence, appears to the subject, thinking man, or where the world—including man—can be regarded in relation to a juxtaposed Deity. Any cogitative objectification of transcendence is unfitting; transcendence eludes objectification. The approach to the deity by virtue of this elusion, the deliberate negation of the fitness of any thought of God, the methodical articulation of the failure of thought with respect to God by means of the execution of such failure, this is the program of negative theology.[47] It is not really in Jaspers's temperament to place any stock in a cogitatively programmatic approach to the assurance of transcendence. Hence it is best to speak of negative theology in relation to Jaspers as a historical effort pointing toward and apposite to what comes to fruition in the conception of cipher. The problem for both the negative theologian and Jaspers as philosopher of ciphers is the same: "Can the chasm between man and transcendence be cleared in forms of thought?"[48] To regard such forms as ciphers of transcendence means to regard "cognition of transcendence" as "impossible," and positively, to have the "right" to "justify" the meaning of such ciphers and "thereby to subject the form of these ciphers to the criteria of philosophical truth."[49] As ciphers, man's assurances of transcendence cannot function as cognitive or dogmatic fixations and are not beyond the movement of criticism; and this criticism will comprise the question of the relevance as tasks and ideals on the part of the ciphers for selves existing as agents in time. And in this regard negative theology can have a "purifying" function: "By means of the 'not', man, in his historic Existenz, can experience the actuality of God as incomprehensible."[50]

It would be interesting to inquire into Jaspers's relationship as philosopher of cipher to some of the many great thinkers in the tradition of negative theology. This sympathy for the negative theology of some of them, even where it is indicated, as for example in the case of Master Eckhart or Nicholas of Cusa, is qualified. Particular regard would have to be paid to his stated admiration, with a hesitant apprehension of kinship, for Indian transcending thought. He says,

> In Asia transcending [*Überschreiten*] occurred not only through vigorous thought but through its realization in a way and practice of life. This occurred in depth with such consequence as perhaps at no other place among men. It is doubtful that we understand much of this. . . . We should understand the astonishing paradox of language cancelling speech.[51]

In his treatment of Thomas Aquinas's negative theology[52] Jaspers fails to mention his theory of analogy. It seems clear that, if he had, he would have noted the discrepancy between 'analogy' and 'cipher'. Thomas rejects a negative theology, such as Maimonides', according to which affirmative substantial attributes of God cannot be predicted in any way whatever.[53] Thomas holds, under the supposition that perfections of creatures reflect perfections of the creator, that perfections known of creatures are also essentially and positively attributable to God.[54] To be sure, this does not mean that we know the divine perfection in its essential fulness, but we know it insofar as it is reflected in the creature which we do know[55] in the manner appropriate to our degree of knowledge. At the same time we know God in his essence to be perfect in this way to a degree unknown and unknowable to us, at least in our earthly state. The two perfections, the perfection known by man, and the unknown perfection which man knows to be of God's essence are neither the same in meaning (*univoce*) nor equivocal, but are attributed to both creatures and God in the manner of an "analogy, i.e., a proportion."[56] The reasons for reversing the enterprise of negative theology at least to the point of regarding affirmative predication about God to be possible analogically are as follows: First, there must be a reason why some attributes are more pertinent to God than others.[57] Secondly, from the viewpoint of what now can be called intellectual thought in distinction from reason, (and thought for Thomas is solely intellectual), the only alternative to strict univocal predication is equivocation, unless it be analogy in the sense of proportion with reference to a standard (in this case God's perfection). It seems clear that in Thomas's view strict negative theology would fall under equivocal predication. But in this case, he observes, nothing could be concluded about God on the basis of man's knowledge of creation. And this is against philosophy as Thomas understands it where, as he maintains, much has demonstratively been proved about God.[58] Finally, and this may be the most decisive reason for Thomas, there are, after all, affirmative propositions of faith concerning God, and faith cannot contain error (*fidei non subest falsum*).[59]

From the viewpoint of the philosophy of ciphers, Maimonides, against whom Thomas turns in proposing the analogical mitigation of negative theology, seems to have proceeded more consequentially. To be sure, Maimonides, like Thomas, was concerned with upholding the authority of revelation, but unlike Thomas did not have to defend the authority of a worldly institutional tradition, namely, the church, as guardian of revelation; also the doctrinal content of his faith did not present such challenges to reason. Moreover, both wished to give philosophical thought, particularly Aristotelianism, the due it demanded; yet Maimonides, unlike Thomas, found a way of philosophizing in the surroundings of his faith without distinguishing between philosophy and faith and subordinating the former to the latter so radically. Understanding, for Maimonides, is a gift man possessed even prior to his Fall, for how can he be expected to follow God's directives unless he can judge what is true and false;[60] and faith is not true unless it comprises a representation which has been examined as to its truth.[61] If faith in God means recognizing that God transcends man's capacity to grasp him, then *a fortiori* it requires the attempt which results in this failure.[62] Accordingly, Maimonides shows that affirmative propositions about the nature of God cannot be made in any mode of attribution.[63] Complete or incomplete essential attribution is impossible because it implies knowledge of determination, and God cannot be thought of as determined; the attribution of accidental qualities entails changeableness which cannot be thought of God; relational attribution requires some kind of equality in the terms of the relation which cannot be said of God with respect to any being to which he may be said to be related. Attribution concerning God can only be negative; only by means of the unending reflection that God's essence is absolutely other than anything we can grasp can we approach an intimation of that essence.[64] Affirmative attribution is not possible with respect to that essence, but only according to the effects of God. By this Maimonides does not mean the same thing as Thomas, for whom such effects are the basis for analogical predications. He means, rather, the reflection, on the part of the creature, upon the absolute dependence of the richness of creatures on the one and simple source of all being. Hence, even in this attribution, the only permissible kind because it does not touch upon the essence of God, there is the element of negation in that the multiplicity of creatures testifies to the otherness of God in his oneness.[65]

Jaspers seems not to have read Maimonides. Yet it should be clear that in conception, if not in its execution and the historic circumstances in which it occurred, Maimonides' negative theology approaches the intention of Jaspers's cipher-philosophy.[66]

The conception of ciphers is related to the historical effort of thinking communicably about transcendence without succumbing to the illusion that what man thinks is appropriate to God, and yet without renouncing the restless movement of thought in favor of a putative mystical vision of deity, or the nihilistic restriction of thought to the as such meaningless objectivities which thought is able to master. This historical relation is even more pronounced in the case of the notion of the hiddenness of God, which Jaspers seeks to realize with singular radicalism. As so often, the central concern is freedom:

> Where I am truly myself I am certain that I am not through myself. The highest freedom consists in regarding oneself independent of the world and at the same time profoundly bound to transcendence.[67]

The consequence of this intimate relation between freedom and transcendent grounding with respect to the hiddenness of transcendence goes in two directions: On the one hand, the consciousness and task of freedom not only require grounding in transcendence, but that this ground be hidden. If it were revealed, freedom would be at an end, and only unquestioning surrender would be possible. Yet freedom knows defiance as well as surrender, moreover surrender which as in Job does not dispense with defiance.[68] On the other hand, the more intensively man is conscious of his freedom and pursues his self-realization in freedom, the more intensively this freedom testifies to the hiddenness of its transcendent source. Thus Jaspers says,

> The deity says nothing directly; but through this possibility of freedom it seems to speak, i.e., to demand that its—to us unfathomable—will be done by which it made man independent in order that he might decide about himself at his own responsibility and thereby gain his dignity.[69]

At another place we read in a like vein:

> The deity has not deprived me of my freedom, and thus relieved me of my responsibility, by showing itself to me.[70]

Thus not only the relation to transcendence but the hiddenness of transcendence is tied to the actuality of freedom. Man's expression of the assurance of his transcendent grounding seems to bring transcendence closer. But man deprives himself of this assurance, and thereby of his freedom and selfhood if he is ensnared by such human expression, if he takes it to be the speech and revelation of God, instead of being constantly prepared to suspend the proximate human expression for the true ground in its distant and hidden transcendence. The expression in whatever form of assurance cannot be taken as determinate objectivity but only as indeterminate cipher.[71] Objectification of such expression, whether it be myth, speculation or embodiment, leads to obedience to something temporal, man-made. Against this, upholding the hiddenness of transcendence can be the refuge of freedom.[72] But in its enlightened version this means the risk and the struggle of reading the ciphers of transcendence. The magnitude of the relentless task of being oneself in freedom with deliberate awareness of the hiddenness and mystery of transcendence, is spelled out by Jaspers in many versions:

> The tension of Existenz toward this hidden transcendence is its life. . . . This tension is the genuine appearance of selfhood but at the same time it is anguish. To escape the anguish man wishes to bring the divinity close, to loosen the stress, to know what really is, what he can go by and what to devote himself to. That which as cipher is a possible truth is then absolutized as Being.[73]

Man, history or God as Personality are ciphers which might be—
and have been—thus absolutized.[74] In another version Jaspers
says:

> In self-dependence Existenz appears more vacillating, ambiva-
> lent and impotent than Existenz which rests assured of and is
> affirmed by objective ties. For in consideration of the weak-
> ness of our nature there is, by virtue of doubt and despair,
> greater danger in freedom: freedom remains a risk.[75]

And most decisively:

> In daily security of God's nearness the relatedness to God
> would be robbed of its profundity, which it possesses in
> doubt. . . . For the hiddenness of God seems to require that
> man labor in doubts and in exigencies.[76]

And in the face of "doubts and exigencies" Jaspers maintains that

> philosophical Existenz can bear not to approach the hidden
> God directly. Only the cipher-script speaks, if I am prepared
> for it.[77]

For,

> Existenz learns of the deity indirectly precisely as much as
> becomes actual for it out of its own freedom.[78]

B. Systematic Main Themes of the Cipher-Philosophy

v. The Cipher as Historicly Valid Symbol

We have shown Jaspers's conception of the ciphers of transcendence insofar as it is rooted in fundamental, historical motives of
thought. Let us now turn to his systematic clarification of the
significance, the interpretation, and the limits of ciphers. First
we shall consider the conception of cipher as symbol.
   We recall that in facing the question of the relation of thought
and being, Jaspers finds the distinction between Being-in-itself,
being-in-its-appearance, and being-oneself particularly fruitful. In
thinking, in our pursuit of being, we never grasp being itself;
being is always being for us. It is split into subject and object,
into being oneself directed toward another and being as it appears to us.[79] And being in its appearance is always in the form

of a determinate objectivity (*Gegenständlichkeit*). Whatever
comes to our attention, whether an appearance proper or an
intimation of what transcends determination, must take the
form of a determinate object of thought; the intellect, as form
and medium of all thought, requires it. Not all that takes the
form of an appearance as determinate object of thought is properly appearance or determinable. Taking this form may be a matter of intimating what cannot appear, cannot be an object, cannot be thought.

Accordingly it is useful to make a distinction between different modes of thought-objects. The determinate object, the object of thought in its proper sense, is the ideal (e.g. mathemati-
cal) or real (i.e. empirical) cognitive object; these thought-objects are either formal determinations or *phenomena of reality*.[80] Quite different are expressions of selfhood and freedom.
To be sure, expressions of this kind may be taken as mere phenomena—as such they are understood only psychologically, with
cognitive indifference and neutrality. Properly regarded, beyond
their general cognitive significance, they are recognized as pointing to possibilities which by virtue of one's freedom one decides
to be or not. Confrontation with such objects does not imply
verification of what is the case but implies decisiveness as to
what one chooses to be. Since these objects of thought point to
possibilities of freedom and selfhood, Jaspers calls them *signa of
Existenz*. Phenomena represent appearing determinations, signa
evoke possibilities of self-determination.[81]

A third mode of thought-objects is the object of metaphysics.
Here the reader of Jaspers may encounter difficulty because
Jaspers calls this object both *symbol* and *cipher*. To wit: in a
section of the Third Book of his *Philosophie* Jaspers comes to
terms with the problem of distinction between symbol and
cipher, and succeeds in delimiting the latter vis-à-vis the former;[82] we shall presently have to take this as the key to our understanding of this topic. Yet at the beginning of this Third
Book, in a section on the "Inconsistency of metaphysical determinate objectivity [*Gegenständlichkeit*]," he speaks of 'symbol'
in the same way as he usually speaks of 'ciphers', without ever
mentioning ciphers. For example:

> The determinate object [*Gegenstand*] which is a symbol is not
> to be fixed as the present actuality of transcendence, but is
> only to be heard as its language.[83]

Inquiry into whether Jaspers wrote this section before he achieved
the distinction of the concept of cipher and before this term oc-

curred to him seems needless, because in works written after the
Philosophie Jaspers shows, by reverting from one term to the
other, that considering the large area in which their conceptions
intersect, they may, in most cases, be used synonymously.[84] But
let us proceed with our account of these concepts.

We coordinated phenomena with being-in-its-appearance, and
signa of Existenz with being-oneself. It is tempting to say that the
third mode of thought-object, the metaphysical object, is being-
in-itself, the third pole of the tripolarity. But being-in-itself cannot
be a determinate object; as such it would be a phenomenon. The
object of thought as metaphysical object does not function as real
object, as what it is; rather it functions as the presence of what is
other than the object and what cannot be object.[85] Being-in-itself
transcends the subject-object dichotomy wherein all being that is
for us makes its determinate appearance; it is 'transcendence', 'encompassing' subject and object. The concept of 'being-in-itself' has
expressed for Jaspers from the earliest the essential mystery of
being.[86] The penetration of this mystery in mystic experience
may possibly be granted one or another man. But this cannot be
represented by thought, nor is it the way of thought, and, in particular, of philosophy. To think, rather, means to let the awareness
of the mystery of Being be the language of Being.

> The world and all that happens in it is secret. . . . Philosophy
> illumines the secret and brings it to consciousness. It begins
> with wonderment and heightens wonderment. . . . Then the
> world shows, as whole and in every one of its features, the
> unending depth. . . . This secret is essential; Being itself speaks
> in it. . . .
> Our wondering enthuses us to plunge through the world into
> transcendence. But we remain in the world and find ourselves
> again, not in transcendence but in heightened presence. What-
> ever is for us becomes more for us than at first it seemed. It
> becomes transparent, it becomes symbol.[87]

It is useful to distinguish 'symbol' and 'sign'. The latter is a clear,
defined, univocal, limited meaning-function, where one determination refers to another determination which can be a sign or a conception or a perception. The sign is the ideal of intellectual
thought, an ideal realized to some degree in notations such as
those used in mathematics and chemistry.[88] Ordinarily we use the
term 'symbol' in a somewhat broader sense, a usage reflected in
Jaspers's *Philosophie* when he speaks not only of "sign" but also
of "metaphor, comparison, representation, [and] model" as "deliberate symbolism [*bewusste Symbolik*]."[89] But the fundamental

restricted meaning of 'deliberate symbol' vis-à-vis Jaspers's usual
terminological use of 'symbol' as "object" of metaphysical
thought remains the same as that indicated for 'sign': It is "the
possession of things in the world by means of reference of one to
another which also exists otherwise."[90] In short, one determinate
object refers to another determinate object. Hence the reference
can be a matter of translation. Cancel the referring sign and the
object remains. None of this is the case with respect to the 'symbol' in Jaspers's sense. The symbol is, as object of thought, a determinate object. But what is meant by it is not, in turn, an object.
Hence, should the symbol be cancelled, what the symbol "refers"
to would vanish. Being as such is not signified, represented or defined by the symbol. According to the criteria of meaning-function the symbol has no object to which it refers; it is as empty as is
the signum of Existenz. But while the latter evokes possibilities of
selfhood, what is 'meant' by the symbol can only be a presence
which is intimated only symbolically and which cannot be de-
noted independently of symbols. The symbol does not stand for a
concept or perception.

The presence which the symbol intimates is not a reality other
than the determinate reality which appears to us in our cognitive
thought. For, as Jaspers says in accord with Kant, "Being is not a
second reality which is behind knowable realities."[91] Rather, the
symbol, insofar as it is significant at all, intimates Being in its indeterminacy which transcends the determinateness of the form in
which it appears to us. This means, first, that the symbol cannot
be regarded as a form of knowledge. So regarded it would be vacuous and illusory.[92] There is no intersubjectively repeatable method whereby symbolic meaning can be confirmed. Second, it means
that the interpretation of symbols must be attuned to the transcendent indeterminacy of Being for whose intimation the symbol
functions as vehicle.

So attuned, the symbol's interpretation will remain incomplet-
able. Its interpretation occurs within the realm of determinate
meaning which is the proper and only arena of our thinking. Only
the restless, constant pursuit of this endless realm of meaning is
adequate to symbolized Being in its indeterminacy to which no
determination is adequate. The symbol, properly regarded, is as
endless as Being is infinite. "No thought is sufficient for Being.
The symbol opens Being for us and shows us all Being."[93]

If its interpretation cannot be completed then a symbol's possible interpretations are endless in number. And if this is so, then
the choice of interpretation is arbitrary or a matter of convention
or habit.[94] Objectively this is indeed the case. In this way one can

classify and compare the endless array of symbols and the endless ways in which they have been understood. Or else one can, by means of the absolutization of a principle of interpretation, seemingly master the endless realm of symbols; Jaspers cites Hegel's dialectic and Freud's theory of the libido as examples of this.[95] Such interpretation is concerned with the determinately objectified precipitation of the historical and personal testimony and articulation of envisaged symbols. It is the inevitable and necessary outward manifestation of symbols but it is not the inner fulfillment of symbols. Jaspers observes that research into the former cannot be divorced from the latter. Strictly speaking, he maintains,

> no research into symbols is possible, only grasp and creation of symbols. Research into the language of historical and past vision of symbols is possible only under subjective conditions in the researcher who is capable of seeing symbols and of being receptive to them prior to any research.[96]

From the view of the possible inner significance of symbols the question of their arbitrariness looks different. And this difference is decisive for the delineation of 'cipher'. The multiplicity of a symbol's interpretation is arbitrary (*beliebig*) only objectively, aside from any obligation to a symbol and its significance. But such obligation obtains only by virtue of a self's commitment to a symbol as the vehicle of its assurance of the transcendent ground of its freedom. It is by virtue of such existential significance that a 'symbol' is what Jaspers calls a 'cipher'. To be sure, there may be as many interpretations of a symbol as there are Existenzen, and therefore the multiplicity of the cipher's significance is no less than the symbol's. However the multiplicity of the cipher's significance is not arbitrary. It results from the multiplicity of Existenzen, each uniquely within the limits of its historicity "incorporating" or "creating" the symbol as it may.[97] But there is no such multiplicity for the self. For the self in its singularity the cipher is singular in meaning:

> The cipher becomes, in an untransferable and . . . unknowable manner, singular in meaning . . . for Existenz only in the moment of its historic presence. This singularity of meaning consists in the unrepresentability of transcendence fulfilling for this Existenz.[98]

As we can see, the distinction between Jaspers's conceptions of 'symbol' and 'cipher' can indeed be made, and the distinction is decisive. For it locates the signficance of 'objects of metaphysics' squarely in the historic self in its concern over the assurance of its freedom and its reach for possibilities of existence. And Jaspers undertakes this labor of locating the import of metaphysics in response to the conclusion of the enlightened critique of meta-physics, which he accepts, according to which metaphysics and its "objects"are cognitively vacuous. The obverse of the enlighten-ment's requirement that whatever does not follow the criteria of cognition not be assigned cognitive significance is that it be placed in its proper import. We can now understand why the use of 'sym-bol' and that of 'cipher' are so often interchangeable, and why, from the enlightened point of view, 'cipher' is preferred by Jaspers:

> We prefer 'cipher' to 'symbol'. Cipher means 'language', lan-guage of actuality which can be heard and addressed only in this way. Symbol, on the other hand, means a representation by another, even if it can exist only symbolically and in no other manner. In symbols we are directed, intending meaning, toward the other which thereby becomes a determinate object and is present in it. But symbols can become moments of cipher-language. Then they are taken into the movement of thought which is directed toward or takes its point of depar-ture from transcendence. Then they lose their misleading sub-stantiality yet avoid being ruined in the pallor of "mere sym-bols."[99]

We can, in fact, regard Jaspers's conception of cipher as a culmi-nation of enlightenment. Nowhere else, it seems, is such a serious attempt made to come to terms with two conflicting motives of thought without danger either of gnostic resolutions or of disre-gard for their tension. One motive is to articulate man's certainty of Being, the other is to grasp Being determinately. The critical achievement of the determinate grasp of Being, particularly in modern science, by means of deliberate methodology attuned to the requirements of determinacy, has paralleled and has even be-come possible by shutting out man's motive of assurance of his ground of Being. And the articulation of the fundamental cer-tainty of Being—on the part of man whose mode of being involves consciousness of his being in Being and with beings—loses the con-crete substantiation according to the progress of critical cognition. Being as determinately known loses its familiarity, its character as the infinite fullness of which we partake, a partaking by which we reach our fulfillment. And Being itself, of whose freedom-giving certainty we seek to assure ourselves, recedes into indeterminable distance.

The radical consequence of this enlightenment is not the abandonment of the motive of the certainty of Being. This would be futile for it would arise again, uncritically. In accordance with Jaspers's thinking on these matters, the alternative to methodical cognition and the reading of ciphers where the two ways of thought are critically distinguished is not the pursuit of science to the exclusion of metaphysics in this enlightened sense. The alternative is, rather, the failure to distinguish scientific from metaphysical thought. This failure may take one of two forms. The first form is the inappropriate entanglement of metaphysical thought in determinate objectivity. There are many examples of this: one is the interjection of a vacuous note of objectivity into what cannot be other than the reading of ciphers, as in scientific metaphysics, the phenomenological vision of essences, or ontology. A different kind of example is the guarantee of certainty as in revelational dogmatics. A further example is to regard a scientifically unverifiable, essentially metaphysical theory of what reality as a whole is like as following from scientific findings, as in dialectical materialism. The second form of failure to distinguish scientific from metaphysical thought is the reverting to a state of consciousness prior to enlightened criticism, a consciousness for which all concreteness is the immanent presence of the source of all Being. It is in the light of these reflections that we must regard the recognition of the cipher as cipher as the culmination of the labor of enlightenment.

vi. Interpretation of Ciphers

We are now able to discuss certain other features and the application of the conception of cipher. The features which we shall consider in the remainder of this chapter are the problems of the interpretation of the cipher, its relation to myth and traditional metaphysics, the 'reading' of the cipher, the significance for it of the communicative struggle and of 'shipwreck', and the question of what is beyond all ciphers.

The whole treatment of the interpretation (*Deuten*) of ciphers depends on the basic insight that Being in its transcendence, as ground of the self's freedom, cannot be interpreted. What is absolutely encompassing cannot be represented by another; neither can it be represented by the cipher. Its presence can only be intimated in the cipher, which as thought-object is inadequate to it. The interpretation of ciphers can heighten the intimation of transcendence precisely by indicating the inadequacy of the cipher.

Stated differently we may say that Being in its transcendence cannot be beheld by man who thinks determinatively in time. To confront transcendence immediately would be mysticism. To man transcendence can only be mediated by an immanence functioning as cipher. But a cipher is a cipher only immediately, and not by virtue of a mediative interpretation. The cipher can only be "seen," not "interpreted," as cipher;[100] it can only be "perceived," not "cognized," as cipher.[101] The impossibility of interpretation is an essential feature of the cipher. For it shows its inadequacy to the infinite presence which is mediated only through the cipher. And the interpretation of the cipher can be a vehicle for eliciting the impossibility of interpretation by virtue of which the cipher is a cipher. In the negative result lies the positive value of interpretation. Interpretation taken as positive achievement is sham and misses the significance of cipher as cipher:

> The meaning [*Bedeuten*] of ciphers is not such that something present means something absent, or something immanent something transcendent. . . . The being of cipher is a meaning which means nothing other. . . .
>
> . . . The cipher is infinite meaning to which no determinate interpretation is adequate; rather, in interpreting, it requires an infinite movement of interpretation. Interpretation is . . . itself an allegorical activity, a game. Interpretation is impossible: Being itself is present, transcendence. It is nameless. When we speak of it, we use endless names and cancel each again. That which is meaning is itself Being.[102]

It is, no doubt, such an allusion to Pseudo-Dionysios's *The Names of God*, under which title negative theology experienced one of its decisive systematic expressions, that leads Xavier Tilliette to observe, quite correctly, that Jaspers incorporates the positive negations of apophatic theology.[103]

To repeat: the significance of the interpretation of ciphers lies in achieving an awareness of the insignificance of man's conceptions by means of which he struggles to assure himself of the transcendent ground of Being and of his freedom.

Hence, first of all, the multiplicity of meaning of a cipher must be upheld as essential to the cipher. Where any interpretation is inadequate, no interpretation can be final. The principle valid for any interpretive penetration of a cipher is: "Transcendence can give notice of itself some other way."[104] Such multiplicity is, of course, not the arbitrary multiplicity of the symbol, endless meanings of which can be gleaned historically or speculatively; rather it is the multiplicity which marks the openness to the presence of transcendence on the part of the historic self who, in its attention to the cipher, by virtue of which this presence is intimated, refuses to absolutize its own finiteness.

Hence, secondly, contradiction, tautology, circularity in thought, as well as dialectic become decisive in metaphysics. Jaspers points out that contradiction, tautology and circularity are, according to the criteria of theoretical thought, vacuous and vicious. They spur research and are avoided or overcome by particular research. However, they are, in Jaspers's observation, inevitable when thought transcends what can be an object of such research. The possibility of assurance of transcendence by means of thought, which is the attempt of thinking the unthinkable, is opened up precisely by pursuing thought to the point of its inevitable failure. As can be seen, this is not a matter of pursuing contradiction and circularity for their own sake. Formal thought is a vehicle of cipher-reading only if pursued with sustained discipline to the point where it genuinely fails, and where this failure is not merely taken as the overreaching of thought into an objectively vacuous region. The achievement of genuine circles and contradictions is, for Jaspers, the "shattering of the conditions of thought as means of transcending."[105] What counts in metaphysical thought is not the shattering of, say, the principle of non-contradiction as condition of thought, but carrying thought itself to its limits as a function of indicating what transcends thought and what eludes man's grasp in his being tied to thought. Thought reaches its limits precisely because its conditions prevail. Formal paradoxes, such as that of the class of all classes, or metaphysical ones, such as those defined by Kant in his critique of the 'antinomy of pure reason' are well-known. In Jaspers's view it is an error to accept contradictions with resignation, or to contrive solutions for them; the former offends thought, the latter is deceptive—the contradiction will appear in another form.[106] And of Jaspers's many expatiations on the metaphysical significance of the circle the following cannot be surpassed in pithiness:

> Every cipher which speaks of the ground of all things, of Being as a whole, necessarily describes a circle. No matter what is supposed to be "the ultimate," since there is nothing before or beside it, it can always be only grounded through itself and not through another. Hence Spinoza's formula: *causa sui*. This is the circle in its simplest form. The circles are differentiated

according to their contents; whether Spinoza's divine substance, or Hegel's spirit, or matter producing the brain that
knows the matter, there is always, at the crucial point, a circle.
It is universal in all philosophy.[107]

The alternative to the pursuit of thought to its limits and by
means of such learned ignorance to be open to Being transcending
human thought, is to take, by means of an absolutization, as transcendence what is less than transcendence.

Hence, furthermore, the traditions of metaphysics, with the apparent chaos of divergent systems, with the juxtapositions of contradictory systems, cancelling each other precisely by virtue of
their equal consistency, become newly significant. Far from being
dismissed as a titanic effort of research into an empty object, an
effort with no result, this tradition is the repository of the historical reading of the cipher-script, of the achievement of that learned
ignorance whose incorporating re-thinking can be the vehicle for a
more profound assurance of freedom's ground in Being. As the
'third language' metaphysical speculation can achieve the highest
clarification of man's essential ignorance concerning transcendence. But while the tradition of metaphysics is recognized as be-
longing to the world of ciphers, this world extends beyond it,
comprising art, myths, perceived nature. For anything can be a
cipher, or at least a means for a more genuine realization of
ciphers. In this sense Jaspers conceives of scientific research as the
indispensable means of gaining a notion of the limits of what can
be known; but such research would have to be actually undertaken, and not be merely a matter of reading what others have
found out. "It is the sense of research," Jaspers maintains,

> to lead in the direction of true ciphers. Cipher-script without
> research is deceptive. Universal research must lead to the limit
> where the highest wonderment and the most penetrating
> cipher-script become possible.[108]

Thus, moreover, as this reference to the importance of one's
own research indicates, the reading of the cipher-script can genuinely only be an experience on the part of a historic self. This can
be clarified by referring to the controversy between Jaspers and
Bultmann about the latter's program of demythologizing the Bible. In Jaspers's view, which Bultmann does not controvert, Bultmann wishes to confirm the contents of faith by means of a
methodical understanding of the mythical idiom of the Bible and
thereby translate it into a non-mythical idiom conforming to modern views and expressing truth literally. Jaspers does not think this
is possible. Truths conveyed by myths are translatable only into

other myths, or symbols or ciphers, and are heard as possible unconditional contents of faith only in such a form. As methodically
determined universal truths they would be merely conditional:

> Not translation, not reinterpretation, not exegesis by means of
> a conceptual universal . . . but entering and lingering in the
> mythical-intuitive presence teach the consummation of the
> clarifying struggles in which no one is destroyed as loser but
> remains as known rejected possibility.[109]
>
> All that is transmitted is valid as a possible language and be-
> comes a true language not in [the form of] universality but in
> historic situations for Existenz which finds itself in it [i.e., in
> such language].[110]
>
> Any myth, so also that of the Christian act of salvation, is to
> be tested, from the standpoint of the seriousness of existential
> actuality, for the power emanating from its language and the
> truth issuing from it in the actuality of life.[111]

It is with respect to this standpoint that Bultmann asks: "Well,
how is this done?"[112] He regards Jaspers's view that expressions
concerning ultimate questions are non-objective as implausible in
consideration of the theologian's need to interpret and to teach
training ministers how to explain biblical passages. In his rejoinder
Jaspers bases himself on the relative value of interpretation. Interpretation can be a vehicle for an objectivity—such as a myth or its
"translation"—to become a cipher, but it does not confirm the
objectivity, nor is it what counts. If interpretation is the focal
point, then it becomes a "vice," then one looks for the mediation
of a methodical "recipe" for what essentially cannot be mediated,
only heard immediately, if heard at all. Can one, after a "paean of
love" ask "how is this done?"[113] One hears the truth, say concerning love, because one learns something one has always known;
Jaspers likes to use the Platonic notion of reminiscence in this
connection. A summary of the relevant thought appears at the
very end of Jaspers's *Von der Wahrheit:* There can be no guidance
for the reading of cipher-script or, which is the same thing, philosophical activity.

> What is decisive is ever unique and cannot be generally antici-
> pated. It is false to think that fulfillment is granted or a pro-
> gram is given or even a consciousness of Being is mediated by
> means of an indication of the ground and the mode of philo-
> sophical movement. . . . Freeing possibilities . . . is not media-
> tion of substance. . . . Philosophy arouses, indicates, shows
> ways, leads a while, makes ready, fosters maturation to experi-
> ence the ultimate.[114]

vii.   The Ultimate Limits of Ciphers

The cipher then is not separable from the historic self who in reading the cipher seeks and expresses its certainty of Being as ground of its freedom. The actuality of the cipher as the resonance of the transcendent source of the self's possibilities is rooted in the self's being itself. This means that no objectivity, no interpretation vouchsafes the truth of the cipher. Being-in-itself transcends and is not representable by the cipher. Lest the cipher be arbitrary only the self can verify its truth as the intimated presence of encompassing Being. And this verification can only be a matter of the testimony of the self's becoming itself:

> Whenever I read a cipher I am responsible, because I read it only by means of my selfhood whose possibility and truthfulness emerge for me in the form of reading ciphers. I verify by means of my being myself without my having any other measure than this selfhood which recognizes itself by the transcendence of the cipher.[115]
>
> In no way is Being for everyone. All remains shrouded for him who is not himself.[116]

In consideration of the responsibility of the self for its cipher-reading it follows, first, that the self is no less the creator than it is the recipient of the ciphers which are the vehicles of its assurance of its ground in Being.[117] Second, reading the cipher-script is an historic activity and thus has the character of a struggle. This aspect of the conception of ciphers does not become a major theme until Jaspers's late publication *Philosophical Faith and Revelation*. Of particular interest is his conception of the communicative struggle for the realization of truth in time as a twofold struggle. On the one hand there is, of course, the struggle between ciphers which is consequent upon the articulation and objectification of ciphers, a struggle which takes many forms and occurs in many strata. Examples are: the struggle of different claims upon us, such as that between erotic love and reason objectified in the deities Aphrodite and Athena; or the struggle for the right realization of the passage in Saint Matthew: "Upon this rock I will build my church," a struggle institutionalized in the Catholic-Protestant schism; or the struggle as to the primacy of will or intellect. On the other hand, there is the struggle for the purity of ciphers, the struggle not to mistake the cipher for a concrete manifestation of transcendence; it is the struggle not only to uphold the possibilities of selfhood in freedom through man's directedness to transcendence, but to do so under the critical standards of the enlightenment.

Hence, finally, the interpretation of ciphers as means of assurance of transcendence must culminate in the multiplicity of the meaning of the cipher, thus becoming a cipher of the foundering of human efforts to realize transcendence in time. And, for Jaspers, such foundering leads to the ultimate cipher of transcendence which is silence before the unfathomable depth of Being. The transcendence of Being is upheld for man's realization precisely by means of man's failure to realize it in his experience, in his conceptions, in his deeds, in relating all of these to a transcending ground of their meaningfulness. Man's foundering and his encounter with foundering can be a cipher of transcendence because the question remains open as to whether foundering is, in the end, merely temporal annihilation or is of transcendent significance. Thus the inevitability of shipwreck might lead to refusal of realization in the world because of its futility only if worldly duration and validity are absolutized.[118] On the other hand to plan or to seek shipwreck is a sham and not a cipher:

> Genuine, revealing foundering is not to be found in any downfall whatever, or in any annihiliation, self-surrender, renunciation or failure. The cipher of eternization in foundering becomes clear only if I do not wish to founder but dare to founder.[119]

Foundering, as cipher of man's effort to realize transcendence in his conceptions and to realize his relation to transcendence by means of his active freedom, has some aspects which lend themselves to interpretation and some which do not. As to the former it might be said, with respect to the actuality of freedom, that foundering is necessary, for it exists by virtue of the actualization of possibilities. Once realized, freedom ceases to be freedom and becomes mundane fact and transience. "What really is, leaps into the world and extinguishes in its actualization."[120] Freedom is a constant task and lives through foundering. We are reminded of two of Faust's last lines:

> Nur der verdient sich Freiheit wie das Leben,
> Der täglich sie erobern muss![121]

Furthermore, freedom is actual only by virtue of the recalcitrance of and the actualization in an other, i.e., nature. But vis-à-vis nature freedom founders: on the one hand by resisting nature it founders in its natural realization; on the other, in its realization it is destroyed.[122] Uninterpretable, for Jaspers, are the ciphers of

senseless destruction, of ruined possibilities, of the passing from
man's historical memory of what had been in the way of human
effort, accomplishment, struggle and greatness.[123] It is in the face
of its uninterpretability that foundering leads to the ultimate
cipher:

> Interpretation finds its limit where speech [*Sprache*] ends. It
> reaches its culmination in silence. But this limit exists only
> through speech. . . . This silence [*Schweigen*] is not conceal-
> ment [*Ver-schweigen*] of something I know and I could tell.
> Rather it is . . . silence fulfilled at the limit of what can be said.[124]

Silence is the ultimate cipher when, upon the collapse of all
insight and expectation consequent upon a lifetime's sweat in
the pursuit of truth, man can recognize his unspeakable ignorance as the indispensable condition for the most profound certainty of transcendence that he can attain. The silence, which in
the actuality of shipwreck becomes a cipher, is both the final
and the simplest expression of the ignorance of faith, a faith
which is not naive or pristine but which is the ability to endure
beyond the possibility of illusion. It would be a mistake to regard Jaspers's conceptions connected with silence of the ultimate cipher as a matter of heroic bearing in the face of the tragedy of man's failure, in particular his ultimate ignorance. For, on
the one hand, in Jaspers's view the tragic obtains precisely by
pointing beyond itself.[125] On the other hand, Jaspers would regard these conceptions of his as being nurtured no less by the Bible than by the experience of philosophical thought. It is no coincidence that his interpretation of Jeremiah's harsh consolation of
Baruch (Jer. 45: 4–5) appears so often in his works where faith in
the incomprehensible transcendence of Being is the topic. For
example, using the idea of God as cipher of transcendence, he
says:

> It is sufficient that God is. In the face of all the terror in this
> world . . . in the face of destruction . . . by implacable con-
> querors . . . in such a state, hopeless for person and nation, it
> sufficed for some Jews . . . that they were certain of God's
> existence. These people's consolation in all despair, their cer-
> tainty in desolate situations, their exultation in the awareness
> of Being was solely this: God is. . . . Certain in this, man de-
> sired no more for himself.[126]

Thought is inadequate to transcendence. But nothing is for us unless we think it. Yet the assurance of transcendence is as vital for
being oneself as freedom. How can thought be the vehicle of the

unthinkable? This is the age-old problem which Jaspers conceives as the task of reading the cipher-script. In his *Philosophie* (1932) this conception culminates in designating silence as the ultimate cipher. However, as Jaspers is concerned to point out and reiterate, the fact that Being itself is for us not immediately but mediately in human language functioning as intimating cipher, this in itself, the very conception of cipher, is a cipher of transcendence. Hence its meaning cannot be fixed. It is not surprising to see Jaspers's last major treatment of cipher[127] culminate in the possibility of confrontation with what is beyond all ciphers. Jaspers takes different soundings of this possibility. He traces the dialectic speculations of negative theologians and of Nicholas of Cusa's *coincidentia oppositorum*, explores Kant's, Leibniz's and Schelling's diverse preoccupations with the problem "why is there something and not nothing?" as a way of transcending, describes the imposing Buddhist temple of Borobodur on Java and Master Eckhart's mystical speculations on God and Deity as "historical examples of the most radical transcending of all ciphers."[128] We may characterize his conclusions as follows: The reading of ciphers, in consideration of its motive, would have to lead beyond all ciphers; to the fullness of Being can correspond only the nothingness of all whereby man attempts to mediate Being. The pursuit of ciphers—be they conceptions or stone monuments to such conceptions—to their negative conclusion, to the point of silence, seems to make what is beyond all ciphers palpable. All ciphers are reduced to insignificance in consideration of what is beyond all ciphers. But thought which dispenses with ciphers would be "thought that voids itself."[129] Seductive as this possibility is, particularly for one who regards man as capable of effecting a mystic union, it is not one which is realized for the being whose mode of being is to think in time:

> Transcending beyond all ciphers—not just beyond the world but beyond the actuality of existing in the here and now—we arrive in the great void, in the All that is Nothingness, in the fullness that remains without revelation.[130]

"The actuality of existing in the here and now [*die Wirklichkeit unserer Existenz im Dasein*]" is the anchor. To realize ourselves as selves in time, and freely, by virtue of faith in our possibilities beyond the determined past, is, for Jaspers, the key to the validity of ciphers. "The will to Existenz in the world" is "the will to read ciphers."[131]

Unless we are vouchsafed a revelation by virtue of a mystic vision or, unless we become lost as selves in freedom, i.e., as values of possible eternal validity, in a world conceived merely positivistically, we remain related to transcendence only by reading the cipher-script.

Alles Vergängliche
Ist nur ein Gleichnis[132]

we read in *Faust*; or in the homelier idiom of Robert Frost:

We dance round in a ring and suppose,
But the Secret sits in the middle and knows.

A positive aspect, however, of the inevitability of ciphers is also reflected in *Faust:*

Am farbigen Abglanz haben wir das Leben.[133]

viii. Postscript: Notes on Tillich and Some Critics

At the beginning of the chapter we noted that some powerful motives of the heritage of thought reverberate in Jaspers's conception of cipher. Thus, though the originality and distinctness of this conception has often been recognized—Tilliette speaks of the theory of ciphers as "la pièce maîtresse de la métaphysique de Jaspers"[134]—it is of interest to note how it has been received by critics. Here we shall restrict ourselves to a few observations. By the nature of the thing those most closely concerned with the theory of ciphers are, first, from the philosophical side, ontologists who uphold the possibility of suprasensible knowledge and quasi-scientific research, and, second, theologians who, in connection with the actuality of revealed faith, consider awareness of transcendence to be more definite than the reading of ciphers. Appropriate, thorough critique of Jaspers's philosophy of ciphers has so far been forthcoming only from the latter camp. Catholic critics have tended to formulate their criticism by way of confronting 'cipher' with the Thomistic notion of 'analogy'. An excellent though brief critical examination of three of these, i.e., Welte, Lotz, and Collins, appears in Lichtigfeld's contribution to the Schilpp volume on Jaspers. Two other particularly noteworthy Catholic critics of the theory of ciphers are Tilliette and Armbruster. Relevant critique from the Protestant side has tended to be more diffuse. The hermeneutic problem has been, by far, the

most important problem in connection with which the Protestant
examination of ciphers has so far occurred; here the names of
Bultmann, Buri, Werner, Fahrenbach, Pennenberg and Lohff are
most important.

Two conceptions, by theologian-philosophers, approach that of
Jaspers's cipher, namely Tillich's 'symbol' and Buber's 'sign'.
Tillich emphasizes that 'symbols' are indispensable and non-trans-
latable, and Buber that 'signs' are existentially immediate and irreducible. However, the congruency of these conceptions with
'cipher' has its limit which, it seems to us, is decisive. The limit is
the absolute conceptual fluidity of Jaspers's conception of cipher.
It will be recalled that in consideration of the absolute transcendence of the ground of Being the notion that it speak through the
code of human awareness in the ciphers is itself a cipher; the
cipher is an invocation, and the ultimate cipher the silence of shipwreck. The cipher is a cipher by virtue of the absence of any supposition that or of how man's relation to transcendence is actualized by means of the cipher. In contrast to this we find Tillich's
concern to give man's operation with—or perhaps better involvement with—symbols an epistemological underpinning. He says,

> An early criticism of Professor Urban of Yale forced me to
> acknowledge that in order to speak of symbolic *knowledge* [!]
> one must delimit the symbolic realm by an unsymbolic state-
> ment. . . . The unsymbolic statement which implies the neces-
> sity of religious symbolism is that God is being itself, and as
> such beyond the subject-object structure of everything that
> is.[135] [Italics mine]

Let us look at the version of the desired "unsymbolic statement" as it appears in Volume One of Tillich's *Systematic Theology:*

> The statement that God is being-itself is a non-symbolic state-
> ment. It does not point beyond itself. It means what it says
> *directly and properly.*[136] [Italics mine]

It is interesting to note that this is followed immediately by this
elaboration: "If we speak of the actuality of God, we first assert
that he is not God if he is not being-itself." Clearly this sets a limit
to the "directness" and "propriety" of the "non-symbolic statement." However, by being somewhat like a negative counterpart
to the positive "statement" it displays something of the symbolic
way which Tillich upholds against Hartshorne's attempt to regard

statements about God as literal.[137] In short, Tillich does not seem to succeed in conceiving of his statement as entirely "unsymbolic." And this is borne out by the continuation of the passage:

> Other assertions about God can be made theologically only on this basis. Of course, religious assertions do not require such a foundation for what they say about God.

This is true in its reflection of the existential, unmediated validity of symbols; yet Tillich maintains that "The foundation is implicit in every religious thought concerning God."

A distinction can thus be made between theology and religious actuality:

> Theologians must make explicit what is implicit in religious thought and expression; and, in order to do this, they must begin with the most abstract and completely unsymbolic statement which is possible, namely, that God is being-itself or the absolute.[138]

This may provide a basis for a magisterial theology which Tillich quite frankly conceives as the "methodical interpretation of the contents of the Christian faith," and whose "apologetic" function vis-à-vis religion is to "show that trends which are immanent in all religions and cultures move toward the Christian answer." However, regarded exoterically, it is not evident that the full immersion exclusively in the symbolic on the part of "religious thought and expression" should prove insufficient for theology even in its magisterial position. Hence Randall's scruples seem justified; he says:

> It seems clear that all these notions are actually used by Tillich as symbols. . . . This is especially true of "being-itself," a concept at which ontological analysis can never arrive. Ontology can find only the "being" which is common to all particular and determinate beings. "Being-itself" in any other sense, seems to be a religious myth or symbol.[139]

In response, Tillich, for the nonce, maintains his positions. First he makes a distinction between the "structure of being" and "being-itself," cautioning that they not be identified. The former is the concern of metaphysics and of the theologian insofar as he is a philosopher. "If, however," Tillich goes on,

> this being-itself becomes a matter of ultimate concern, . . . words like "ground" or "power" of being appear which express both the theoretical and existential relation of the mind to being-itself.[140]

There seems to be a loosening of this position, and a greater sensitivity for the limits of the distinctions Tillich makes between philosophy and theology, and between the "theoretical" theological and the "existential" religious "relation of the mind to being-itself" in the Second Volume of his *Systematic Theology.* [141] Here the "question" again "arises . . . as to whether there is a point at which a non-symbolic assertion about God must be made," and "there is such a point." But the point is located differently, namely, that "the statement that everything we say about God is symbolic." It is with respect to this new version of the "non-symbolic statement" "delimiting the symbolic realm," that Richli correctly points out that the very notion of ciphers precludes that it be conceived on the basis of presupposed concepts:

> What would happen if we could grasp the being of ciphers directly? Woud not, then, the being of ciphers have to be that which is immediate? Does not the very brokenness of ciphers—vis-à-vis the objectivity of determinate objects—mean that the being of ciphers is a cipher? . . . The cipher would not be possible if its being were not at least a cipher. [142]

From the same passage in Tillich one can sense that he was not unaware of considerations which are the basis of a conception of symbol which accords with Jaspers's 'cipher'. Hence Richli's observations are correct but it is problematical how strongly they stand as valid criticism of Tillich's ultimate position. For Tillich goes on to say,

> Such a statement is an assertion about God which itself is not symbolic. Otherwise we would fall into a circular argument.

It would seem that the whole issue is the result of Tillich becoming embroiled in a purely formal consideration. However, more is at stake for Tillich, namely, the "theoretical" position of "theology" vis-à-vis the "existential" relation of "religion" to "being-itself." Interestingly enough, Tillich is running up against precisely the sort of aporetic circularity which, in Jaspers, is the point of departure for the conception of "ultimate concern" as the reading of ciphers, and for regarding the proper existential significance of 'symbols' in their being 'ciphers'. We see hints of this in Tillich, particularly when he continues the cited passage as follows, after identifying the "non-symbolic statement" as a formal requirement to avoid "circularity":

> On the other hand, if we make *one* non-symbolic assertion about God, his ecstatic-transcendent character seems to be

endangered. This dialectical difficulty is a mirror of the human situation with respect to the divine ground of being. . . . The state of being ultimately concerned . . . is the point at which we must speak non-symbolically about God, but in terms of a quest for him.[143]

Clearly the issue, for Tillich, is one of alternatives: on the one hand is the recognition of the "dialectical difficulty . . . of the human situation with respect to the ground of being"; this recognition is engendered by God's "ecstatic-transcendent character" and entails man's radical risk of reading ciphers in ignorance of *what* they convey and *whether* they convey "the ground of being" to which man is directed. On the other hand is the urge for assurance that this enterprise have substance; this urge appears in the form of a formal requirement for criteriology. Tillich opts for the former but will not abandon the latter. The logic of symbols, however, requires such abandonment, and that 'symbols' be consequentially regarded as 'ciphers'. Herein lies the difference between Tillich and Jaspers.

The realization of "ultimate concern" as radically existential is more successfully reflected in Buber than in Tillich. Hence his 'sign' is more akin to Jaspers's 'cipher' than Tillich's 'symbol'. And Buber recognizes this similarity. However, in a juxtaposition of 'sign' and 'cipher' Buber observes that

If the concept 'cipher-script' is to have a unitary significance, then one has to presuppose an "encipherer" [*chiffrierende Instanz*] who wills that I correctly decipher the script assigned to me for my life, and who makes it possible, though difficult for me.[144]

For Buber the problem hinges on the conception of transcendence as personal God. Since for Jaspers this is a cipher, and a questionable one at that, Buber must reject Jaspers as one who eliminates the intimate relation between dialogue with fellow creature and dialogue with God by virtue of his lack of "existential rootedness in the actuality of a religion."[145] For Jaspers, without doubt, the problem is one of taking seriously the second commandment; with respect to Lichtigfeld's contribution to the Schilpp volume Jaspers says,

I am grateful to Lichtigfeld that, in meeting the theologians' objections to my philosophizing, he recognizes approvingly the movement [in my philosophizing] toward the image-less biblical notion of God, toward the fulfillment of the commandment: "Thou shalt not make unto thee any image or likeness."[146]

Chapter Eight

The Problem of Evil

i. The Concern over Evil in Jaspers's Thought

Expressions of contents of faith truly evoke and reflect faith in its communicative and testimonial actuality if they are recognized as ciphers rather than taken as the cognitive content whose form they use. One can find exemplifications of this in the many works of Jaspers with respect to a great diversity of possible contents of faith which concern the fundamental questions man raises about God, freedom, nature, history. Of these we have chosen the example of the notions connected with the awareness of evil. The cogency of Jaspers's exemplification of the content of faith regarded as cipher is not greater in the case of evil than in any of the other notions. Yet ours is not a random choice. There are several reasons for it.

First, fathoming evil as a fundamental phenomenon of the human condition is a red thread running through the web of Jaspers's philosophical thinking, from beginning to end. Thus in the proto-philosophical *Psychologie der Weltanschauungen* (1919) he identifies the 'limit-situations', one of the most distinctive contributions of this early work, and a lasting one. In this work, unlike later works, he characterizes limit-situations as being essentially suffering; other limit-situations—such as death, failure, struggle—are here regarded as instances of suffering.[1] The last major philosophical work contains Jaspers's major treatment of the problem of evil in its metaphysical universality;[2] this treatise is the result of Jaspers's lengthy preoccupation with the problem and of several attempts at its treatment.[3]

Another reason for our choice is the fact that particularly through Jasper's treatment of evil we can gain insight into his thinking about a great number of basic problems, such as the import of metaphysical thought, of the conception of 'Existenz', and of theological doctrines. But above all the problem of evil, involving the conception of freedom and thereby that of the transcendent ground of the possibility of freedom, is for Jaspers a touchstone of man's ability and willingness to be free. Whichever way man conceives of the problem of evil, whichever way he comes to terms with this problem or even envisages solutions thereto, has bearing on his view of his position in the scheme of things, his responsibility in his position and his ability to bear the burden of the evil of his own guilt. The problem of evil is a matter of reading ciphers of evil which reflect in what way man can or does exist. Hence the examination of Jaspers's treatment of evil affords us entrance into the chambers of his most central philosophical motives.

M. K. Malhorta, discerning the centrality of Jaspers's concern over 'limit-situations', especially suffering, also points to the pervasive connection of this motive with other major strands of his philosophising.[4] In this he sees strong parallels to Indian thought, which in turn suggests to him, particularly in light of Jaspers's few occasional writings on Indian thought and philosophers, that Jaspers's thinking may bespeak the influence of Indian thought. It seems Malhorta goes too far in two respects. On the one hand, the concern over evil, fundamental as it is in Jaspers, cannot be said to be the origin of Jaspers's philosophising any more than other concerns, as we have made sufficiently clear earlier. On the other hand, knowledge of Indian thought came to Jaspers after his philosophical activity had matured. This is borne out in particular with respect to the problem of evil, as will be seen. The ciphers of evil which Jaspers considers are, with the exception of the doctrine of karma and some Chinese doctrines, Western in development and formulation. It is, of course, a deliberate motive of Jaspers's 'philosophizing' that his thinking, which is self-consciously nourished primarily by Western tradition, is communicatively open and responsive to other traditions, including the Indian. However, reduction of any thinking to the influence of another would not accord with Jaspers's conception of the historic significance of philosophical thought. In this sense such reduction would, in Jaspers's case, be a misunderstanding of the philosopher, aside from being factually false.

Before we can face the problem of evil, we must be aware of the facts of evil. Before we can identify such facts, we must be clear about what constitutes evil, about the conditions under which evil is an actuality. This is our concern in section ii, where we shall trace Jaspers's connection of the conception of evil to freedom and to willing; here we shall also see how the *problem* of evil is contained within this connection of freedom and evil. In section iii we shall see, on the basis of the connection of freedom and evil, in what sense we can and what sense we cannot speak of *facts* of evil. We shall also see how the problem of evil is a problem of the possibility of freedom. In section iv we shall see how Jaspers, regarding the problem in this way, understands the major historical testimonies of the concern over this problem as ciphers of evil, and how they can possibly function as viable ciphers. In a final section (v) we shall summarize Jaspers's treatment of the problem of evil in its import for philosophical activity as he understands it.

ii. Freedom the Condition of Evil

What are the circumstances in which there can be evil? 'Good and evil' fits the pattern 'value and disvalue'. In Jaspers's sense it would be a mistake to regard 'good and evil' as the most general exemplification of this pattern. Jaspers says,

> In being all things have a rank, but to rank low is not evil. In existence ugliness repels us, but ugliness is not evil. Selfhood can fall—it is in fact constituted by rising from its fallen state— but straying, becoming empty, dissipating are, as such, not evil. Not even untruth is the same as evil, and neither are urges and drives, or the calamities which cramp and destroy existence. . . . Evil is not peculiar to any existent, not to any empirical reality or an ideal efficacy.[5]

Jaspers rejects any conception of evil as existing independently of and thus prior to the actuality of freedom.[6] There can be evil only where there is responsibility and accountability. Hence actualities in their disvalue are not as such evil. They can be said to be evil insofar as their disvalue is connected with responsibility. Here alone resides evil. Disvaluable actualities

> are mere means in the hands of evil, which animates them with its negative willing. . . . There is evil because there is freedom. *The will alone can be evil.*[7]

There are, then, two related main features of Jaspers's conception of the location of evil. First, there is no specific value-content which is, as such, good, such that they are alternatives for choice. We do not choose between what presents itself to our choice as either good or evil. And neither are the objective results as such good or evil. Jaspers says, "Good and evil are thus not determinable as to content, but all content-possibilities lie in both." Specific works are not as such good or evil.[8]

Second, good and evil, not residing in *what* is willed, resides *in* the freedom and responsibility of willing itself. This conception of evil is not popular and can be misunderstood, but it belongs to the mainstream of the philosophy of evil. Ashton, a translator of Jaspers, misses this point when he is at a loss as to the meaning of "das Böse ist durch Freiheit."[9] Ashton understands this to mean "we are free to be evil."[10] This is, to be sure, in accord with what Jaspers thinks. Here, however, Jaspers expresses the idea that "evil exists through freedom." This view expresses Jaspers's affinity with similar views in which the notion of the radical transcendence of God is connected with the affirmation of man's historicity and its constituent freedom and responsibility. This is, in particular, a red thread running through the web of Jewish thought for which Jaspers displays in many respects a decided penchant. Such similar views on evil are, for example, reflected in Buber, who, in his interpretation of the biblical myth of the 'fall of man' and the 'tree of knowledge', says:

> In themselves, naturally, neither the concept of clothed- and unclothedness, nor that of man and woman before one another, have anything whatsoever to do with good and evil; human "recognition" of opposites alone brings with it the fact of their relatedness to good and evil.[11]

And with respect to the second of the two related points, the relation of evil to freedom, we read the following in *I and Thou:*

> It is not decision to do the one and leave the other inert. . . . He alone who directs the whole strength of this other into the doing of the former, who lets the unabated passion of the unchosen enter the actualization of the chosen—he alone who "serves God with the evil impulse"—makes decision, decides the event. . . . If there were a devil it would not be one who decided against God, but one who, in eternity, came to no decision.[12]

For,

> He who decides is free.[13]

It is only when man fails to be fully man, when he fails to exercise his freedom with respect to what is other than the realm of spirit that the latter has the force of evil. As such it is not evil. Buber says,

> The primary word I-It is not from evil—as matter is not from evil. It is from evil—as matter is, if it presumes to be that

which is. If man permits it to prevail, the relentlessly growing world of It overruns him, his own I is drained from him of its actuality.[14]

Similarly we read in Kant that only a will can be said to be good—and evil—without qualification. The reason is that anything else which may be said to be good or evil, and here this is associated with 'desirable-undesirable', is "qualified" by the goodness—or evil—of the willing whose object it is.[15] We shall soon see that Jaspers's affinity to Kant in this respect is not accidental.

The location of good and evil in the will, in freedom, does not as such solve the problems connected with the question of the origin of evil. There is a problem in the position that "the will does not choose between good and evil, but becomes good or evil in choosing."[16] The problem is how the will, in its freedom, can choose to be evil, how the will, by virtue of its choice, can choose to become evil, to become guilty. Jaspers attempts to illuminate this problem by a number of considerations, some of which are historical.

Jaspers, for example, interprets Plato's consideration of the Socratic dictum that no man does injustice voluntarily, particularly as it appears in *The Laws*, Book IX; it says there (Stephanus 860):

If any contentious or disputatious person says that men are unjust against their will, and yet that many do injustice willingly, I do not agree with him.[17]

Jaspers takes this to mean that to do injustice is a matter of ignorance, yet not absolute ignorance. For, on the one hand, the will is exercised with respect to an object, and this is known. Yet this is either knowledge of what fulfills one's passionate motivation, or it is knowledge of what is just, regardless of one's desires. It is only in ignorance of the latter that one can speak of doing injustice involuntarily. For to speak of 'knowing' in the latter sense is tantamount to saying that to know what is good means to will good:

The true will is the knowing will. The desire that overpowers is not will but ignorance. Only he wills . . . who wills the good. Only he who does what is right acts freely. In original knowledge, the good and the right are one.[18]

Precisely because such genuine knowledge is 'original', what one knows and what one wills are one; and it is 'original' precisely because it is "not an acquisition of something other, but the unfolding of one's own essence."[19] To will evil is, then, not a positive act of freedom, but a failure to be knowing in willing. In a like vein, and extending the import of knowledge for freedom in its struggle against its potentiality of evil, Jaspers says:

> It is guilt not to know what I could know insofar as such knowledge is essential for the realm of my action. In all action there is guilt of ignorance of what it was possible to know.[20]

A second example is Jaspers's consideration of the circumstance that the self-reflection upon one's good willing contains the seed of the evil of self-contentment. Here Jaspers refers to Saint Paul and Lieh-ztse. The righteousness with respect to the good carries with it righteousness with respect to oneself. To be sure, we can make the following distinction proposed by Kant, namely,

> between the justified contentment with my objective act and the self-contentment that makes me untruthful, since I can never quite see through my ultimate motive.[21]

Yet deliberate moral rightness contains the trap of moralistic righteousness.

A third consideration in Jaspers's attempt to find how the will can be evil is that of 'self-will'.[22] Here the arbitrary willing of one's empirical existence (*Dasein*) is absolute. Nothing else is binding, neither the unconditional and universal imperatives of morality, nor the loyalty to ideas of spiritual community, nor the awesome demands imposed on becoming selfhood by the possibility of one's eternal validity, nor the transcending bonds of reason. The self-willed person is isolated from any realm of being—and meaning—which would enlarge the range and modes of validity for him beyond his self-willing. And he remains so isolated even if he acknowledges such realms insofar as they serve his self-willing, because they exist for him as his means and not as realities making claims upon him. Self-willing reveals its fundamentally nihilistic tendency when it takes place by virtue of deliberate self-awareness. Its essential hatred of all that is other than one's own willing reaches its logical conclusion in destruction as confirmation of all that it holds to be of disvalue. In this way self-willing, regarded as the basis of evil willing, is the perversion of love, which is the renunciation of self-willing and its isolation. Thus it is also a perversion of freedom which essentially is "freedom toward Being," not "freedom from something."[23] We read in John 12:24–25:

> Except a grain of wheat fall into the ground and die, it abideth alone; but if it die, it bringeth forth much fruit. He that loveth his life shall lose it; and he that hateth his life in this world shall keep it unto life eternal.

In a like vein Jaspers points out that the "individual, regarded as Existenz, is not separated," i.e., "not arbitrary self-will."[24] Yet a kind of self-will may also be ascribed to possible Existenz. Existenz may be so intent on an uncompromising realization of truth, that it withholds its full identification with all concretion which, as such, is a compromise with perfection. Such "dignity of defiance" is not to be confused with self-willing which occurs in isolation from any binding sources of meaning and obligation.[25]

Our final example of Jaspers's consideration of the basis of evil is that of Kant's notion of "radical evil"[26] as expounded in the latter's *Religion within the Limits of Reason Alone* (1793). Kant distinguishes between man's—morally neutral—natural inclination toward happiness and the unconditional enactment of moral imperatives which man demands of himself as creature of reason. In case the two conflict man either gives his reason the precedence which he, as rational creature, demands, or else fails to do so. Therein, in producing good by his willing or failing to do so, lies man's freedom. Man is not as such good, but has an "original predisposition" (*Anlage*) to good. Similarly, man is not as such evil, but has a "propensity" (*Hang*) to evil.[27] In the enactment of this propensity Kant distinguishes three levels.[28] By his "fraility" man chooses evil because his moral motivation is is not as great as his natural inclination. By his "improbity" a man's actions appear to be morally right; but these actions disguise the fact which only he knows, namely that they were executed not purely out of moral motivation but, partly or wholly, out of the desire to satisfy his appetites. Man's "radical evil" consists in a man's exploiting, by his depravity, the dictates of moral conviction as a means to nonmoral ends. Kant also refers to this as "perversity" because, as he says, "It reverses the moral order among the motives of a volition that is free."[29] It is the perversity of this reversal that Jaspers stresses in his interpretations:

> To rank the will to happiness, which dominates among man's motives, above the unconditioned law that shows in reason— that is the root of evil, the 'propensity' which Kant calls 'radical evil'.[30]

The stress on this reversal is most significant. It points to the fact that man's evil is not diabolical in the sense that evil is willed as evil, for the sake of evil. It means moreover that, as we have seen, evil does not lie in what is willed, and that evil is not grounded in the nature of man. For, finally, evil is simply grounded in the freedom of willing. Thus it remains, like freedom, unexplained.

Our problem was, how is it possible for a will that chooses

freely, to choose evil? Of the many possible answers to this problem which Jaspers considers we referred to four: man is evil out of self-inflicted ignorance; out of self-contentment; out of egotism; out of perversity. The reference to other thinkers of all times and all places in connection with these four considerations shows the universal persistence of the problem at hand. The multiplicity of attempted solutions of the problem shows the limitation of each solution with respect to the others.[31] All these attempts bespeak the self-awareness of guilt which inextricably accompanies the self-awareness of freedom. One cannot be without the other. Let us mention some ways in which this is expressed in Jaspers.

First, in the realm where whatever happens is in some way determined by man's presence, no borderline can be drawn between what is a matter of man's freedom and what is not: "I carry the guilt for the conditions of my life, if I continue to live under these conditions."[32] It is the task of freedom to invest that which is unfree with the responsibility of freedom. In particular, a man's realization of his freedom hinges on his responsiveness not only to the unfreedom which he finds within him but also that of the world which he accepts as the arena of his realization.[33]

Similarly no sharp line can be drawn between specific guilt incurred as the result of one's clear choice and the guilt with which one is burdened prior to such clarity of choice. The person who affirms his freedom will accept both. One will accept the former guilt out of freedom's motive of responsibility and that of avoiding its incurrence. One will accept the latter guilt as the unavoidable basis of the continuous unfolding in the course of time of one's being as one who chooses freely. "From this guilt I cannot escape without incurring another: the guilt of denying my freedom itself."[34] One is oneself, both free and guilty, because one does not exercise deliberate choice and one does not choose oneself prior to the incurrence of guilt. One deliberately chooses oneself not prior to but in the changing moments of one's temporal career. Man is associated with the evil of which he is guilty by virtue of his freedom not only as the result of the exercise of freedom but because of his very being as free.

In a like vein Jaspers speaks of a matter reminiscent of Kierkegaard's characterization of 'despair' (i.e., lack of attaining selfhood) viewed with respect to 'finitude/infinitude' and 'possibility/necessity'.[35] Self-realization requires the actualization of possibilities. A man's possibilities are beyond measure. What can be actualized is limited and implies a restrictive choice amongst, and hence an irretrievable rejection and sacrifice of possibilities. In one's freedom one is responsible not only for making choices, not

only for the choices made but for the alternatives thereby rejected. If the choice be sound, its soundness is not without the evil
of the sacrifice. This circumstance was mentioned peripherally in
the following passage in Buber cited earlier in this section:

> It is not decision to do the one and leave the other inert. . . .
> He alone who directs the whole strength of the other into the
> doing of the former, who lets the unabated passion of the un-
> chosen enter the actualization of the chosen . . . makes deci-
> sion.[36]

Is there a suggestion, in this passage, that the evil of rejecting other
possibilities in choosing the actualization of one is mitigated by
directing the thrust of the former into the performance of the
latter? If there is not, then the evil of deciding against possibilities
would be secondary to the evil which consists of lack of decisiveness; but then, since each is important in its own way, its significance as characterizing the situation of freedom would be trivialized. But if it is suggested, then the claim of infinite possibilities
upon our limited powers of realization would become trivial, and
lost as moments of the situation of freedom. This can be seen
when we find that alternative possibilities of choice can be actualities in their own right. Consider the example of a person who has
the means, the opportunity, and the desire to adopt a child, and
chooses one of many whose need for a home comes to his attention. Let us suppose that the person is able to love this child and
give him care in the way he would love and take care of all of
them, if he, stepping beyond human limitation, had not rejected
any of them. This still leaves the others rejected, unloved and un-
cared for—at least by him.

In Jaspers's view such considerations underscore the associations
of guilt and freedom, serve in the characterization of man's situation and as a point of departure for a further penetration of the
problem of evil. "Man may choose to act or not to act; in either
case he will be guilty."[37] This "inevitability of guilt" is, for Jaspers, a feature of man's situation that is fundamental. The fundamental nature of this circumstance shows the incomprehensibility
of the association of evil and freedom.[38] By virtue of his freedom
man regards himself as imperfect. And nothing can be adduced as
the explanation or the source of his guilt, for that would vitiate his
freedom. Also, even as man, incomprehensibly, finds his freedom
to lead to evil, so evil is no actuality without freedom, and man
knows of no freedom other than his own. The fundamental nature
of the inevitability of guilt is, for Jaspers, also an instance of a
'limit-situation'. Jaspers conceives limit-situations as inescapable

conditions of man's existence. The clear confrontation with such situations is the indispensable point of departure for man's deliberate decisiveness in making the choices by which he becomes himself. In this way what is known as the 'problem of evil' is, for Jaspers, basically a problem of man who, in pursuit of the problem, is concerned over the fulfillment of his potential selfhood in view of his incomprehensible guilt. What is metaphysically or mythically adduced as the foundation of evil is then a matter of the reading of ciphers. Before we proceed to Jaspers's treatment of some ciphers of evil it is necessary to consider the question of the facts of evil in the light of the foregoing account of the association of evil and freedom.

iii. The Facts of Evil

Facts of evil which are unquestionable are facts pertaining to the acts of man because here the association of evil with freedom is manifest. The recital of these facts of man's inhumanity to man, whether directed to his own person or to his fellow man, is the starting point of reflection for Jaspers no less than for other thinkers. Details need not be cited; they are well-known. However, Jaspers's characterization of some types of human evil are of special interest: The cruelty veiled or justified by reference to principles or higher purposes, e.g., mass murder because "orders are orders." Or "the confusion of faith and crime," e.g. "the Crusaders in Jerusalem murdering, wading in blood and kneeling with curious humility before the grave of Christ." Or the evil that is connected with the claim of knowing God's will, and which does not only lie in the evil actions resulting from this claim but which consists, for Jaspers, in this claim itself. Or, action based on erroneous appraisals of reality coupled with a delusive knowledge which is really a faith; e.g., "men will fool themselves about a good world order, and plan a just society in which the state has withered away and force is unnecessary, and will seek to accomplish this by the worst terrorism." Or the failure to sufficiently anticipate the possible consequences of one's decisions and actions, consequences which have careers beyond one's plans and which can be dire for a multitude and for generations; it does not take much hard thinking to recall appropriate examples of a technological, economic, military or political nature.[39]

This typology of the facts of evil perpetrated by man by virtue of his freedom shows the discrepancy between man as realized and man as he might aspire to be, i.e., man in his goodness. Even though this distinction implies a reference to an image of man transcending man's actuality, it does not carry the problem of evil beyond man. To carry it beyond man requires the presupposition that the disvalue we perceive beyond man's guilt is, like man's evil, associated with freedom, albeit a freedom which we do not know, which we project in anology with man's freedom which we do know.

What might be indicated as realms of facts of evil beyond man's guilt? There are, first of all, the facts of nature viewed from the standpoint of value. For example, we characterize living nature with reference to purposiveness. The notion of purpose lends itself to function as a value category. In this sense we can, on the one hand, observe how living beings, in displaying purposiveness, are destructive of other life. On the other hand we notice the calamities which befall living beings by virtue of the blind course of nature beyond all purposive direction. In still another way we experience how the humanity of human beings is destroyed by organic processes.[40] All this, however, is not yet evil proper; rather, it is, as was said, nature viewed from the standpoint of value without attributing what we view as disvaluable to the efficacy of responsible choice. In English we call this 'natural evil' in distinction from 'moral evil', in German *Übel* in distinction from *Böse*. Man can know himself as being both creature of nature and free. The problem of man's guilt involves the fact that he is both; yet, as we have seen, it can not be resolved by attributing man's evil to man viewed as nature, but only as freedom. Similarly with nature at large, its evil proper does not lie in its being of disvalue to us. The 'natural evil' of nature becomes an aspect of the problem of evil only if we consider whether its occurrence is willed. If it is, how can its occurrence be reconciled with or even display purpose? If not, what is the basis of purpose and meaning? The involvement of the purposiveness of nature in theodicy constitutes a major chapter in theological thought, particularly in connection with the 'argument from design'.

A realm of facts of evil beyond man's guilt which is of greater concern than that of 'natural evil' involves man directly. We have seen that even if man can be imagined as animated by an ingenuous motive of responsible freedom, he inevitably incurs guilt. The question can then arise whether the *inevitability of man's guilt* does not lie in man but has its source in a will beyond man:

Does the guilt for man's capability or even the necessity of becoming guilty lie, prior to him, in an other [being]? Who is then guilty? A supersensory being? A cosmic source? Something that God created? God himself?[41]

From the viewpoint of Jaspers's philosophy of freedom it is no accident that reflection on the inevitability of guilt provokes the problem of evil regarded as the problem of the transcendent justification of evil. The reason is that awareness of guilt is awareness of freedom. And awareness of freedom is awareness of the transcendent ground of freedom. The awareness of freedom, where it reaches fullest clarity, has a negative and a positive side. Negatively freedom means independence from determining natural necessity. If this negative side of the concept of freedom were all that there is to it, the concept would be fruitless, as Kant says,[42] and no doubt freedom itself as well. Positively, Kant and Jaspers offer corresponding concepts of freedom; Kant that of autonomous causative willing, Jaspers that of self-originating decisiveness in action. According to Jaspers it is precisely the self-awareness as free *and* independent that entails the free self's grounding in a transcendent source. For even though I become myself by virtue of the excercise of my freedom, I do not choose my being as free self prior to its enactment within the limits of the course of time. Jaspers expresses this in dialectical variations with particular reference to the problem of evil as follows:[43]

If there were no transcendence, the question would be why I ought to will; there would be only volition without guilt. . . . If there were transcendence pure and simple, however, my will would vanish in automatic obedience. . . . In being free I experience transcendence in freedom and only through freedom. . . . It is precisely in the *origin* of my self-being, in which I mean to reach beyond the necessities of laws of nature and obligation, that I am aware of *not* having created myself. . . .[44] *Wherever I am fully myself I am no longer myself alone.* . . . Wherever, in willing, I am truly myself, I am, at the same time, given to me in my freedom. . . . What I am *from* within myself that I cannot be *only* through myself. Since I am that from within myself, I am guilty. Since I am that not only through myself, I am what I willed as something that has been bestowed upon me. . . . In taking hold of my self out of my freedom, I took hold of my transcendence whose evanscent phenomenon is *I myself in my freedom.* . . . To decide— for freedom and independence—against all forms of wordly reality, against any authority, does not mean to decide against transcendence.

For Jaspers it is natural, then, that the awareness of guilt, as expression of man's freedom, leads to the problem of evil, as concerning the ground of freedom. It is equally natural for Jaspers that the pursuit of the problem of evil is a way of deciding the significance and scope of man's guilt. Man's becoming himself by virtue of his awareness of guilt and his pursuit of the apparently transcendental problems of evil are two sides of the same thing. We cited earlier Jaspers's formulation of the problem with respect to the guilt for the inevitability of man's guilt. But this is followed by a parallel human problem: "May man ease his own guilt, shift it, exonerate himself because he is not its ultimate source?"[45]

And there is another realm of facts of evil beyond man's guilt which intensifies the problem of evil. This does not involve man but concerns him. It is the discrepancy between man's merit and his rewards which is brought to light under the supposition that the course of affairs is guided by transcendent justice:

Good men fare badly, evil men fare well. The connection is random or accidental. The sun shines on the just and the unjust alike. How is it possible that human existence be so unjustly directed.[46]

Here again Jaspers adds a corresponding question reflecting man's problem: "May man advance accusations against the ground of things . . . that it is unjust?"[47]

We see that the main thrust of Jaspers's way of identifying the facts of evil and of the consequent formulation of the problem of evil lies in his regarding man's concern over the problem of evil as at heart the concern over how it is possible for him to live. The questions are: Is it possible to bear the facts of evil without sinking into the destruction of nihilism, or the paralysis of cynicism? Is it possible to maintain faith without blurring one's vision of the facts? Can one be strong enough to maintain the posture of truthfulness and not surrender to comforting illusions? Is it possible to pursue Truth in its ultimateness without losing oneself in the diffuseness of immanent truth? Is it possible to risk failure in the search for the meaning of it all in favor of accepting plausible though ultimately questionable theories, myths, traditions? The significant questions arise from the exigencies of actual life. And the answers to these questions, be they dogmas, metaphysical visions or invocations of assurance, are verified by the sort of life

they make possible. It is in this sense that they function as and are
to be interpreted as ciphers.

iv. Ciphers of Evil

Ciphers are human language intimating transcendence in which
man seeks the ground of his freedom. Ciphers of evil are ciphers of
transcendence related to man's questions concerning the ultimate
ground of the evil he apprehends. In this way ciphers of evil are,
for the most part, equivalent to man's efforts at theodicy.

Jaspers considers theodicy in general and the different major
theodicies in each of the three main works of his philosophical
maturity. In his *Philosophy* he regards theodicy as arising from the
tensions between two basic, opposing existential relations to transcendence, i.e., defiance and surrender. Theodicy is defiance in the
service of surrender. Theodicies not only do not represent cogent
knowledge, but are bound to fail as comprehensive convictions
concerning man's grounding in transcendence. It is here that, for
Jaspers, their full significance can arise. On the one hand, they
can, in this failure, indicate the ultimate incomprehensibility of
the facts of evil in confrontation with transcendence. On the other
hand, this failure can be an appeal to freedom, for without this
failure, i.e., if the problem of evil would lend itself to solution,
then the problem would not constitute a limit-situation. Man experiences such situations only in freedom, only if they involve his
decisiveness with respect to what he is to become. Radical surrender is surrender in ignorance, ignorance clarified by the failure of
certainty. In the *Philosophy*, theodicy is of direct existential significance.

The basically existential significance of theodicy is also shown in
Jaspers's treatment of it in *Von der Wahrheit;* however the problem is approached from the question of the truth of Being and the
truthfulness of thought. The realization of evil which gives rise to
theodicy is here seen within the broader problem of the fragmentation of Being as it confronts man. Thought will retain its
integrity in its pursuit of the one and ultimate truth of Being if it
does not anticipate this truth, if it intensifies the incomprehensibility of this truth in the failure of its attempts at comprehension,
if it remains open and in dialectical tension, if it questions and
searches at the risk of failure and is able to apprehend an indica-

tion of what it seeks in this failure. The earnestness of the search for truth is nourished by the experience of failure. This experience is vital:

> Only the integration of the questions with the soul produces the movement of being human . . . and seems to us the only way in which man still has possibilities . . . and also the only way in which he can remain truthful without abandoning the supreme aspiration.[48]

Theodicy, relating the world man knows to the ground of things, and seemingly universal in the speculations of mankind, is a main form of this vital experience. A reflection on the different theodicies can intensify the urgency of the nature of man's search for ultimate truth. Accordingly, in *Von der Wahrheit*, Jaspers arranges and evaluates different historical theodicies in an order of increasing clarity concerning the insurmountably problematic nature of the fact of evil.

The significance and the interpretation of theodicies as ciphers are thus indicated in both the cited works, and in them Jaspers has ample occasion to interpret some theodicies in this way. The full force of such interpretation, however, is reached in the third of the three relevant main works, in *Philosophical Faith and Revelation*. Here Jaspers penetrates the different theodicies as ciphers of evil according to what sort of human existence is possible by the consciousness of transcendent grounding the ciphers bespeak, and what sort of active testimony they require.

Let us examine Jaspers's treatment of the ciphers of evil, keeping in mind that Jaspers's considerations of theodicy in the three works form a continuity of significance to which we shall explicitly return.

At first we must mention the world of polytheistic ciphers which is essentially naive with respect to the problem of evil. It is so because in it the question of the unity of all things remains in the background. In the apotheosis of irreconcilables and of conflicting forces the problem how it is possible for them to exist side by side does not arise to any degree of decisive seriousness. The life that is possible here is to give, ingenuously, all that lays claim to sanctification its due, and in its season: "Aphrodite and Artemis," Hera and Athena, so also good and evil; conflicts of claims are out of man's hands, beyond his question or decision.[49]

Certain forms of dualism are midway between the unquestioned multiplicity of polytheism and the full problematic of the unified view that the problem of evil presupposes. The question of the possibility of evil co-existing with the good is resolved by the cipher of the being of two original forces for which the world is their field of battle. Each lays claim upon man, neither can save man from the other. Man must choose whose side to take in this life, even if the ultimate victory of the good force is assured. For Jaspers the straightforward simplicity of the dualistic cipher has the power of readily placing the immanent struggle on a transcendent foundation. However, aside from the conceptual difficulties of such Zoroastrian dualism, Jaspers regards the lack of dynamism of this cipher as capable of essentially no more than a dogmatic repetition and of no vital development.[50]

Sharing these faults but displaying a more profound realization of the problems of evil, are, according to Jaspers, the ciphers of certain gnostic dualisms and of the Indian doctrine of karma. Neither of these views is content with a simple explanation of evil; both of them seek the reason for and man's reconciliation with evil with respect to the ultimate ground of things. In gnostic dualism the world is the product of an evil creator who is distinguished from the transcendent divinity; man is justified in his resistance to the world's evil by virtue of carrying with him a spark of the divinity. In the doctrine of karma the reincarnation of all beings, including man, is unalterably determined by their merit in the prior life. This explains and makes it possible to bear suffering; and it impels the motive of leading a more meritorious life as well as the hope of liberation from the circle of rebirths.[51]

Jaspers considers several other pre- and extra-biblical ciphers of evil, so the consciousness on the part of certain pre-Socratics that the scheme of things runs in accordance with a supra-human order; so the many attempts with respect to the problem on the part of Plato, all of which exonerate the divinity and reaffirm man's responsibility for the evil that befalls man; so the implacable vision of man's lot on the part of the ancient tragedians and of Shakespeare; so also the "complaint without accusation"[52] in the ancient Chinese Shiking, without doctrine of sin or salvation, without tragic consciousness, but in accord with the course of nature.

In the West, according to Jaspers, decisive profundity in the realization of the problem of evil and a richness of vital ciphers of evil have been connected with the biblical conception of the personal God and Creator. Jaspers considers four groups of ciphers, those of the Fall and original sin, those of harmony and the denial of evil, those of divine predestination, and those connected with the book of Job.

The conception of Creation being in a fallen state has appeared in many places, at many times and in many forms. However, the myth of the Fall of man is, in its many versions, primarily associated with biblical consciousness. From it arose the myth of original sin. Jaspers seems to associate the latter exclusively with Christianity by speaking of it in connection with the incarnation, grace, justification by faith. However, this is not quite correct. The notion arose among the Jews in post-biblical, 'intertestamental' times, albeit in Judaism it has never been widely accepted and, unlike in Christianity, it does not function as a doctrine.

How does Jaspers view the Fall? How the somewhat similar myth of Prometheus? And what sense does he see in original sin?

The story of the Fall[53] is directly responsive to what for Jaspers are the two basic aspects of the problem of evil. How is it that man inevitably becomes guilty? How is it that justice and merit have no bearing on man's lot? For the Bible there are no two ultimate forces, one good, one evil; there is only God, and God is good.

Hence, on the one hand, the myth's answer to both questions is that evil, whether it be man's guilt or his saving lot, is the consequence of man's doing, not God's. God wanted man, in his paradisiacal existence, to obey Him freely. But this entails the ability to disobey. Man's disobedience, as reflected in the Fall, is not necessarily original sin; but it is the primal disobedience that constitutes man's existence as he knows it, i.e., knowing, viewing things with respect to the distinction 'good and bad' and 'good and evil'. Man's existence as knowing constitutes his Fall, his disobedience of and insurrection against God.

Hence, on the other hand, even as the myth connects man's grounding in God with man's blame for his fallen state, so it heightens the incomprehensible mystery of evil. For what makes man man, his fallen state, knowing good and evil, constitutes his God-likeness. Man's knowledge in view of the distinction 'good-evil' ultimately shatters against the incomprehensible transcendent omnipotence of God. Yet this omnipotence desired man's freedom whose actuality consists in defiance of this omnipotence.

The myth of the Fall expresses man's awareness of the discrepancy between the facts of his condition and the standard of goodness and fulfillment against which he measures his lot. It seeks to explain the facts of evil while heightening the sense of ultimate rootedness in a divine source. At the same time it points the way to man's task within his condition, the task of cognition and the active use of knowledge for the sake of the betterment of his lot, "by the sweat of his brow," not safe but free and conscious of his God-likeness.

In these respects the myth functions as a powerful cipher, and in other respects as well: in its challenging appeal to the mythical as well as the doctrinal and the enlightened consciousness; in its evocation of interpretation and in its defiance of any finality thereof. It is a cipher in bringing to consciousness, by means of an historical happening, what is not such a happening and is misunderstood if regarded merely as such a happening; what is nothing other than a fundamental feature of man's being and his relation to the ground of things, and yet not expressible or even present without the determinate idiom such as the story of an historical event. Moreover such consciousness is not in the manner of cognition but of the testimony of one's own realizations. Finally it is a cipher by virtue of its failure to illumine the mystery that one seeks to heighten by means of it.

The guilt of defiance against the divinity as the condition of man's greatness and dignity is, in Jaspers's view, even more intensely symbolized in the myth of Prometheus.[54] To be sure, man's defiant realization of his knowing freedom is here represented by the rebellious Titan Prometheus. However, as Jaspers interprets it, this is, on the one hand, an analogy of the divine rootedness of man. On the other hand, in this myth the horrible thought of man's direct insurrection against the divinity is eschewed.

The myth of the Fall can be a forceful cipher precisely because it arises from an appraisal of man's condition and enables man to live without illusion about and without detracting from the ultimate mystery of this condition. It is otherwise, for Jaspers, in the case of original sin.[55] Man's possibility of living is here taken from him in the realization of his inevitable guilt as inherent; he is completely and directly dependent upon God's grace. This saving grace is manifest in man's faith in it, and such faith is itself possible only as a gift of grace. Jaspers finds this "closed circle of faith" highly questionable as a viable cipher of the ultimate meaningfulness of man's misery. The same faith that offers hope of salvation from my general and irremediable sinfulness requires my regarding the inevitability of guilt as a general and inherent sinfulness. Also, the cipher of inevitable guilt that man experiences is shifted, by a movement of doctrinalizaton, into the very substance of man, along with other ciphers. Jaspers regards the notion of justification by faith as a failure of original sin as a cipher:

> How can it be meritorious to believe in something laid down in a creed, in statements about an objective occurrence? Where the reality of revelation loses even the voice of a possible cipher, we sense a disturbing limit.[56]

And finally, the cipher of original sin is capable of obscuring realities:

> To be truthful, we must insist on recognizing the full extent of misfortune, of misery, of dire need. To be truthful, we must not expect to be freed from guilt otherwise than by expiation and a posture in this world that can be trusted.[57]

This means that men can forgive each other, but cannot mediate God's forgiveness; neither can expectation of God's forgiveness absolve men from responsibility to fellow man.

Yet Jaspers also notes some positive possibilities in the cipher of original sin. First, it can be the presence of the "accusing voice" that reminds man of the self-righteousness that lies in the notion that he can, out of his own self, create good—provided that it does not provoke "moral passivity" by virtue of the expectation of grace. Neither the cipher of original sin nor its opposite, that of man's inherent nobility, can function as "total ciphers." Second, the cipher can remind man that even in the independence of his freedom his being springs from ineffable sources—provided that it does not seduce him into accepting himself as he happens to be and into taking recourse to merciful grace.

The cipher of original sin is full of pitfalls. It can make it impossible to live in responsible freedom, and it can misconstrue the transcendent ground of freedom and of the meaningfulness of evil as something that is objectively palpable. It can thereby take from human life its feature of a struggling striving for the active realization of what is essentially unknowable, and cause the acquiescence in human fallibility even to the extent of moral lassitude. A cipher ceases to be a cipher if its idiom is taken as the objective presence of transcendence.

Accordingly, no doubt, the crucial aspect of Jaspers's criticism of original sin is that it tends not only not to locate man's way to truth in communication but to obviate it. This can also be regarded as the main feature of Jaspers's many appraisals of harmony and the concommitant ultimate denial of evil. This sort of thinking appears in numerous forms, and in biblical, especially Christian, thought it accommodates the apparently incompatible doctrine of original sin.

The doctrine under consideration springs from what Jaspers considers to be the most profound of the basic motives of philosophical thought, i.e., that of the oneness of truth, of the realization of the ultimate unity of Being. The question is how we are to regard the palpable dissonances of being—the oppositions and tensions, the counterpurposive and evil—in consideration of the motive of unity. Doctrines of ultimate harmony do not deny these dissonances, but regard them as realities which appear only within a narrow human perspective. In a wider perspective or ultimately they are an essential feature of the realization of unity and harmony, and from this view they do not exist or at least do not prevail in their negativity.

In the light of Jaspers's treatment of the unity of truth[58] we can well understand that Jaspers largely rejects the doctrine of harmony and the denial of evil as ciphers of unity.

He rejects it on principle. For example, realized unity—no matter how comprehensive, no matter how dialectically potent, no matter how extensive its basis on what is known and knowable—is a unity of human realization and in this way not the all-encompassing unity but a moment within it.[59]

He rejects it on the basis of the conception of man's pursuit of truth as a communicative struggle. Possession of putative insight into the ultimate nature of things—in this case its harmonious unity where evil is a mere appearance of factors that are means of the good—removes the urgency of questioning and questing which impels what Jaspers regards as man's way to truth. In the harmonious view, man merely needs to acquiesce; the realization of truth does not depend essentially on him and on his becoming himself by virtue of joining the decisive struggle for truth. Jaspers goes so far as to say that the avoidance of harmony is presupposed for communication.[60]

He rejects harmony because where it is taken seriously, where one's situation is appraised in the light of it, it tends to promote passivity, moral resignation, the deference to authority to the extent of the extinction of freedom.[61]

He rejects it above all because it trivializes palpabilities while objectifying what cannot be known. It fails to take the facts of evil seriously, it fails to take these facts as the irremediable condition of man's search for truth and unity, it fails to realize the profound transcendence of truth and unity in the light of these facts, and in the contemplative realization of goodness it fails to impel toward its remedial, active realization. Against the vision of harmony Jaspers contraposes the cry of indignation which, to him, is most persuasively voiced by Ivan Karamazov: No ultimate harmony can justify the least suffering of the innocent even if all, including the innocent, joyfully acknowledge this harmony.[62] It is as dishonest not to hear or to silence the cry of indignation, and to veil palpable realities by virtue of a conviction of harmony, as it is to absolutize either harmony denying the earnestness of evil or indignation denying harmonies in the world such as they are. Only in their contraposition, only in mutual challenge and struggle, only in shattering against undeniable realities, only in failing as *total* visions can doctrines be ciphers of transcendence. And so it is with harmony in confrontation with indignation and the facts on which it is based. Harmony and the denial of evil spring from the motive of tranquillity in the certainty concerning the ultimate meaning, unity and goodness of things, the motive of optimism. As the epitome of theodicy, it can be a genuine cipher in the failure of its vision, and in this way a challenge to man in his freedom to testify by *active* realization his surrender to the ground of things whose profundity is intimated precisely by the failure of that vision.[63] In this sense Jaspers follows the thoughts Kant expresses in the essay of his old age on the failure of all theodicy. For Kant this failure throws man from the justification of God, which is beyond his ken, back to the concern over his own justification by virtue of his moral conduct.[64]

For Jaspers the primary, though not the only, example of harmony is idealism. However, it is clear that his criticism also concerns thinkers with whom the idealistic motive is not deliberately pronounced, such as Thomas Aquinas and Leibniz. The venerable Leibniz is able to carry through his theodicy as a profound expression of groundedness in God, with due attention to logical consistency, with stringent and effective simplicity, with encompassing sweep, without illusion about the given realities, and with a forceful indication of man's task of reconciliation by the work of reason. For Jaspers the will to nonillusion is not immune to the trivialization of the facts of senseless evil and misery if the realization of meaningfulness is more than a task, is a certainty. Even if Leibniz himself cannot be adduced as an example of this, the eighteenth-century proponents of Leibnizian optimism, whom Voltaire laughed out of court, can. And the work of reason, for Jaspers, is that of the creation of conciliating meaning in confrontation with concrete disharmonies, rather than the application of an ultimate harmony that is essentially known. The latter, whether desired or not, in the end involves authoritarianism and fanaticism, and the end of freedom. In a vital and true cipher the labor of enlightenment raises negative theology to its highest pitch: God remains hidden. No human vision is substituted for God in his transcendence. Nothing that man can understand is interposed between man and God. God is not made to speak in human idioms. God is not made to appear in human form, in humanly palpable form. And the fabric of time and its palpabilities, including the facts of evil, are not rendered trivial or illusory by transposing man to a vantage point where he is not as long as he is in time. It remains the world where man must be and is free to decide eternal validity; he does not know the eternal validity that determines what happens in time.

The effectiveness of consistency and simplicity are, as such, no virtues for Jaspers; in metaphysics they can be deceptive. This can be seen from his probing for the capability of the doctrine of divine predestination to function as cipher.[65] He likens the effective clarity of this doctrine to that of dualism and the doctrine of karma. In contrast to these doctrines he regards predestination as an intensification to a high degree of the problem of evil. The reason is that this doctrine is founded on the consciousness of man's complete dependence on God who predetermines man's destiny, his salvation or doom, regardless of man's merit or will.

For Jaspers there is something positive and negative in the Christian doctrine of predestination as propounded by Paul, Augustine, and Luther, and perfected by Calvin. And there is something highly questionable in the sort of life that it makes possible.

Predestination can be a cipher of the human incomprehensibility of the fact of evil, of the insolubility of the problem of evil, of the failure of theodicy. It can be a cipher of the ineffableness of God's ways. It can be a cipher of the abysmal depth at which we are grounded in our condition and with our lot. It is a cipher for man's being as springing from a source of destiny, and not resulting from blind chance.

And yet there are sides to this doctrine that detract from and even destroy the dignity of human freedom. The incomprehensibility of the problem of evil is here comprehended. But then, comprehension is not integral to the life process of penetrating the questions that engagement in the tasks of freedom raises. Rather, the incomprehensibility is comprehended in a dogmatic elaboration which is epitomized in Calvin's doctrine of God's "horrible decree." Transcendence makes its appearance as a tyrant, subject to moral evaluation yet beyond its obligation, inspiring fear and terror as well as awe. Nothing in life has value or merit in its own right, neither science nor culture, neither art nor even morality. Since salvation or damnation is a matter of God's decree, the value of life's activities lies in their being signs of God's election. Certainty of election makes for a sense of possession where everything should be in question, and for dismissal and intolerance of finding one's unconditional commitments in the restless movement of time. This certainty is the basis of the pride of righteousness and the justification by reference to God's will, even of acts that from the viewpoint of pure morality are wrong. Jaspers speaks from his experience with theologians when he condemns such corruption of man's dignity of freedom and search as a "witch's brew of humility, fatalism, activism, fanaticism."[66]

Precisely because predestination marks the intensification of the cipher of evil that is connected to the biblical conception of the personal God, and precisely because it has been an historically effective cipher for those who partook of the dogmatic contents integral to its Christian elaboration, Jaspers is concerned to come to terms with it and to enter into a critical dialogue with it. For his part, however, he sees in it a realization of truth radically different from what he can regard as valid. In his view, truth for man and the reading of ciphers cannot be sustained if decision in time is voided.[67] And, as we have seen, this occurs in an acceptance of the cipher of predestination that is carried over into a way of life. Surrender to incomprehensible and implacable transcendence is, to be sure, a possible way of man's relation to transcendence, according to Jaspers. However, it is an existential and not a doctrinal relation; if it is genuine it arises from the experience of life, of its vicissitudes, its dashed hopes, the failures to understand ultimate meanings in proximate realities. Surrender as an existential possibility is a relation to transcendence precisely where transcendence is cognitively and doctrinally questionable. And, understood in this way, it is not an exclusive possibility; it stands in tension to its opposite, namely, defiance. In existential relation to transcendence the defiant indignation over manifest evil is no less honest than humble surrender to what is beyond comprehension.

In Jaspers's philosophy the failing of the cipher of predestination lies in its reflecting only surrender. Among the ciphers of evil that are connected with the biblical conception of the personal God there is one which reflects both defiance and surrender. Jaspers regards it as the most potent cipher of evil. It is the cipher of Job.

The poetry of the Book of Job is, for Jaspers, the cipher, or rather: a world of ciphers, expressive of the most intense urgency of the problem of evil. His discussion of it is one of the pre-eminent examples of a functioning cipher that can be found in his writings. Hence in our consideration of Jaspers's treatment of the Book of Job we shall not so much concentrate on the highlights of his interpretation, much less on merely giving an account of it. Rather we shall try to pay attention to how he probes Job as a cipher of transcendence.

One of the basic features of a cipher is that indeterminable transcendence appears in it in the determinate idiom of human realization. We can see this in Jaspers's interpretation of Job. Job's pious faith in God is unshakeable, even "childlike." But within the framework of this faith Job seeks God with his understanding. He persists with integrity in his knowledge concerning the world, rejecting deceptions that would adulterate, by means of pious explanations, what he knows by virtue of his experience. He sees the facts of the evil and injustice of his lot. If the certainty of God is related to these facts, then it is in spite of and not in explanation of the facts. For even as the conduct of his life has been largely blameless and his extreme misfortune is unrelated to it, so it is everywhere manifest that evil and injustice prevail without rhyme or reason. In this way, man's understanding, unclouded in its nourishment by experience, sees the problem of evil in its irremediable grimness.

Moreover Job rejects the consolations of his friends as well as the exhortations of Elihu, all of whom Jaspers designates as the 'theologians'. Job is told by them that no man is pure, the sons were slain as punishment, the extent of his misfortune bespeaks transgressions which it is meet to atone for, and more. Job is not unwilling to accept such reasons, if they are reasons that pertain, and not merely as general propositions of faith. If there had been transgressions what were they? His protesting his innocence is not the moral perversity of moral righteousness for what is at stake is the question of God's justice. This is the reason why he also rejects the suggestion that misfortunes may be sent as incentives. The 'theologians' ' consolation and advice with pious words are deceptions, gainsaying truth. The wicked are not punished and prosper, the good are not spared and suffer—as Job's own lot exemplifies; no pious faith in God's ultimate justice can adulterate this truth. It is truth that Job means to hold on to, not deception. He does not doubt God, but even as he knows the disorder and injustice of man's existence he means to understand God's justice in it. Consolation that is an adulteration of the sense of truth and justice compounds the suffering: "Honest, straight talk would help, and truth alone can comfort."[68]

In Job the problem of evil is articulated in such a way that no human solution of the problem is possible without perversion of the sense of truth and justice. In Jaspers's interpretation, therefore, the counterpart to Job's futile desire for 'communication' with fellow men is his turning to God for understanding of evil. Job's desire for understanding, for both God and truth, reaches its highest pitch when, in spite of his impotence before God which he asseverates, he "appeals to God against God":

God, who lets truth prevail, the oath helper, the witness, the defender, against God the despot who inspires fear and dread.[69]

But God remains silent. And, it seems that in Jaspers's interpretation, this is man's situation. The more intensive the yearning for understanding of evil, the more intense the despair over the juxtaposition of the fact of evil and certainty of God, the more are the traditional answers revealed as merely human, the less can these take the place of God's, the more can man's experience of his ignorance be the measure of the magnitude of the truth he seeks. The sense of Jaspers's interpretation is that Job is the cipher of man's endurance in the face of grim reality, with his veracity—his sense of truth and justice, in the silence of God, and against the temptation of comforting sham—in particular the sort that is associated with doctrines and dogmas whose only strengh is tradition and theological authority:

He wants God himself, not human wisdom. He insists on taking the primacy of his own experience seriously.[70] His concern is not with theology but with God. This is his rebellion.[71]

What of the cipher of the theophany? Jaspers stresses that God's appearance is sudden, and not in response to a specific one of Job's many invocations; that God disdains Job's questions and implicit demands to show His justice, and that He humbles Job with questions which Job cannot answer. The cipher of the theophany is a confirmation of God's transcendance, of man's irremediable inability to comprehend the ground of things. It reminds man of the limits of his grasp and precisely thereby vouchsafes a glimpse of the ineffable reaches of transcendence. Essential, in Jaspers's view, is the circumstance that, even though God rejects Job's questioning beyond his reach, he favors the stubborn veracity which led to this questioning over the pretention of the 'theologians' to know where man cannot even question. The theologians are condemned and Job is upheld:

God wants truthfulness, not blind obedience. God wants freedom, not unquestioning surrender.[72]

Jaspers points to a danger in this sort of interpretation of Job, according to which the conclusion of the book is man's essential ignorance of God, his ways, his justice. Even though the confirmation of this insight—through the sufferings and the stubborn integrity of Job and through the rebuke of God in His epiphany—is gained in opposition to the 'theologians' ' doctrine, it can itself become a doctrine, even a theological, and moreover an ecclesiastical doctrine. No doubt an endless number of examples for this can be adduced. Gregory the Great, for one, regards Job as designating the Catholic Church, and his comforters, the heretics.[73] "How is it," Gregory asks,

> that blessed Job . . . is praised to the enemy, and reproved in his own person . . . unless it be that the holy man surpassed all men by the virtue of his merits, and yet, inasmuch as he was man, could not possibly be without blame before the eyes of God. For in a holy man sojourning in this temporary state, the rule of Divine judgment has still something to judge.[74]

Indeed, Jaspers points out, don't the 'theologians' in Job say the same thing as God? "They ask whether Job heard God's secret, and God asks where Job was when the earth was made."[75] For Jaspers, then, the danger is that man's knowledge of man's nonknowledge of God can be dogmatized, as is the case in the doctrine of predestination. As we have seen, any such dogmatization can be the instrument of an authoritative realization of ultimate concern with all that this may and invariably will entail, the failure and loss of freedom, the weakening of thought, moral lassitude—all within the framework of deference to temporal power.

Against this Jaspers maintains Job as a powerful cipher, where the humbling of Job in his ignorance does not lead to cogitative acquiescence to such ignorance, but where the arrival of ignorance is risked in the relentless, continuously renewed movement of questioning with integrity:

> The cipher of God's humbling Job . . . bespeaks the faithful Job's inner action in coming to himself, constantly reborn of question and defiance. It does not terminate this movement by means of a dogmatized knowledge of ignorance. . . . The cipher raises the movement of knowledge to the fulfillment of encompassing ignorance.[76]

Such fulfillment, as we have seen in chapter 1, requires, if it is genuine, the enactment of the will to know and the pursuit of knowledge to the point where it founders. It is by virtue of the experience with evil and the concerned penetration of this mystery that comprehension of the incomprehensibility of evil is actual and that it can become the intimation of the transcendent grounding of freedom. The humbling of Job is not a cipher as a *doctrine* of man's ignorance concerning the transcendent meaning of evil. It is a cipher as the reverberation and intonation of a life that is engaged in the ongoing search for such meaning and that is able to renew its strength in the failure of such searching. The "destruction of reflection on truth and justice" is not, in Jaspers's words, the point of the cipher, but its "overcoming," its active transcending:

> God, unlike the theologians, accepts these reflections on account of their integrity. But he leads Job beyond the point where thinking circles about itself and congeals—he leads him to a sphere where thinking does indeed cease, but in a luminosity that would be impossible except for the thoughts that have been overcome.[77]

Thus for man in his finitude relentlessly pursuing truth, spurning comforting claims that do not harmonize with life's bitter experience, questioning with defiant freedom and passionate integrity are the ways of assuring himself of his transcendent grounding. The intensity of Job's defiant integrity is the measure of such assurance.

Jaspers points out, as we have said, that the most potent ciphers of evil are associated with the biblical cipher of God as person to whom man relates as an I to a Thou. And it is precisely in Job that he sees this conception of God as a cipher. It is in the address of God as Thou that the incomprehensibility of evil becomes overwhelming and the insolubility of the problem of evil acute. And it is in Job's defiant wrangling with God and the consequent breaking of the imagery of the 'Thou' into God who is invoked and God against whom He is invoked that Jaspers sees the cipher in its foundering and in its foundering pointing beyond itself.[78] Because the personal God is, in Job, revealed as a cipher, Jaspers, in his interpretation, is at odds with orthodox interpretations which associate with the 'Thou' of the personal God a literal and embodied meaning and hence an "apparent solution" of Job's problem. Thus orthodox Judaism offers the solution of God's revelation embodied in the Law. Against this Jaspers upholds the Judaism of the prophets,[79] particularly Isaiah, Jeremiah and Amos, and of Ruth, the Psalms, Ecclesiastes and Job, albeit a Job[80] that cancels the emphasis on those aspects of the ancient editorial modifications which bespeak the work of the orthodoxy of the "religion of the Law." In Christianity Job's problem is solved because no charges can be levelled against "a God who took all suffering upon himself."[81] Both solutions are rejected by Jaspers, and perhaps for no reason more so than that they miss the sense of ultimate insolubilities as a way of faith that is so decisively conveyed precisely in the books of the Bible which Jaspers favors, and so also in Job as he interprets it. Hence we see him speaking for biblical faith against the orthodoxies which are based on the Bible.[82] Hence we also see him interpreting Job, not always at variance with the 'theologian', but at decisive points departing from orthodox interpretations and going independent ways.

The large topic of Jaspers's dialogue with the theologians exceeds our present scope. We mention it in order to point to an important aspect of Jaspers's interpretation of Job as the cipher of evil that is most penetrating and most powerful. Job is for Jaspers the cipher for the circumstance that man's assurance of the ultimate ground of his being in freedom is a matter of reading ciphers. Transcendence makes its appearance in a determinate mode whose meaning does not lie in what it means literally but in its intimating force. Cancel the cipher and the intimation vanishes, as in the case of the doctrinalizations; what remains is the immanent doctrine and the mediating authority. Such intimation of transcendence is not a matter of knowledge but of the endless movement of interpretation which is pursued to its foundering. The multiplicity of, the endlessness of, the combat between interpretations are functions of such foundering, as is the circumstance that the interpretations of ciphers are themselves ciphers and not as such the presence of transcendence. Moreover ciphers are actual as ciphers only historicly, i.e. as the testimony of assurance on the part of the self who in his interpretation becomes himself and is as much creator as recipient of the cipher. To read ciphers means neither to mistake finitude for the embodied presence of transcendence nor to absolutize finitude. It is the courage to pursue the cipher to the foundering whose uninterpretability is the ultimate cipher of silence. The reading of ciphers leads beyond all ciphers. Its defiant pursuit is endurance beyond illusion. In the light of this reminder of the philosophy of ciphers it can be seen how for Jaspers, whose interpretation of Job runs like a thread through the whole web of his philosophy, Job is the cipher of ciphers.

In the cipher of Job, Jaspers finds the most intense consciousness of God in the light of the facts of evil. The pursuit of the ciphers of evil reaches a culmination in his interpretation of Job. The philosophical sense and the existential actuality of this pursuit is summarized as follows:

> It has proved impossible to solve the question of evil in a way that would be both logically consistent and borne out by all the facts. Every construction of Being in a cipher of totality will founder as it claims to comprehend this totality. All that remains is to comprehend the incomprehensibility.[83]

v. The Final Issue: Guilt and Freedom

Jaspers's conception of metaphysics as the reading of the cipher-script is founded upon a radical consciousness of the requirements of freedom. Inasmuch as human freedom is enacted with the limit-situation of inevitable guilt, this is eminently exemplified in his treatment of the problem of evil.

In Jaspers's view the motive of freedom requires that neither the world nor transcendence nor indeed freedom itself be absolutized.

The absolutization of the world with its necessity, of the course of nature in accordance with laws, to which man himself is subject insofar as he is a being in the world and part of nature—all this of course denies freedom. But against this absolutization there asserts itself the consciousness of freedom. This is not to be regarded as a theoretical consciousness based on the adduction of evidence; in this sense freedom would be vacuous and questionable. What is meant is the original consciousness of responsibility, of the course of things in the exigency of a situation depending on my decisiveness and on my action, an action which is other than the epiphenomenal concurrence of natural necessitation. What is also meant is that in acting or failing to act man can be aware of the incurrence of guilt by virtue of what he recognizes as incumbent upon him, of the discrepancy between what he ought to be and what he realizes in acting.

If freedom were absolute, freedom would not be actual—only possible, or else it would be random activity, without responsible decisiveness, and as such the self-denial of freedom in its actualization. The reason for this is that without nature as a mode of being other than freedom and in its own right, there would be nothing to challenge the options of freedom, nothing to provoke the actualization of possibilities, no reason to act one way rather than another. Without the constraints of situations, without the discipline of time, of irretrievable chances at realization, there would be no burden of guilt but also no actuality of responsibility. This insight is not unusual. It is reflected, for example, in the commandment that Jews eat, at their family Passover celebration, a bite of *matzoh* (unleavened bread)—a symbol of liberation—with a piece of *maror* (bitter herb)—a symbol of the slavery and oppression suffered at the hands of the Egyptians; this can be a cipher of the link of freedom with the world of nature, history and situations.

Similarly there would be no actuality of freedom if freedom were absolutized vis-à-vis transcendence. Without transcendence it makes no difference whether or not I act or how I act. There would only be choice of the moment, without anything transcending the moment being involved that is realized in the moment and that marks its significance. What I am as freedom would be constituted solely by the flow of my temporal career from one momentary present to another, and no vision of my transtemporal validity would hold me to account for my choices. I would be responsible to my present which is determined by my choice; there would be no guilt connected with such choice, and thus no selfhood.

The absolutization of transcendence cancels freedom by reducing willing to pure obedience. Where God's will is absolute—and for man this means that it is known—there is only submission beyond the burden of responsibility, beyond the risk of guilt.

Man's freedom, for Jaspers, is real only if there are all three, world, freedom, transcendence:

the world as the concrete here and now that is the only arena of the actualization of man as free self;

freedom as the mode of being that becomes what it is in a time-bound career by virtue of its decisions and actions;

transcendence that is, beyond the self's consciousness of the insufficiency of reality that is merely world and beyond the self's recognition of its own limitations, the intimation of and impulsion toward pervasive unity and fulness.

Moreover, man is free by virtue of his incurrence of guilt, by virtue of his risking such incurrence, by virtue of his recognition of his guilt. But this inevitable and ineluctable association of guilt with freedom is, in the last analysis, incomprehensible. As we have seen, for Jaspers this is the basis and the motive of the problem of evil which is seen as concerned over the ground of freedom. There were two specific questions: Is perhaps not man himself but the ground of his freedom at fault for his culpability? What is to be decided in facing this question is whether man is exonerated for his guilt and what sort of life is possible with a sense of redemption. The other question is whether accusations of injustice can be raised against the ground of man's freedom on account of the discrepancy between man's guilt and merit on the one hand, and man's lot on the other. What is at stake here is also what life is possible if we deny what we know or deny that we know, if we forbid such questioning or make it the principle of freedom.

It is this problem of the possibility of a life of freedom that is the motive for Jaspers's joining the battle of ciphers. It is, as we have seen, a twofold battle, a battle between ciphers and a battle

for the purity of ciphers.[84] Both are essential and they are intertwined. The former is a matter of eliciting through interpretation and through the testimony of action what ciphers one
chooses to assure oneself of the ground of one's being, how one
reads the ciphers, and what life for oneself and for mankind one
deems to be humanly possible by virtue of this assurance and
this reading. The latter is a matter of upholding the cipher as
cipher, and thus of not mistaking transcendance for human visions thereof, of not confusing metaphysical assurance with cognitive certitude, of not conflating the options and risks of freedom with divine authority. Accordingly, with respect to the
battle between ciphers, Jaspers probes for the existential significance of ciphers, so also the ciphers of evil, i.e., not only for the
kind of actions they engender but for the frame of mind they
bespeak:

> Ciphers of the root of evil are not universally valid as matters
> of fact; they are ideas that clarify or produce an inner disposi-
> tion on the part of the thinker. We do not think of them with
> the neutrality we feel toward factual hypotheses. . . . By our
> way of conceiving them, we share responsibility for our-
> selves.[85]

With respect to the battle for the purity of ciphers, Jaspers fights
against conceptions of the ciphers as the "embodied" presence of
transcendence. As such, whether in the form of the literal acceptance of an imagery, or a gnostic vision, or a systematic extension
of an idea, or a revelation regarded as historic event, or a doctrin-
alization of an expression of faith—whether it be the idea of harmony, the Zoroastrian dualism, the vision of God's grim decree of
predestination—the result that Jaspers sees is "delusion of cor-
poreality," "talking away and thinking away of facts" out of a
desire for "the comfort of definite answers," and in the end "a
way out of the seriousness of evil" and of the actuality of human
guilt.[86]

But earnestness with regard to guilt is for Jaspers the touchstone
of the validity of ciphers and of the reading of ciphers of evil.
Where guilt is taken as the sign of the depravity of man's freedom,
there is a disposition to leave all to God's grace. Possessed by one's
worthlessness, one's redemption is not a matter of redeeming redirection and action but a matter of waiting for, hoping for, or
even expecting God's gracious act of redemption. Both freedom
and its incurrence of guilt are thereby trivialized. It is otherwise
where the ciphers of evil are read with a consciousness of man's
"nobility." Here man in his freedom regards himself with expecta-

tions and faces himself with tasks. He must act out of his resources in situations he cannot anticipate and whose ultimate meaning he does not know. Incurred guilt can be borne not as a confirmation of the total dependence on God's undeserved grace, but with unmitigated responsibility, with an uncompromising and undissembling realization of failure, with the redoubled urgency to recall oneself to one's task of realizing what cannot be without one's decisive action, and perhaps to do good where one has incurred the guilt of evil before. Redemption lies in what one enacts, not in a cognitive guarantee or a transcendence that is unconnected with the demands upon man in the present. The siginificance of the recognition of one's guilt and of what is brought to consciousness in ciphers of evil lies in what difference it makes here and now, at the moment of decision and action, in the decision and action of the moment, where one counts, where the becoming of what is to be depends on me, where one fails if one leaves the unfolding of good and evil to God because one's freedom may be the instrument of this unfolding.

This idea of freedom is no less directed towards transcendence than the idea of freedom regarded as man's depravity. Even as the cipher of man's need for grace is connected with the latter, so Jaspers formulates imagery befitting the former. The cipher we find in Jaspers so often—it is at the heart of his personal faith—is that of man being given to himself as a gift in his freedom. It is as if transcendence, by remaining hidden, wants man to be in and through his freedom, unknowing of the origin and the goal of his being. To speak in biblical idiom: God wants man to be free; and freedom is possible precisely by man's ignorance concerning what transcends his limitation. In man's being free in his ignorance lies the proclamation of God's will. It is appropriate to recall at this point a memorable passage toward the end Kant's second *Critique* that made a deep impression on Jaspers:

> Thus what the study of nature and of man has sufficiently shown elsewhere may well be true here, viz., that the inscrutable wisdom through which we exist is not less worthy of veneration in respect to what it denies than in what is has granted.[87]

Chapter Nine

Questions

i. The Question of Jaspers's Historical Significance

Kant is one of the only three philosophers in history to whose greatness Jaspers can give the pre-eminent characterization of "seminal founders of philosophizing." Yet he makes this evaluation with caution:

> Kant is close to us in time, from a historical and human standpoint the closest of the three. Like Plato and Augustine, he stands before us as an unsurpassed whole, questioning and creative. But two hundred years are very little beside fifteen hundred or twenty-three hundred, and this must not be forgotten when making historical judgments.[1]

Karl Jaspers is dead. He belongs to history. His philosophical thought is now part of the history of philosophy. "Historical judgments" about his thinking will now be made. This is to say that no such judgment can any more be made with the idea in mind that it is possibly part of a dispute, that it may be evocative of a deliberate response. There is still the chance of communication with the spiritual actuality of Jaspers's thought, but this actuality is contingent on our understanding. Not Karl Jaspers but Jaspers's work is the participant that enters this hermeneutic circle.

Yet for the present generations and those soon to come Karl Jaspers is a contemporary or nearly so. Hence it is fitting to observe the same caution in making historical judgments about him that he attempted to observe in judging Kant. After all, Jaspers directs his attention to prevailing actualities which are profoundly related to our commitments. This circumstance may cloud dispassionate historical judgment even where such judgment is recognized as requisite for commitment that is both sound and passionate. For example, Jaspers probes actualities—whether they are institutions or persons, traditions or tendencies, problems or works, movements or testimonies, ideas or actions—for their promise of freedom. Some, such as Lukács, may hear in this the tattoo of a parasitical individualism that is destructive of reason and social conscience. Others may hear in it the clarion call to man's liberation for true community. Methodological clarification, to which Jaspers contributed to no small degree, shows that knowledge of historical persons is correlative with the confession of the knower and requires that research aim at the distinction of the two. The danger to truth that consists in conflating the two exists particularly with respect to contemporaries or near-contemporaries whose provocative involvement in our own vital actualities was so great. Let us hope that the Jaspers whose historical stature is being and will be judged will not be a Jaspers assassinated post mortem.

Another respect in which temporal proximity imposes a difficulty in appraising the historical significance of a philosopher is that of examining his work according to the criterion of originality. Hence, the critical examiner will be at a loss how to operate with this criterion in the case of Jaspers. From a wide historical perspective we can reduce the operation with this criterion to tracing a conception to its first formulation or its most significant modifications and its most creative integration with philosophical motives. In this way we can find the first consistent use of the *natura naturans-natura naturata* distinction in Eckhart, but find its formulation in his contemporary, Saint Bonaventura, and allusions to it in a translation of Averroës's commentary on Aristotle's *De Caelo*, all in the thirteenth century. Yet who would deny that more than mere adumbration of this distinction is involved in Scotus Erigena's (ninth century) fourfold distinction of nature in which we find the relevant conceptions of nature uncreated but creating and nature created but uncreating; these conceptions are, in turn, outgrowths of neo-Platonic motives. *Mutatis mutandis* who would deny the distinctness and power in the unfolding of the metaphysical scope of this distinction at the hands of Spinoza (in the seventeenth century) such that it is most appropriately associated with him. We cannot deny originality to any of these men, precisely by virtue of a wide historical perspective.

So many faces and facets of reality merited Jaspers's attention, so universally open was his thinking to all that lays claim to being true that perhaps, to take up a suggestion of Saner, therein, in the unprecedented scope, lay Jaspers's originality. But precisely because of the scope of what his thinking tried to embrace do we find, especially by virtue of the as yet necessarily narrow historical perspective, themes, even main themes, in Jaspers which seem familiar from elsewhere. In this sense I have tried to show the reverberation of age-old motives and the continuity of specific problematics in Jaspers. With respect to the question of originality one can also show, as I have tried, the influence of specific philosophers on Jaspers.

For example, Jaspers's theory of the political import of philosophical ideas is surely not unrelated to Max Weber's relation of historical events, practices and movements to underlying spiritual realities and beliefs.

Another instance is Jaspers's pervasive and deliberate penchant for Kant. In fact, finding in Jaspers the resonance of Kantian themes could constitute a most promising approach to Jaspers. In this vein Professor Salmony, the successor to Jaspers's Basel colleague Heinrich Barth, said, when I told him that I was writing a book on Jaspers, that if he ever wrote such a book he would call it "Karl Jaspers: The first and last Kantian." Kantian is Jaspers's transcendental method, the consistent use of the distinction between being and its appearance, the non-identification of thought and existence, the transcendence-consciousness, and in all of this the primacy of freedom. In the larger features of Jaspers's philosophical enterprise we can also recognize the Kantian strain. Jaspers, like Kant, sees the fulfillment of thought in its cognitive employment, seeks to stake out the range of cognition—both to liberate science from metaphysical encumbrances and to liberate metaphysical motives from illusion, and, identifying these motives as central to the vitality of freedom, he opens up ways and realms of metaphysical validity founded on practice. Unlike Kant, however, Jaspers considers that scientific thought comprises the human studies and history; metaphysical thought is more than postulation, is of symbolic signifiance and in its validity is the reading of ciphers; the sense of the practical actualization of freedom is, with respect to its temporality, intensified to a consciousness of historicity, and, with respect to its moral content, enlarged to an awareness of the tragic and of the risk of faith and commitment; and in Jaspers Kant's consciousness of the sovereignty of reason is enlarged to disclose its essentially communicative mode of concretion.

A final example is Jaspers's debt to Kierkegaard, which is immeasurable in spite of his rejection of Kierkegaard's conception of the Christianity of martyrdom and negative decision as the highest possibility of selfhood. Kierkegaardian in Jaspers is the awareness that Existenz—the existence of selfhood—involves choice, decision, responsibility, and does not consist of mere reflection. Kierkegaardian is the insight that reflection about selfhood can only be exploration of possibilities and not insight into the nature of man, and, on the other hand, that the possibility of existence, and its being constituted by reflection, is a vital moment of selfhood. Kierkegaardian is the conception of selfhood as the wholeness of disparate validities and claims upon man that are enacted and not suffered by the individual. Kierkegaardian is the consciousness of the transcendent foundation of freedom, selfhood, Existenz. Kierkegaardian is the notion that the factors of selfhood such as choice and responsibility cannot be mediated. The instances of Jaspers's leaning on Kierkegaard can be multiplied. Many and complex are the ways also in which his thinking is distinct from Kierkegaard's. For example, distinct from and yet an outgrowth of that Kiekegaardian insight into the unmediatableness of the factors of selfhood is Jaspers's conception of communication as man's way to truth.

But as we recall such examples of influences and continuities we also take note of a curious thing: Jaspers is the first to point out these affinities, the first to acknowledge his debt to those who "nourished" his thinking. No malice is meant towards anyone in voicing the conjecture that perhaps there is originality also in this acknowledgement on the part of Jaspers.

However, there is something unsatisfactory in characterizing Jaspers's stature within the history of philosophy merely by tracing the influences upon him, as if the question of his originality were exhausted by the procedure even in a narrow historical perspective. His relation to tradition was, after all, not passive but deliberate, not simply receptive but profoundly transformative. There is a distinct attempt in his philosophical activity to identify the exigencies of the situation at this juncture in the history of thought. There are distinct features in this attempt of his to discover and impel the vitality of the tradition of thought, to make it amenable to what may yet come, to uncover in it the humus on which new seed can take hold, can find nourishment, can flourish. The appropriate criterion of originality here is not so much to discover what is new but what efforts, conceptions and achievements are distinctive or characteristic of his work. This we have tried to show throughout this book.

Some of the most distinctive accomplishments of Jaspers's work were not sufficiently considered in this book. The most important of these are two related distinctions, i.e., his delimitation of the respective validities of science and philosophy, and his position of the self-assertion of philosophy vis-à-vis the relation of philosophy and religion. These are no mean accomplishments, and their potential significance is immense. Like all historians of science and philosophy, Jaspers knew of the difficult problems and the vehement struggles that accompanied the rise of modern science, and in the light of this rise, the conception of the scope of human knowledge, both in its grasp and its power of forming reality. And unlike many such historians he knew this from personal experience in the practice of both science and philosophy. Jaspers's ingenuous assertion of the originality of philosophy with respect to ultimate questions vis-à-vis revealed religion without gainsaying the originality of the latter may prove to be seminal. I hope to have occasion to consider the significance of Jaspers's proposal that the old distinction between reason and faith be supplanted by the distinction science-philosophy-theology in future studies of Jaspers. In Jaspers's self-understanding the systematic development of this distinction ranks as one of his most important achievements, and arose from what he regarded as one of the most pressing exigencies of the philosophical situation of his time.

The notion of a philosopher's 'self-understanding' and the eliciting of such 'self-understanding' in the study of philosophers was developed by Jaspers into a revealing tool of historical research. And Jaspers himself practiced self-understanding at every stage of his work, a feature that is related to his requirement of awareness of the methodical character of thought. In appraising the originality of a philosopher's place in history the philosopher's self-understanding can be a relevant criterion. We have had occasion to indicate Jaspers's self-understanding, and even though it may be of interest to see how he appraised the over-all significance of his work we shall not give an account of it here. Instead we shall try to see whether there is a significant implicit self-understanding in Jaspers's grouping of the great philosophers.

ii. A Question of Jaspers's Self-Understanding

Does Jaspers's arrangement of his work *The Great Philosophers* imply a self-understanding on his part of his possible significance as a philosopher? The treatment of this problem must proceed in two stages: first we shall interpret the arrangement of the great philosophers under the supposition that it reflects Jaspers's conception of the philosophical enterprise. Then we shall try to see in what way Jaspers's own philosophizing can be said to be mirrored in this conception.

a. The Philosophical Enterprise

The conception and design of *The Great Philosophers* stresses the
"uniqueness" of human beings and particularly that of the great
men. It upholds the "unity" of the philosophical enterprise of
each thinker and of the truth at which all of them aim.

In examining Jaspers's grouping of the great philosophers[2] two
things must be noted: the marks by which each main group and
subgroup of greats is distinguished from the others, and, with few
exceptions, the order in which the groupings appear. There are
three main groups: first, the "exemplary men";[3] secondly, the
"great thinkers"; finally, men "concerned with philosophical
thinking" in various realms of human endeavor. As one can see,
only the second main group comprises men who are 'philosophers'
in the ordinary sense. All of these, even the most eminent ones,
namely, Plato, Augustine, and Kant, are in a position second to
the exemplary "men who by being what they were did more than
other men to determine the history of men." We are thereby
shown two things about Jaspers's views on philosophy. For one
thing, the examples of actual men, exalted by mankind, can serve
better as measures of what man could and ought to be than the
philosophers' visions of ideals. And, secondly, the human actuality
in which the exemplary lives of Socrates, Buddha, Confucius, and
Jesus can be and have been lived is the alpha and omega of philosophy.

The interweaving of the actualities of life and philosophy is also
apparent in the relation between the second and third main
groups. The order of these two groups is not meant to indicate a
difference in rank between philosophers proper and men who,
though they contribute to philosophy, do so in the pursuit of non-
philosophical callings. The reason for the order is primarily practical: in a history of philosophy the philosophers should occupy a
central position. Beyond this we may consider the relation of
these two groups as a juxtaposition rather than an ordering by
rank.

By means of this juxtaposition Jaspers shows that we would be
taking "too narrow a view of philosophy" if we were to "reduce it
to the exclusive preserve of rationality." Moreover, philosophical
thought requires for its efficacy "something which is more than
philosophy," i.e., the actuality of such human endeavors as
"poetry, science, politics, literature, practical affairs, theology and
the teaching of philosophy."

The fact that science and politics appear near the beginning of
this list is, for Jaspers, significant, as is, perhaps, also the listing of

theology as next to last. Most significant, however, is the position of the professors: they appear last. In this manner Jaspers rejects the identification of the great philosopher with the professor of philosophy and the restriction of philosophical thought to academic philosophy. The professor's task of "turning the great enterprise into a learned profession indispensable to tradition and education" is "the humblest of tasks." The concrete realms of science, literature, and public affairs are closer to philosophy as living reality.

In the second main group we are dealing with philosophers proper; therefore, Jaspers's arrangement of this group into subgroups is intrinsic to his conception of philosophy. Each of the four subgroups is distinctly conceived; yet the conception of each is keyed to that of the others. Now, insofar as these conceptions reflect Jaspers's idea of philosophy the assignment of a great philosopher to one of the subgroups reflects Jaspers's position vis-à-vis that philosopher and Jaspers's judgment of his philosophical significance. Let us now explicate this fact by taking a look at each subgroup in turn and in relation to the others.

The first subgroup comprises the already mentioned "seminal founders of philosophizing." This is the most restricted group, for which in Jaspers's view only three qualify, namely, Plato, Saint Augustine, and Kant.

The second subgroup includes a selection of the great metaphysicians of the East and West. They are men of "visions of thought." The group is so large that it requires subdivision, the detailing of which would exceed the scope of this discussion. Let us mention the first, however, because it is particularly telling. They are the "original metaphysicians," i.e., those "who think from the sources" of metaphysical thought and who "have arrived at and lead to serenity." With such thinkers as Parmenides, Plotinus, Lao-Tsu, the emphasis is on the positive metaphysical thought which, fulfilled by visions of Being, tends to harden into doctrine.

Here we can make our first comparison. In the seminal founders there are also the potentials of doctrinal dogmatism; but these potentials are not actualized in Plato, Augustine, and Kant because they remain masters of their visions. Like the original metaphysicians the seminal founders aim at the fulfillment of the movement of thought in "serenity." But the founders do not "arrive at serenity." The men in both subgroups are "creative" but in different ways: The metaphysicians in the formation of their thoughts; the founders in "generating the ideas of those who come after them." Hence the founders, unlike the metaphysicians, do not "lead to serenity." They are founders of philosophizing precisely by virtue of this seminal influence. Of course, the metaphysicians are also influential. But there is a difference in their influence. Their thinking can be reiterated, ramified, distorted, rejected, or assimilated. The reason for this is that their thinking is a project which has been brought to a recognizable conclusion. In distinction for them, the seminal founders are "not an end" but perennially "a beginning of inexhaustible possibilities."

The third subgroup of "disturbers" consists of the "probing negators" Abelard, Descartes, and Hume, and the "radical awakeners" Pascal, Lessing, Kierkegaard, and Nietzsche. The subgroup of disturbers is conceived vis-à-vis the metaphysicians and the founders. The example of the founders shows the mainly affirmative thinking of the metaphysicians to be an anticipative vision of ultimates. It is the primary task and contribution of great disturbers to recall human thought from such premature fulfillment and the concomitant hardening into doctrine. However, lest the impression be gained that Jaspers makes his distinction of subgroups as if he were playing off one philosophical party against another, we must mention a relevant cautionary note which appears in the original version of the work but has been left out of the translation. Jaspers holds that great philosophical thought is neither fulfillment of vision nor questioning reservation of final judgment, but both in their polar relation. Hence, the difference between the subgroups is a matter of emphasis rather than of exclusive alternatives.[4] Founders, like Plato and Kant, maintain the dialectical tension between the two poles, whereas metaphysicians place the accent on "visions of thought," and disturbers on criticism, as the way to clarity.

The last of the four subgroups of philosophers is that of the "creative orderers," among whom Jaspers includes Aristotle, Thomas Aquinas and Hegel, Shankara and Chu Hsi. Vis-à-vis the "thinking out of affirmation" displayed in the "visions of thought" and the "thinking out of negation" of the disturbers, these orderers, like the founders, comprise both poles, the *sic* and the *non*, the thesis and the antithesis. The influence of Aristotle, Thomas Aquinas, and Hegel is immense and, as Jaspers attests, only that of the founders (Plato, Augustine, and Kant) is comparable to theirs. But Jaspers insists upon a radical distinction between the kinds of influence exerted by the members of these two subgroups. The impact of the founders makes itself felt in the independence of the thinking of those who came later. On the other hand, the influence of the orderers is "embodied in schools, doctrines, and propositions that can be learned."[5] This contrast is most significant. No doubt Jaspers recognizes the universal range of thought of each of these six by virtue of which they are the pinnacles of Western philosophy. In this he agrees with the judgment of history. Yet, venturing beyond this judgment and the fact of their comparable influence, he considers three of them to be the founders of philosophy and the other three to be, in a certain sense, detractors from philosophy.

This distinction is not a matter of where Jaspers's sympathies lie. What is at stake for Jaspers is the promotion of philosophy as the vital concern to penetrate to the sources of truth by means of one's own thinking. If the unexamined life is not worth living, then, since lives are individual and personal, this examination should be original in each life. Plato, Augustine, and Kant are siminal founders of philosophy precisely because they impel such philosophical originality. In his view of the nature of philosophical thought, the examination of life cannot be a reiteration of others' examinations nor can it be constituted by a systematic composite of the testimony of past thinking. However, Jaspers cautions his readers that there is more to Aristotle, Thomas Aquinas, and Hegel than their emphasis on ordering. He deplores this emphasis, finds especially in Thomas Aquinas a way of thinking alien to his own, shares Kierkegaard's harsh judgment of Hegel's system, and displays the modern scientist's mistrust of Aristotle. Yet Jaspers often speaks of these three with ungrudging admiration and profits from particular aspects of their thinking, denying that in ordering they merely "reiterate" and "incorporate."

The reflection of Jaspers's conception of philosophy culminates in this contrast of the founders and the orderers, providing additional emphasis on some of the other purposes of *The Great Philosophers*. He means to separate philosophy from academic philosophy, i.e., philosophic thought from schools and doctrines. He also means to promote the relevance of critical and independent thought for all manner of men in all manner of concerns.

b. The Irony of Jaspers's Self-Understanding

In a conversation which I once had with Jaspers the question was raised whether he was able to characterize his own philosophical efforts with respect to the groupings by means of which he distinguishes between the great philosophers. Disclaiming any association with "greatness" for himself, and rejecting other alternatives, he thought he could best be grouped amongst the teachers of philosophy. From our discussion of his *The Great Philosophers* we recall that this group of the professors of philosophy is purposely and significantly last. Can his opinion as to what group he might belong to be regarded as an instance of self-understanding? There are reasons to doubt this. A professor and researcher in philosophy he was, as were, for example, Kant, Hegel and Thomas Aquinas, the primary significance of none of whom lies, for Jaspers, in their researching activity. It would be no doubt bewildering had Jaspers designated their prime significance by grouping them with the teachers. And, it seems to us, Jaspers's self-understanding as primarily a teacher is similarly bewildering, because it is inadequate.

Yet, what are the alternatives? There are, first of all, the other designations of the third main grouping of philosophers among which we also find that of the *professors*. We cannot count Jaspers as a *theologian*. Even though he provoked and engaged in dialogue with them, he viewed revelational theology as reflective of a source of truth that is of concern to but distinct from philosophy. He was bemused by occasional suggestions that he was a theologian in disguise. Similarly we can clearly dismiss for him the designation of philosophizing within the framework of *practical affairs*. It is different with the designations of *political thinker* and *scientist*. Jaspers laid claim, and rightly so, to being a scientist, and for him it was a principle of his scientific activity to engage in that activity with philosophical clarity as to its scope and limits, even before he became explicitly a philosopher. Yet Jaspers's significance is not restricted to this, hence this designation fails as an indication of his primary significance. His political thinking may in the future prove to be of lasting significance. However, with respect to his self-understanding it is nothing other than the explication of the potential political import that, Jaspers insists, is implicit in any philosophical thought; his thinking is also political, it is not political in its primary significance. Finally, Jaspers is certainly not a philosophical *poet*, but he is a *literary* figure in the sense that his philosophical work is intimately associated with a deliberately developed mode of linguistic expression that is distinct in vocabulary, in the use of the linguistic materials, in style, power, and fluency. Yet philosophical thought is here not the fellow traveller of linguistic giftedness or intoxication, but the master for whom language had to be bent into a suitable tool.

In our attempt to elicit Jaspers's self-understanding from his schema of *The Great Philosophers* we are left with the distinctions of the second main group, that of the philosophers proper. We have shown how the conception of this grouping bespeaks Jaspers's conception of philosophy. Can we apply the distinctions of this group to a characterization of Jaspers's main historical significance? Much can be said in favor of designating Jaspers as an 'orderer', as he calls Aristotle, Thomas Aquinas and Hegel. The principle of systematic order is strikingly apparent in his *General Psychopathology*, the *Psychologie der Weltanschauungen*, and his *Von der Wahrheit*. The first version of the *Psychopathology* was written years before the possibility of a career in philosphy ever occurred to Jaspers. Upon reading it his friend Erich Frank, a scholar of classical philosophy, saw a motif familiar to him in this work. He remarked to Jaspers that he regarded the finesse with which he ordered and systematized according to conceptual and logical distinctions as Aristotelian in character. In the conversation in which he related this incident Jaspers also recalled how strange it had seemed to him to be likened to a philosophical mentality which he even then regarded as decisively at odds with his conception of the philosophical enterprise. We have shown in what way Jaspers regards the activity of massive summary ordering to have a stifling effect on philosophy. And as we examine in particular his primarily systematic works we cannot fail to affirm the justification in his self-characterization according to which the "synthesis" he aims at is not bounded by or prejudicial to the historic diversity of apprehending truth and Being, but "ingenuous," and open to such historicity. He says:

> I regard my thinking as the natural and necessary conclusion of Western thought until now, the ingenuous synthesis by virtue of a principle that enables us to admit all that is true in any sense whatever.[6]

The resuscitation and vitality of metaphysics is at the heart of Jaspers's philosophical concern. And the 'metaphysicians' appear near the head of the groupings of great philosophers; they are second only to the 'seminal founders'. Some of the metaphysicians whom Jaspers regards as seers of most profound visions of truth appear as the main witnesses of his philosophical career. In his teens Spinoza was his philosopher. And Spinoza together with Plotinus, Schelling, and Bruno are invoked, in the preface of his *Philosophy*, as among those who in particular nourished his thinking. Yet how far removed from them he considered himself! He says, for example:

> Today's metaphysical thinking, if it is honest, can neither in form nor in content have the same character as the old. Today anyone who skips Kant's critical clarity and the realm of cogent scientific insight can only end in confusion. In today's intellectual situations metaphysics in the old style—considered as knowledge of Being, as proclamation of what is and what happens, basically and comprehensively—can only stray into a

brand of magic which to be sure follows, though uncritically, the thought habits of the old metaphysics, but without its earnestness. Preconceived patterns which are not subjected to the methodological scrutiny that has become indispensable leads to artificial thinking without roots in Existenz. . . . It is a specter which seduces, then vanishes. It is not an actuality which becomes luminous in the Existenz that thinks it.[7]

One of the things we have tried to show in this book is how for Jaspers the legitimacy and vitality of metaphysics can now only be existential, and that metaphysics conceived in this way must incorporate the movement of critical doubt and cognitive skepticism. We have also had occasion to indicate Jaspers's affinity to philosophers whose main significance he sees in their having been 'disturbers', particularly the 'radical awakeners', and among these Kierkegaard and Nietzsche. Nevertheless, the groundswell of his philosophical motives, as powerful as the weight of critical skepticism which it carries, is that of affirmation, resolution, vision of ultimate and comprehensive unity:

> Severed from all that is definite we search for firm footing, in diremption we seek the tie, in dispersion concentration, in the many the one, in the relative the absolute.[8]

Jaspers's affinity to the 'disturbers' does not signify that his main theme is in their mode, even as the rejection of the idiom of the 'metaphysicians' does not signify the denial of the eminent significance of their motive. Rather the critical doubt pre-eminent in the 'disturbers' becomes, for him, the condition sustaining regard for the finitude of the one who in thinking pursues his ultimate metaphysical concerns.

Philosophizing that proceeds with such regard is, for Jaspers, communicative rather than doctrinal, periechontologic rather than ontologic. It is a thinking understood as faith in search of understanding rather than a disclosure of, or derivation from, absolute transsubjective insights, a way of thinking that is prepared to recover from the objectifications of formulated assurances. It is also a thinking that remains steadfastly itinerant lest the historicity of its vision usurp the place of truth in its transcendent oneness, and hence a thinking that remains open for and that promotes the realization of truth beyond the finitude of its own vision. These are features of the kind of thinking for which the 'seminal founders of philosophizing' are historically most significant:

> In reading the works of Plato, Augustine, Kant, we experience the productivity of thinking itself, of the truth of Kant's re-

mark that one cannot learn philosophy but only how to philosophize. . . . In them nothing is finished, and yet everything
is at all times finished in the possible presence of the essential. . . . There was something inexhaustible in their manner of
thinking. They open up worlds whose extent they themselves
seem unable to fathom. They are as wide as reality and as the
soul of man. . . . They themselves are never at an end and, having grown old they cease to speak, they seem to be able to
start all over again.[9]

It would be wrong to view the kinship of Jaspers's conception of
the pre-eminent significance of the 'seminal founders' and that of
the possibility of philosophy in the wake of the Enlightenment as
an instance of deliberate self-understanding, and a clandestine one
at that. The relation exists, but must be characterized as follows.
First, both conceptions are moments in an hermeneutic circle, as is
Jaspers's interpretive assimilation of the texts and traditions of the
philosophers. The first moment is a historical judgment, the second the conception of a present task, the third the communicative
presence of what is past. From the perspective of the circle the
possible historical significance of Jaspers's philosophical program,
as he himself may be thought to have understood it, arises no
more from his conception of the 'seminal founders' in their pre-
eminent significance, than the other way around. Moreover, the
alignment of Jaspers's conception of the philosophical enterprise
that is possible today, and so of his, with the conception of the
scheme of distinction between the 'philosophers' among the great
philosophers, involves all four of the subgroups of these 'philosophers', i.e., 'seminal founders', 'metaphysicians', 'disturbers', and
'orderers'. It is the arrangement of these four subgroups that was
characterized as intrinsic to Jaspers's conception of philosophy.
To be sure, the arrangement is such that the 'seminal founders' are
pre-eminent, that only three could be identified as such, and that
they stand, not by virtue of a difference in philosophical scope
and power or in historical effectiveness, but by virtue of their conception of the philosophical enterprise as elicited from their philosophical realization, in polar distinction from the 'orderers', whose
program and role Jaspers rejects for himself.

What then can be said about the position of the 'founders' as a
possible mark of Jaspers's self-understanding? First of all, no one
can want to be a 'founder'. The very conception of the 'seminal
founders', more so than that of any of the other groupings, involves historical effectiveness and the temporal distance this presupposes. Yet in Jaspers's conception, in its truest realization
philosophizing—whatever philosophical motive it emphasizes,

whatever field of human endeavor it animates—must be evocative of precisely that whereby Plato, Augustine and Kant are 'seminal founders': the intensification of one's *own* active struggle towards truth, at the risk of one's own faith and freedom, in one's own time and situation on the part of him who stands in communicative relation to the testimony of this philosophizing. Whether Jaspers can be effective in this way and whether his historical significance can ever be characterized by such effectiveness may be subject to the sort of doubts I shall raise in the next section. But it is a moot question which Jaspers both provokes and leaves unanswered. For by the nature of the kind of effectiveness with which we are faced here, its actuality cannot depend on any intention to be effective but on the will to be affected. And this means the will to be free and oneself.

Paradoxically, then, by the nature of the thing, Jaspers's scheme of *The Great Philosophers* cannot be a pattern for self-understanding, yet it mirrors the self-understanding of his philosophizing.

No philosophizing can, in the deliberateness of its execution, be seminal of philosophizing in others present and yet to come. Yet all philosophizing is here seen as true in proportion to its power of evoking precisely that. This too is paradoxical.

Hence, paradoxically, the judgment of self-understanding waits on a judgment of history that would consist not so much in an appraisal of Jaspers's work but in an enactment of one's own historicity.

The juxtaposition of Jaspers's self-understanding as 'teacher' with the aim of philosophy to be seminally communicative is also paradoxical, unless the "humble" task of teaching and philosophical research is at heart nothing other than the appeal to 'think oneself free'.[10] "Not philosophy, only philosophizing can be taught." It was Kant who said that. And what, after all, were not only Kant but also Plato and Augustine?

Paradoxically, Jaspers's judgment that his significance was that of the professor of philosophy is both an expression of simple, modest factuality and an ironic challenge to posterity.

iii. The Question of Criticism

A challenging philosopher does not go unchallenged. Criticism of Jaspers—sympathetic and inimical, sound and aberrant, understanding and confused, sincere and invidious—has been very extensive. We have had some occasions to refer to some of it. A good guide to the critical literature up to the year 1964 is Werner Schneider's *Karl Jaspers in der Kritik.*[11]

Many vital questions can be raised with respect to Jaspers in addition to those already considered earlier. For example, if one wishes to use traditional metaphysical concepts one would characterize Jaspers's position as a transcendental monism that is at the same time an immanent pluralism, where each is the basis of the other. Aside from the systematic promises and pitfalls of this position, one can, with respect to the immanent pluralism, raise the question whether this is not a matter of making a virtue out of chaos. One can ask whether it might not be possible to melt down the distinctions, particularly between modes of 'encompassing' being, and operate with a more accessible monism.

Another question is that of the effect of the radical transcendentalization of the unity of Being and truth in Jaspers. We are told that it has the effect of liberation from the methods of authority, from the stagnation of inquiry, for the recognition of the dignity of the next man who in his own finitude founds his life on a vision of truth other than one's own, for the communication with such another, and for the recovery of the temporality of existence from the transtemporal fixation of thought. Yet is not the effect of this transcendentalization with all that goes with it—the import of faith, the reading of ciphers, the sense of historicity—none other than that ostensibly there is no effect at all? All remains as it has been, each has his own belief, each goes his own way.

It may also seem that the acceptability of Jaspers's conception of the possibility of metaphysics is questionable. It may well be imagined that for many philosophers concerned over this problem its professed virtues are its vices. It upholds the significance of metaphysics against positivism but denies it the objectivity of the sciences. It directs itself against mystical and authoritative resolutions of ultimate questions, insists on the all-pervasiveness of critical thought, yet it speaks of philosophical faith and takes from it the certainty which the religious believer enjoys. It makes metaphysical thought a matter of individual risk, denies its aim of universal agreement and takes from it the promise of a community of the likeminded. Instead it offers the notion of metaphysics as a struggle for truth and only asks that it be a loving struggle.

The possibility of a metaphysics capable of commanding both free and universal assent is remote, even utopian. But it should not be discounted. What it would be like can hardly be imagined. Per-

haps a way of thought can be devised which can again dispense
with the rift of scientific and ultimate concerns, and the related
distinctions between appearance and reality, the 'is' and the
'ought', immanence and transcendence.

But perhaps the strongest challenge to Jaspers is existential. It is
his conception of man that gives his philosophy the special vigor
which no doubt affects even the most critical reader of Jaspers.
But before we are carried away, if we follow Jaspers's conception
of man, are we not saddled with an overwhelming burden, the
burden of freedom, the burden of reason, the burden of historicity?

At the heart of Jaspers's philosophy of man is the illumination
of possible Existenz, not 'knowledge' but 'illumination' of, not
'Existenz' but 'possible Existenz'. This means that what man is in
his becoming is more than what can be known about man and is
actual beyond his knowledge. It also means that with reference to
existential actuality we can only sketch out possibilities, we cannot adumbrate or characterize that which is in the vicissitudes of
time and by virtue of the spontaneity of freedom. Where Jaspers
speaks of man he speaks of man in his possibility vis-à-vis his cognitive and existential actuality. He speaks of man as he ought to
be, as he might be, as he can be, not as he is.

Thus Jaspers speaks of the possibility of freedom, of the originality of man's essential being regarded as self, of the decisiveness
of his choice, of the consequentialness of his action, of the responsibility of his agency, of the earnestness of guilt.

Thus Jaspers speaks of the possibility of man's assurance of the
transcendent grounding of his wholeness without determinative,
cognitive certainty, beyond divisive and self-destructive objectification.

Thus Jaspers speaks of the possibility of the realization of eternal validity in time and not beyond time, of redemption within
man's decisive action in time's moment and not in the hope of
grace that is enacted without man's freedom, of the grace of man's
temporal being and not of his salvation at the end of time.

In consideration of this look towards possibility, man's actuality
is measured, becomes a project, indeterminate in its being ongoing,
and man himself the task and the taskmaster, and indeterminate
finitude. "Man is imperfectible," we read in Jaspers. This is said
with reference to man's finitude. But does it not also mean that
man is not perfect, not finished as he is, that man is itinerant on
the road to perfection, that we cannot set any limits to what constitutes man's completion, that however man finds himself, whatever he accomplishes and as what he realizes himself there is
always new time, there are always new tasks, higher visions, deeper

chasms between what is done and what might be done, that what may yet be possible for man is beyond his vision, and what he is is perennially short of what he can be?

What is the import of holding the mirror of the possibility of freedom to man in his actuality? That man has been called to something higher, truer, better, that man has discovered within himself the lure of ultimate truth and for himself the call to its service, this is not new. But in Jaspers we are reminded of this without promises, without guarantees. All enactment is at our own risk whose outcome is shipwreck in which alone lies the chance of our assurance of the transcendent meaningfulness of an itinerary whose origin and goal lie hidden. There is no trace here of Faustian storming of the gates of revelation. To Mephistophles's mockery:

> Möchte selbst solch einen Herrn kennen:
> Würd ihn Herrn Mikrokosmus nennen,*[12]

Faust states his central question:

> Was bin ich denn, wenn es nicht möglich ist,
> Der Menschheit Krone zu erringen,
> Nach der sich alle Sinne dringen?†[13]

This is the Faust who shortly before expressed in his famous curse the ultimate anguish of a shipwrecked search for 'mankind's crown', which is to glimpse, to see himself as one with the creative force of the 'infinite':

> So fluch ich allem, was die Seele
> Mit Lock-und Gaukelwerk umspannt
> Und sie in diese Trauerhöhle
> Mit Blend- und Schmeichelkräften bannt!
> Verflucht voraus die hohe Meinung,
> Womit der Geist sich selbst umfängt!‡[14]

Where the effort of the search is unrequited, there the virtues which sustain the effort become themselves a burden:

---

*Such a person—*I'd* like to meet him; 'Mr. Microcosm' is how I'd greet him (MacNeice translation [New York: Oxford University Press, 1960], p. 62).
†"What am I then, if it is impossible to attain the crown of humanity toward which all my senses strain?" (my translation).
‡I now curse all things that encompass
  The soul with lures and jugglery
  And bind it in this dungeon of grief
  With trickery and flattery.
  Cursed in advance be the high opinion
  That serves our spirit for a cloak! (MacNeice translation, p. 56).

> Fluch sei der Hoffnung! Fluch dem Glauben,
> Und Fluch vor allen der Geduld!*[15]

As long as the shipwrecked striving for the 'crown of humanity' is thought to imply the curse then the answer to Faust's question is:

> Du bist am Ende—was du bist.†[16]

This cold piece of factuality is given by Mephistopheles. But it might also be offered by the minister to souls. Neither considers striving for "nearness" to the "infinite"—this is for Faust the "crown of humanity"—a proper pursuit for man; the former because mankind is "that little world of fools," the latter because it is overweaning. The former offers man the distraction of earthly delights; the latter, mediation.

There is none of this in Jaspers. Man is not flung back to what he is. And the shipwreck experienced in man's reach for the 'crown of humanity' does not lead to a curse of the motives arising from the 'spirit's' 'high opinions', of 'hope', 'faith', and 'patience'. For Jaspers the 'nearness to infinity' lies in free activity in the finitude of time, lies precisely in 'patience', in 'endurance' of man's finitude.

But there is power in Mephistopheles's answer, "You are in the end . . . what you are," a power that extends beyond its austere factuality. This answer expresses what is also adumbrated in Faust's curse, that freedom is an unbearable burden, that to call man beyond his finitude, beyond his actuality, is an imposition. The weightiest criticism that can be levelled against Jaspers is that tackling the question of man, not by restriction to a look at man's actuality but by the illumination of the possibilities for man, leads to excessive expectations of man. In this way the philosophy of man—the heart of Jaspers's thought—may show itself as unrealistic and may be regarded as being false. Accordingly, criticisms such as the following might be advanced.

Man in his finitude incurs guilt. But man becomes himself by taking on the burden of guilt, and the extent of his redemption lies in what difference the recognition of his guilt can make in the ever new challenges to his freedom. This is held up to us, by Jaspers, as the measure of man. But can one live with this? Is it not more cogent to follow the realistic view that man is delivered, on the one hand to the forces which make the incursion of guilt in-

---

*A curse on hope! A curse on faith!
  And a curse on patience most of all! (Ibid.).
†"You are in the end—what you are" (my translation).

evitable, on the other to the forces by which he may be redeemed of his guilt. Man is what he is, and he becomes what he must become. To live under the supposition that man is essentially involved in the incursion of and redemption from his guilt does not enhance but destroys life.

Is it not an exaction to expect to live believing that grace may consist of the gift of freedom? How can a being that is finite, that can imagine but can hardly see beyond the next moment, much less see the import of his actions, live as if he participated in the determination of the eternal validity of his actions and of his destiny?

Is it not an exaction to live believing that there can be dignity for man, that man can be related to the ground of his meaningfulness without some form of mediation? The power and authority of churches, and more tellingly the submission and deference thereto, particularly on the part of untold multitudes of worthy people throughout the ages for whom the alternative of independence has been and is available and a live option, speak against the need for and possibility of the immediacy of the risk of personal freedom for man's dignity.

Is it not an exaction to expect man to live by enacting assurance of the meaning of existence, without knowledge or revelation or mysticism or authority? The mainstream of mankind has eschewed the risks of uncertainty by virtue of the evidence of miracles, the cogency of proofs, the perpetuation of traditions, the guarantee of dogmas, the experience of ecstasy, the reception of theophany, the comfort of the confirmed and the familiar, the admonitions of the ascendant, the soothsaying of the consecrated. Against such reality what is the lure of freedom, with its restless, never-ending round of confirming truth by ever new search for sources of strength!

Is it not an exaction to expect man to live with the idea that true community is so essentially a matter of the communicative commitment of the multitude of individuals, that tutelage and specific, publicly agreed and promulgated regulation are merely the framework but not of the essence? Almost everything speaks against community conceived in this way. Man neither expects nor grants to fellow man the sort of dignity that this presupposes. Neither is man prepared nor able to live in any way that is not primarily a matter of tutelage and regulation. Man, in fact, prefers the authority of law and leaders to the uncertainty, the effort, the risks and the chaos of freedom whether in his own person or that of fellow man. The impulse of freedom is a danger, not only to others but to oneself. It is destructive of, and does not promise the fulfillment of man as we know him.

Is it not indeed remarkable to hear a philosopher in all seriousness challenge each and every man to become himself, to live as if all had not yet been determined, to do as if what counts may depend on him, to regard himself as the essentially participating instrument of truth, goodness, justice, to consider that every moment counts, that any situation may require the utmost, all the while not to be sure of any of this but to believe and enact it out of his own resources on the chance that it may be true, and with the consciousness that in case it is true he must not fail, and since it may be true he must live with the burden of having failed. The overburdening immensity of this exaction can be seen by comparing Jaspers with Nietzsche. Nietzsche measures man as he is against the Übermensch, 'superman'. Nietzsche does not doubt the coming of the superman. But superman—the being who like a 'lion' creates out of his own willing, and like a 'child' is ever a new beginning—is not a model for man, not a goad for man. Rather, superman is an overcoming of man, and man a mere "bridge" on the way to the coming of superman. The coming of superman is not a matter of man reaching his measure; man cannot become superman. The purpose of man, even of 'higher man', is to pave the way for the coming of superman. It is different in Jaspers. When he says that man is finite and imperfectible, he does not mean that what we propose as the measure of man exceeds man in such a way that he is condemned to be and must content himself with being the mere bridge to such a higher realization of freedom. Jaspers means rather that when it comes to the tasks of freedom we can never set man's goals so high that it exceeds his possibility, nor is man's actualization so profound that no higher goals are possible.

What is man, Jaspers asks? And he answers, man is what can be known of him, the actualities of his psycho-physical nature, the works of the spirit, the discipline of his intellect. This is real and indispensable, but it is not all. What man is essentially is his Existenz, and the possibilities of his Existenz. This we cannot know, but we can illuminate it. Against the lure of possibility the realist can uphold a conception of the life of man and structure it in accordance with observed actualities, as we have seen. Human reality seems to give the lie to Jaspers. Do we recognize ourselves as possible Existenzen, do we accept the travails of freedom as our own task, can we carry the burden of guilt, can we take on the risk of faith beyond the certainty of knowledge and the guarantee of dogma, do we dare and do we have the courage to testify, by means of our actions, to the truth of our beliefs without gainsaying that of the other's to which he testifies at his own risk?

In such questions lies the thrust of the most significant criticism that can be levelled against Jaspers, and the import of the communicative aspect of his work which otherwise is nothing other than the confession of a mind. What does it mean to criticize Jaspers? The same as it means to follow Jaspers: to show what one believes, in Jaspers's sense of 'faith'.

Appendix One

Jaspers's Books and Monographs

Note: Where there have been several editions of a work, the latest is cited at the end of the entry.

A. In German

1. *Allgemeine Psychopathologie: Ein Leitfaden fur Studierende, Ärzte und Psychologen.* Berlin: Springer Verlag, 1913.
2. *Allgemeine Psychopathologie.* 2nd rev. ed. Berlin: Springer Verlag, 1920.
3. *Allgemeine Psychopathologie.* 3rd augmented and improved ed. Berlin: Springer Verlag, 1923.
4. *Allgemeine Psychopatholgie.* 4th completely rev. ed. Berlin, Göttingen, Heidelberg: Springer Verlag, 1946. 8th ed., 1965.
5. "Zur Analyse der Trugwahrnehmungen (Leibhaftigkeit und Realitäts-urteil)." *Zeitschrift für die gesammte Neurologie und Psychiatrie, Origi-nalien* 6:460—535. (Also published in item 17.)
6. *Aneignung und Polemik: Gesammelte Reden und Aufsätze zur Geschichte der Philosophie.* Edited by Hans Saner. Munich: R. Piper & Co., 1968.
7. *Antwort: Zur Kritik Meiner Schrift "Wohin treibt die Bundesrepublik?"* Munich: R. Piper & Co., 1967.
8. *Die Atombombe und die Zukunft des Menschen: Politisches Bewusstsein unserer Zeit.* Munich: R. Piper & Co., 1958. 5th ed., 1962.
9. *Chiffren der Transzendenz.* Edited by Hans Saner. Munich: R. Piper & Co., 1970.
10. *Descartes und die Philosophie.* Berlin: W. de Gruyter & Co., 1937. 4th ed., 1966.
11. "Eifersuchtswahn: Ein Beitrag zur Frage: 'Entwicklung einer Persönlich-keit' odor 'Prozess'?" *Zeitschrift für die gesammte Neurologie und Psy-chiatrie, Originalien* 1: 567—637. (Also published in item 17.)
12. *Einführung in die Philosophie: Zwölf Radiovorträge.* Zurich: Artemis Verlag, 1950 and Munich, R. Piper & Co., 1953. 10th ed., Munich, 1965.
13. *Existenzphilosophie: Drei Vorlesungen.* Berlin: W. de Gruyter & Co., 1938. 3rd ed., 1964.
14. *Die Frage der Entmythologisierung* (with contributions by Jaspers and Rudolf Bultmann). Munich: R. Piper & Co., 1954.
15. *Freiheit und Wiedervereinigung.* Munich: R. Piper & Co., 1960. (Also published in item 20).
16. *Die geistige Situation der Zeit.* Berlin: W. de Gruyter & Co., 1931. 11th ed. 1965.
17. *Gesammelte Schriften zur Psychopathologie.* Berlin, Göttingen, Heidel-berg: Springer Verlag, 1963.
18. *Die Grossen Philosophen: Erster Band, Die massgebenden Menschen: Sokrates, Buddha, Konfuzius, Jesus; Die fortzeugenden Gründer des Philo-*

sophierens: Plato, Augustin, Kant; Aus dem Ursprung denkende Meta-physiker: Anaximander, Heraklit, Parmenides, Plotin, Anselm, Spinoza, Laotse, Nagarjuna. Munich: R. Piper & Co., 1957.

19. "Heimweh und Verbrechen." *Gross' Archiv für krim.-Anthropol.* 35, no. 1: 1 ff. (Also published in item 17.)

20. *Hoffnung und Sorge: Schriften zur deutschen Politik, 1945-1965.* Munich: R. Piper & Co., 1965.

21. *Die Idee der Universität.* Berlin: Springer Verlag, 1923.

22. *Die Idee der Universität* (Not the same as item 21). Berlin, Heidelberg: Springer Verlag, 1946.

23. *Die Idee der Universität* (Not the same as items 21 or 22; written in conjunction with K. Rossmann). Berlin, Göttingen, Heidelberg: Springer Verlag, 1961.

24. "Kausale und 'verständliche' Zusammenhänge zwischen Schicksal und Psychose bei der Dementia praecox (Schizophrenie)." *Zeitschrift für die gesammte Neurologie und Psychiatrie, Originalien* 14: 158-263. (Also published in item 17.)

25. *Kleine Schule des philosophischen Denkens.* Munich: R. Piper & Co., 1965. 3rd ed., 1969.

26. *Lionardo als Philosoph.* Bern: A. Francke A. G., 1953. (Also published in items 6 and 34.)

27. *Max Weber: Politiker-Forscher-Philosoph.* Oldenburg: Stolling, 1932. 3rd ed., Munich: R. Piper & Co., 1958. (Also published in item 6.)

28. "Die Methoden der Intelligenzprüfung und der Begriff der Demenz: Kritisches Referat." *Zeitschrift für die gesammte Neurologie und Psychiatrie, Referate und Ergebnisse* 1: 402-52. (Also published in item 17.)

29. *Nietzsche: Einführung in das Verständnis seines Philosophierens.* Berlin: W. de Gruyter & Co., 1936. 3rd ed., 1950.

30. *Nietzsche und das Christentum.* Hameln: Bücherstube Seifert [1946] and Munich: R. Piper & Co., 1952. (Also published in item 6.)

31. *Nikolaus Cusanus.* Munich: R. Piper & Co., 1964.

32. a. *Philosophie.* Vol. I, *Philosophische Weltorientierung.*
    b. *Philosophie.* Vol. II, *Existenzerhellung.*
    c. *Philosophie.* Vol. III, *Metaphysik.*
Berlin: Springer Verlag, 1932.

33. *Philosophie.* 3 vols. 3rd ed. with a "Nachwort" in vol. I. Berlin, Göttingen, Heidelberg: Springer Verlag, 1956.

34. *Philosophie und Welt: Reden und Aufsätze.* Munich: R. Piper & Co., 1958. 2nd ed., 1963.

35. "Philosophische Autobiographie." In *Karl Jaspers,* ed. P. A. Schilpp. Stuttgart: Kohlhammer, 1957. (Also published in item 34.)

36. "Der philosophische Glaube angesichts der christlichen Offenbarung." In *Philosophie und christliche Existenz: Festschrift für Heinrich Barth,* ed. G. Huber. Basel, Stuttgart: Verlag Helbing & Lichtenhahn, 1960.

37. *Der philosophische Glaube angesichts der Offenbarung.* Munich: R. Piper & Co., 1962. 2nd ed., 1963.

38. *Der philosophische Glaube: Gastvorlesungen.* Zurich: Artemis Verlag, 1948 and Munich: R. Piper & Co., 1948. 5th ed., Munich: R. Piper & Co., 1963.

39. *Provokationen: Gespräche und Interviews.* Edited by Hans Saner. Munich: R. Piper & Co., 1969.

40. *Psychologie der Weltanschauungen.* Berlin: Springer Verlag, 1919. 5th ed., Berlin, Göttingen, Heidelberg: Springer Verlag, 1960.
41. *Rechenschaft und Ausblick: Reden und Aufsätze.* Munich: R. Piper & Co., 1951. 2nd ed. 1958.
42. *Schelling: Grösse und Verhängnis.* Munich: R. Piper & Co., 1955.
43. *Schicksal und Wille: Autobiographische Schriften.* Edited by Hans Saner. Munich: R. Piper & Co., 1967.
44. *Die Schuldfrage.* Heidelberg: L. Schneider Verlag, 1946 and Zurich: Artemis Verlag, 1946. (Also published in item 20.)
45. *Strindberg und van Gogh: Versuch einer pathographischen Analyse unter vergleichender Heranziehung von Swedenborg und Hölderlin.* Bern: Bincher, 1922. 3rd ed., Munich: R. Piper & Co., 1951.
46. "Die Trugwahrnehmungen." *Zeitschrift für die gesammte Neurologie und Psychologie, Referate und Ergebnisse* 4: 289–354. (Also published in item 17.)
47. *Vernunft und Existenz: Fünf Vorlesungen.* Groningen: J. B. Wolters, 1935. 4th ed., Munich: R. Piper & Co., 1960.
48. *Vernunft und Widervernunft in unserer Zeit: Drei Gastvorlesungen.* Munich: R. Piper & Co., 1950. 2nd ed., 1952.
49. *Vom europäischem Geist.* Munich: R. Piper & Co., 1947. Appeared originally in French translation by J. Hersch. *L'Espirit européen.* Paris: La presse française et étrangère, O. Zeluck, 1946.
50. *Vom Ursprung und Ziel der Geschichte.* Zurich: Artemis Verlag, 1949 and Munich: R. Piper & Co., 1949. 4th ed., Munich, 1963.
51. *Von der Wahrheit: Philosophische Logik, Erster Band.* Munich: R. Piper & Co., 1947. 2nd. ed., 1958.
52. *Wohin treibt die Bundesrepublik? Tatsachen-Gefahren-Chancen.* Munich: R. Piper & Co., 1966.

B. In English Translation

53. *The European Spirit.* Translated by R. G. Smith. London: SCM Press, 1948 and New York, 1949. (Translation of item 49.)
54. *The Future of Mankind.* Translated by E. B. Ashton. Chicago: University of Chicago Press, 1961. (Translation of item 8.)
55. *General Psychopathology.* Translated by J. Hoening and M. W. Hamilton. Chicago: University of Chicago Press, 1963. (Translation of item 4.)
56. *The Great Philosophers: The Foundations, The Paradigmatic Individuals: Socrates, Buddha, Confucius, Jesus; The Seminal Founders of Philosophical Thought: Plato, Augustine, Kant.* Edited by H. Arendt. Translated by R. Manheim. New York: Harcourt, Brace & World, 1962. (Translation of part of item 18.)
57. *The Great Philosophers: The Original Thinkers: Anaximander, Heraclitus, Parmenides, Plotinus, Anselm, Nicholas of Cusa, Spinoza, Lao-Tzu, Nagarjuna.* Edited by H. Arendt. Translated by R. Manheim. New York: Harcourt, Brace & World, 1966. (Translation of part of item 18 and of item 31.)

58. *The Idea of the University.* Edited by K. W. Deutsch. Translated by H. A. T. Reiche and H. F. Vanderschmidt. Boston: Beacon Press, 1959 and London: P. Owen, 1960. (Translation of item 22.)

59. *Kant.* New York: Harcourt, Brace and World, n.d. (Excerpt from item 56.)

60. *Man in the Modern Age.* Translated by E. Paul and C. Paul. London: Routledge & Kegan Paul, 1953; New York: Henry Holt & Co., 1933; and New York: Doubleday & Co., 1957. (Translation of item 16, 5th ed.)

61. *Myth and Christianity.* New York: Noonday Press, 1958. (Translation of item 14.)

62. *Nietzsche and Christianity.* Translated by E. B. Ashton. Chicago: Henry Regnery Co., 1961. (Translation of item 30.)

63. *Nietzsche: An Introduction to the Understanding of His Philosophical Activity.* Translated by C. F. Wallraff and F. J. Schmitz. Tucson: University of Arizona Press, 1965. (Translation of item 29.)

64. *The Origin and Goal of History.* Translated by M. Bullock. New Haven: Yale University Press, and London: Routledge and Kegan Paul, 1953. (Translation of item 50.)

65. *The Perennial Scope of Philosophy.* Translated by R. Manheim. New York: Philosophical Library, 1949 and London: Routledge & Kegan Paul, 1950. (Translation of item 38.)

66. *Philosophical Faith and Revelation.* Translated by E. B. Ashton. Chicago: University of Chicago Press, 1967. (Translation of item 37.)

67. *Philosophy.* 3 vols. Translated by E. B. Ashton. Chicago and London: University of Chicago Press, 1969–71. (Translation of item 33.)

68. *Philosophy and The World: Selected Essays and Lectures.* Translated by E. B. Ashton. Chicago: Henry Regnery Co., 1963. (Translation of item 34.)

69. *Philosophy is for Everyman: A Short Course in Philosophical Thinking.* Translated by R. F. C. Hull and G. Wels. New York: Harcourt, Brace & World, 1967. (Translation of item 25.)

70. *Philosophy of Existence.* Translated by R. F. Grabau. Philadelphia: University of Pennsylvania Press, 1971. (Translation of item 13, 3rd ed.)

71. *Plato and Augustine.* New York: Harcourt, Brace & World, n.d. (Excerpt from item 56.)

72. *The Question of German Guilt.* Translated by E. B. Ashton. New York: Dial Press, 1947. (Translation of item 44.)

73. *Reason and Anti-Reason in our Time.* Translated by S. Goodman. New Haven: Yale University Press, and London: SCM Press, 1952. (Translation of item 48.)

74. *Reason and Existenz.* Translated by W. Earle. London, Toronto, and New York, 1955. (Translation of item 47, 3rd ed.)

75. *Socrates, Buddha, Confucius, Jesus.* New York: Harcourt, Brace & World, n.d. (Excerpt from item 56.)

76. *Three Essays: Leonardo, Descartes, Max Weber.* Translated by R. Manheim. New York: Harcourt, Brace & World, 1964. (Translation of items 26, 10, and 27, 3rd ed.)

77. *Tragedy is not Enough.* Translated by H. A. T. Reiche, H. T. Moore, and K. W. Deutsch. Boston: Beacon Press, 1952 and London: V. Gollancz, 1953. (Translation of excerpt from item 51.)

78. *Truth and Symbol.* Translated by J. T. Wilde, W. Kluback, W. Kimmel. New York: Twayne Publishers, and London: Vision Press, 1959. (Translation of excerpt from item 51.)

79. *Way to Wisdom.* Translated by R. Manheim. London, Toronto, and New Haven, 1951. (Translation of item 12.)

C. Chronological List

1909 "Heimweh und Verbrechen"
1910 "Eifersuchtswahn"
1910 "Die Methoden der Intelligenzprüfung und der Begriff der Demenz"
1911 "Zur Analyse der Trugwahrnehmungen"
1912 "Die Trugwahrnehmungen"
1913 "Kausale und 'verständliche' Zusammenhänge zwischen Schicksal und Psychose bei der Dementia praecox (Schizophrenie)"
1913 *Allgemeine Psychopathologie*
1919 *Psychologie der Weltanschauungen*
1922 *Strindberg und van Gogh*
1923 *Die Idee der Universität*
1931 *Die geistige Situation der Zeit*
1932 *Philosophie* (3 vols.)
1933 *Max Weber: Politiker-Forscher-Philosoph*
1935 *Vernunft und Existenz*
1936 *Nietzsche: Einführung in das Verständnis seines Philosophierens*
1937 *Descartes und die Philosophie*
1938 *Existenzphilosophie*
1946 *Allgemeine Psychopathologie* (4th ed.)
1946 *Die Idee der Universität* (2nd version)
1946 *Nietzsche und das Christentum*
1946 *Die Schuldfrage*
1947 *Vom europäischen Geist*
1947 *Von der Wahrheit*
1948 *Der philosophische Glaube*
1949 *Vom Ursprung und Ziel der Geschichte*
1950 *Einführung in die Philosophie*
1950 *Vernunft und Widervernunft in unserer Zeit*
1951 *Rechenschaft und Ausblick*
1953 *Lionardo als Philosoph*
1954 *Die Frage der Entmythologisierung*
1955 *Schelling: Grösse und Verhängnis*
1957 *Die Grossen Philosophen: Erster Band*
1957 "Philosophische Autobiographie"
1958 *Die Atombombe und die Zukunft*
1960 *Freiheit und Wiedervereinigung*
1960 "Der philosophische Glaube angesichts der christlichen Offenbarung"
1961 *Die Idee der Universität* (3rd version; together with K. Rossmann)
1962 *Der philosophische Glaube angesichts der Offenbarung*
1963 *Gesammelte Schriften zur Psychopathologie*
1964 *Nikolaus Cusanus*
1965 *Kleine Schule des philosophischen Denkens*
1965 *Hoffnung und Sorge*
1966 *Wohin treibt die Bundesrepublik?*
1967 *Antwort: Zur Kritik meiner Schrift* "Wohin treibt die Bundesrepublik?"
1967 *Schicksal und Wille*
1968 *Aneignung und Polemik.*
1969 *Provokationen*
1970 *Chiffren der Transzendenz*

Appendix Two

Abbreviations of Frequent References

Note: The numbers in parentheses following the titles refer to Appendix 1.

An & Pol	*Aneignung und Polemik* (6)		
Atom	*Die Atombombe und die Zukunft des Menschen* (8)	*Mankind*	*The Future of Mankind* (54)
Chiffren	*Chiffren der Transzendenz* (9)		
Descartes	*Descartes und die Philosophie* (10)		
Einführung	*Einführung in die Philosophie.* Zurich, 1950 (12)	*Wisdom*	*Way to Wisdom* (79)
Entmyth	*Die Frage der Entmythologisierung* (14)	*Myth*	*Myth and Christianity* (61)
Gr Ph	*Die Grossen Philosophen* (18)	*Gr Ph* I	*The Great Philosophers.* Vol. I (56)
		Gr Ph II	*The Great Philosophers.* Vol. II (57)
Kleine Schule	*Kleine Schule des philosophischen Denkens* (25)	*Everyman*	*Philosophy is for Everyman* (69)
Nietzsche	*Nietzsche: Einführung in das Verständnis seines Philosophierens* (29)	*Nietzsche*	*Nietzsche: An Introduction to the Understanding of his Philosophical Activity* (62)
Ph I	*Philosophie.* 3rd ed. Vol. I (33)	*Ph* I	*Philosophy.* Vol. I (67)
Ph II	*Philosophie.* Vol. II (33)	*Ph* II	*Philosophy.* Vol. II (67)
Ph III	*Philosophie.* Vol. III (33)	*Ph* III	*Philosophy.* Vol. III (67)
Ph & W	*Philosophie und Welt* (34)	*Ph & W*	*Philosophy and the World* (68)
Ph Gl	*Der Philosophische Glaube.* Zurich, 1948 (36)	*Scope*	*The Perennial Scope of Philosophy* (65)

Ph Gl Off	*Der Philosophische Glaube angesichts der Offenbarung* (38)	*Ph F Rev*	*Philosophical Faith and Revelation* (66)
Ps WA	*Psychologie der Weltanschauungen* (40)		
R & A	*Rechenschaft und Ausblick* (41)		
Sch & W	*Schicksal und Wille* (43)		
Schilpp: *Jaspers*	P. A. Schilpp, ed., *Karl Jaspers.* Stuttgart: Kohlhammer, 1957	Schilpp: *Jaspers*	P. A. Schilpp, ed., *The Philosophy of Karl Jaspers.* New York: Tudor Publishing Co., 1957
		Three Essays	*Three Essays: Leonardo, Descartes, Max Weber* (76)
U Z Gesch	*Vom Ursprung und Ziel der Geschichte* (50)	*History*	*The Origin and Goal of History* (64)
Vn & Wvn	*Vernunft und Widervernunft in unserer Zeit* (48)	*Rea & Anti*	*Reason and Anti-Reason in Our Time* (73)
W	*Von der Wahrheit* (51)		

Notes

Reference to most of Jaspers's books are made by means of the abbreviations indicated in Appendix 2, followed by the page or chapter number. In references to both the original and the English translation the former will precede the latter and they will be separated by means of '/'; for example: "*An & Pol, 425/Three Essays, 189*" means "*Aneignung und Polemik*, p. 425; in English: *Three Essays*, p. 189." Another example: "*Ph*, I, 321/319" means: "*Philosophie*, vol. I, p. 321; in English: *Philosophy*, vol. I, p. 319." References to Schilpp, *Jaspers* will be made in a similar manner regardless of whether they are to Jaspers's contributions to this volume or to the contributions of other authors.

Notes to Introduction

1. See H. A. Wolfson, *The Philosophy of the Church Fathers*, vol. I, *Faith, Trinity, Incarnation* (Cambridge, Massachusetts: Harvard University Press, 1956), chapter on "Faith and Reason"; and idem, *Religious Philosophy* (New York: Atheneum Publishers, 1965), pp. 106 ff.
2. In English translation these lectures have been published under the title *The Perennial Scope of Philosophy* (see Appendix 1, item 65).
3. The English translation appeared under the title *Philosophical Faith and Revelation* (see Appendix 1, item 66).
4. Schilpp, *Jaspers*, 63/77. My translation.

Notes to Chapter 1

1. *W*, 915.
2. *Ph*, I, 34/73.
3. *W*, 915.
4. *Einführung*, 84/*Wisdom*,89.
5. *Einführung*, 85/*Wisdom*, 89–90. Italics and variant translation are mine.
6. *U Z Gesch*, 273/*History*, 213.
7. *Ph Gl*, 10/*Scope*,10.
8. *W*, 676.
9. *W*, 675.
10. *W*, 676.

11. *W*, 675–76.

12. Ibid.

13. *Ph*, I, 303/304. My translation of: "Was ich beweisen kann, das brauche ich nicht noch zu glauben. Wenn ich den Glaubensinhalt als objektive Gewissheit suche, habe ich meinen Glauben schon verloren." Ashton's translation is not quite correct: "What I can prove I need not believe any more. If I seek objective assurance about a tenet of faith, I have already lost my faith."

14. *Ph*, I, 304/304.

15. Dieter Henrich is right in pointing out that it is not in accordance with the concept of 'antinomy' and with Kant's use thereof to speak of his paradoxes as "antinomies." He also doubts that this misuse is reversible. See his *Der Ontologische Gottesbeweis* (Tübingen: Mohr, 1960), p. 153.

16. This distinction—between 'faith in something' and 'faith as which it exists'—which is traditional in Christian theology, is discussed at several points in Jaspers's works; e.g., *Ph*, II, 280–81/244–45; *Ph Gl Off*, 49/*Ph F Rev*, 18.

17. *Ph*, I, 304–5/304–5.

18. See *Ph*, II, 281–82/245–46.

19. The use of 'intellect' has to be understood in the following context. All thought is determinative by virtue of the forms of thought which are explored in formal sciences such as logic and the theory of knowledge. Jaspers, like Kant, calls this 'consciousness as such'. Some human thinking fulfills the requirements of the universal forms of thought, for other human thought the forms of thought are as inadequate as they are unavoidable. Instances of the former are scientific knowledge and everyday experience. It is this that Kant and Jaspers call 'Verstand', and Locke and Hume, for example, the 'understanding'. However, 'understanding' has too many uses, particularly when speaking of Jaspers in the English language. To avoid confusion I use 'intellect' where Jaspers speaks of 'Verstand' or equivalent German expressions. There are precedents for this use of 'intellect', not the least significant the meaning of 'intellectus' among medieval thinkers such as Thomas Aquinas and Anselm. Anselm's use of 'intellectus' is exemplified in the well-known phrase 'fides quaerens intellectum'.

20. See especially the section "Handeln in der Welt" in *Ph*, II, 329 ff./286 ff.

21. For example, in the United States the conflict between the duty of military service and a person's "conscientious objection" against bearing arms is generally and even officially recognized, and is usually resolved by releasing the person from the kind of service which is connected with the bearing of arms.

22. *Ph*, II, 331/288.

23. *Ph*, II, 330/287. My translation; my italics.

24. *Ph*, II, 331/288. My variant translation.

25. *Ph*, II, 331/288. Ashton seems to misunderstand the relation between the rule of law and existential commitment, as can be seen by his erroneous translation of the passage: "Allgemein ist nur das Gesetz der Gesetzlichkeit überhaupt als die Forderung, seine jeweilige Unbedingtheit im Gesetz zu verstehen." Ashton understands this to say: "Only the law of legality at large, the demand that my unconditionality of the moment be understood in the form of a law, is general." Actually Jaspers is saying the following: "Only the law of the rule of law as such is universal [i.e., the law of rule of law], regarded as the demand to understand one's particular unconditionality within the framework of law." (The bracketed repetition is provided for the purpose

of clarity). Ashton translates "jeweilig" as "of the moment"—rather than as the concept opposed to "allgemein," i.e., "universal." Moreover, he translates "im Gesetz" as "in the form of the law"—rather than as the demand of the law in its sovereignty to place the particularity of unconditionality within itself. As a result, he has Jaspers say that the law of the rule of law is nothing other than a mask behind which a hypocrite may hide by having his shifting, capricious interests parade as the conformance to law.

26. *Ph*, II, 282/246.

27. *Ph*, I, 305/305. My variant translation.

28. Ibid.

29. See F. Buri's contribution to *Kerygma und Mythos*, vol. III, ed. H. W. Bartsch (Hamburg-Volksdorf: Reich, 1952), pp. 83–91.

30. *Ph*, I, 307/307. My variant translation.

31. *Einführung*, 138/*Wisdom*, 169. My variant translation.

32. *Ph*, I, 141 ff./167 ff.

33. See *Ph*, I, 142–43/168.

34. *Ph*, I, 143/168. My variant translation.

35. *Ph*, I, 143–44/169.

36. *Ph*, I, 144–45/170. My translation of the following:
sapere aude, eine Unbedingheit des Wissenwollens, die sich doch aus der Richtigkeitsgeltung nicht herleiten kann. Das ursprüngliche Wissenwollen ist Wagnis, weil es die Gefahr der Verzweiflung im Gefolge hat.
In Ashton's translation I find particularly the confusion of 'unconditionality' and 'absoluteness' unacceptable:
sapere aude, an absoluteness of the will to know that cannot come from a validity of the accurate. The original will to know is a hazardous venture because it involves the risk of despair.

37. *Ph*, I, 144/169. My variant translation.

38. *Ph*, I, 246–47/255–56.

39. *Ph*, II, 281/245. See also *Ph*, I, 40–41/79–80.

40. *Ph*, II, 281/245.

41. *Ph*, I, 247/256.

42. I. Kant, *Critique of Pure Reason*, B xxx. My translation.

43. *Critique of Pure Reason*, A vii. Kemp-Smith translation.

44. Op. cit., B. xx. Kemp-Smith translation.

45. Op. cit., B xxi. Kemp-Smith translation.

46. *W*, 725.

47. Ibid.

48. Quoted in Jaspers's *Nietzsche*, 211–12/210; this passage appears in Nietzsche's *Human, All-Too-Human*, pt. II, sec. 1, no. 20.

49. Op. cit., 213/211.

50. Op. cit., 234/228. 'Historical' and 'historic' are used differently in this book. 'Historical' is correlative with the noun 'history', meaning the course, the account and the interpretation of events; it corresponds to the German 'Geschichte'. 'Historic', on the other hand, is correlative with the noun 'historicity', in German 'Geschichtlichkeit', meaning the circumstance that realities transcending the temporality of events—such as ideas, purposes, selfhood—become actual only in time and by virtue of deliberate human activity.

51. *Ph Gl Off*, 141 ff./*Ph F Rev*, 83 ff.

52. *W*, 729 ff.

53. *W*, 743.

54. *Ph Gl Off*, 144/*Ph F Rev*, 85–86. My variant translation.

55. *Ph Gl Off*, 144/*Ph F Rev*, 86. My variant translation.

56. Gabriel Marcel, *The Mystery of Being*, vol. II, *Faith and Reality* (Chicago: Henry Regnery Co., 1960), pp. 77–79.

57. Ibid., 86.

58. Ibid., 87.

59. Ibid., 88.

60. *Ph*, I, 133–34/160.

61. *Ph*, II, 261–62/228–29.

62. *W*, 532.

63. *Ph*, II, 262/229.

64. Ibid.

65. *W*, 954.

66. See *W*, 936 ff.; the quoted phrase appears on p. 943.

67. *Ph*, II, 262/229.

68. *Ph*, II, 191/167 and 183–84/160–61.

69. *Ph*, II, 263/230.

70. Ibid.

71. *Ph*, I, 54/91.

72. *Ph*, I, 323/320. My variant translation.

73. *Ph Gl Off*, 423/*Ph F Rev*, 281.

74. See *Ph Gl Off*, 423/*Ph F Rev*, 281; and *Ph*, III, 234–35/206–7.

75. *Ph*, II, 263/230.

76. *Ph*, I, 234/244. See also *Ph*, I, 218/231; *W*, 463–64.; and *Ph Gl Off*, 283–84/*Ph F Rev*, 184 ff.

Notes to Chapter 2

1. *Ph*, I, 246/255.

2. *Ph*, I, 247 ff./256 ff.

3. *Ph*, I, 252 ff./260–61.

4. *Ph*, I, 250–51/259–60.

5. *Ph*, III, 11–12/12–13.

6. *Ph*, I, 251–52/260. My translation.

7. *Ph*, I, 253/261. My variant translation. My colleague, Peter Heller, pointed out to me that the original passage appears in "Israel in der Wüste" which is one of the essays Goethe appended to his *Der West-Östliche Divan;* in the Artemis edition the relevant passage appears in vol. 3, pp. 504–5.

8. See *Ph*, I, 254–55/261–2.

9. *Ph*, II, 305–6/266–67.

10. *Ph*, III, 81/72.

11. *W*, 153. My translation of the following:
Wenn wir uns nicht binden an Endlichkeit, bleiben wir in blosser Möglichkeit leer und bodenlos. . . . Aber in der Endlichkeit geht das was durch sie sprach, verloren, sofern die Endlichkeit als solche absolut genommen wurde.

12. Ibid.

13. *Ph*, I, 178–79/199.

14. *W*, 135.

15. *W*, 894.

16. *Ph*, III, 11–12/12–13.

17. *Ph*, III, 13. In the English edition see *Ph* III, 13.

18. *U Z Gesch*, 124. My translation. The Bullock translation of this passage, on p. 95 of *History*, contains some grave and misleading errors.

19. See Jaspers's *Descartes/Three Essays*, especially 95 ff./173 ff.

20. *U Z Gesch*, 124/*History*, 95. My variant translation.

21. *U Z Gesch*, 123–24/*History*, 94–95.

22. *W*, 789.

23. *W*, 789.

24. *W*, 806–7. My translation.

25. See *W*, 635.

26. *W*, 137.

27. *W*, 702.

28. *W*, 897–98. My translation. About the lasting impact of Jaspers's childhood experience of the ocean in the Frisian Islands see *Sch & W*, 15–16.

29. *W*, 898; my translation.

30. E. Hederer, ed., *Deutsche Dichtung des Barock* (Munich: Carl Hansen Verlag, n.d.), p. 7.

31. *W*, 307.

32. Ibid.

33. *W*, 702.

34. *W*, 393.

35. Cf. F. Wulf, "Mystik," in *Handbuch Theologischer Grundbegriffe*, vol. II (Munich: Kösel Verlag, 1963), especially pp. 187 ff.

36. See S. J. Day, O.F.M., *Intuitive Cognition: A Key to the Significance of Later Scholastics* (Saint Bonaventure, New York: Franciscan Institute, 1947).

37. *Critique of Pure Reason*, B 139.

38. For example, ibid., B 71–72.

39. Ibid., B 43.

40. Cf. Day, op. cit., pp. 55 ff., 67–68, 72–73, 91, 101 ff.

41. Ibid., pp. 101 ff.

42. See, for example, *Critique of Pure Reason*, B 723.

43. Ibid. Kemp-Smith Translation, p. 135.

44. Ibid., B 145.

45. "Vorrede zu Reinhold Bernhard Jachmanns Prüfung der Kantischen Religionsphilosophie," *Sämtliche Werke*, vol. 6 (Leipzig: Inselverlag, 1921), p. 676.

46. *Ph*, II, 208/183.

47. *W*, 393.

48. *Ph*, II, 280/244–45.

49. *W*, 1005–6.

50. *W*, 393.

51. Preface to the *Proslogium* in Saint Anselm, *Basic Writings: Proslogium; Monologium; Gaunilon's On Behalf of the Fool; Cur Deus Homo*, trans. S. W. Deane (La Salle, Illinois: Open Court Publishing Co., 1962), p. 1. Anselm uses this phrase to describe his *Monologium* but it is clear that it can also refer to the *Proslogium*.

52. *Gr Ph*, 737/*Gr Ph*, II, 104. My quotation follows the Manheim translation except for the insertion of the words "of certainty of God" which appear in the original but not in the Manheim translation.

53. On prophecy cf. *Quaestiones Disputates de Veritate*, q. 12, and *Summa*

Theologica, II-II, qq. 171–74. This portion of the *Summa* does not appear in the most comprehensive of the popular editions of Thomas, namely *Basic Writings of St. Thomas Aquinas*, ed. A. C. Pegis (New York: Random House, 1945).

54. *Summa Contra Gentiles*, III, q. 154, art 1, trans. *On the Truth of the Catholic Faith* by A. C. Pegis (Garden City, New York: Image Books, 1956), pp. 239–40.

55. *Summa Theologica*, I, q. 89, art. 4, in Pegis, *Basic Writings*, 1:857.

56. On rapture see *Quaestiones Disputates de Veritate*, q. 13; and *Summa Theologica*, II-II, q. 175 and q. 180, art 5. Thomas's treatment of rapture is to be found neither in the popular editions of his writings nor in *Basic Writings*.

57. *Quaestiones Disputates de Veritate*, q. 15, art. 1, trans. *Truth*, vol. II (Chicago: Henry Regnery Co., 1953), p. 183.

58. Ibid., q. 10, art. 11, p. 62.

59. *Gr Ph*, 738/*Gr Ph*, II, 105.

60. Ibid.

61. G. E. M. Anscombe, *An Introduction to Wittgenstein's Tractatus* (London: Hutchinson University Library, 1959), p. 170.

62. Max Black, *A Companion to Wittgenstein's Tractatus* (Cambridge: At the University Press, 1964), p. 374.

63. This translation is mine. The Pears and McGuinness translation of this passage is not accurate as to meaning and as to nuance of expression. This seems due to a tendency to determine the translation of words by the translation of the same words in other parts of the book. Thus, in our passage, Wittgenstein says "dies zeigt sich. . . ." The translators refrain from using 'to show' in this context, even though they used this translation for the occurrence of this key word many times before. Now, while this use of 'to show' is not in accord with the previous uses, Wittgenstein must have been aware of this, and it is not the translator's job to deprive the student of Wittgenstein of a problem by supplying a putative emendation. Stegmüller quite rightly sees that we are confronted here with a distinct and deliberate use of the word 'to show'. See Wolfgang Stegmüller, *Hauptströmungen der Gegenwartsphilosophie*, 3rd ed. (Stuttgart: A. Kröner, 1965), p. 559.

64. Max Black, *Companion to Wittgenstein's Tractatus*, p. 374.

65. Pears and McGuiness translate "darüber muss man schweigen" as "we must pass over in silence." "To be silent" and "to pass over in silence" do not mean the same thing. And the latter phrase is neither an accurate translation, nor, in the light of the *Tractatus*, a possible one.

66. Stegmüller, *Hauptströmungen*, p. 560.

67. Gabriel Marcel, *Metaphysical Journal* (Chicago: Henry Regnery Co., 1952), p. 161.

68. Ibid, p. 303.

69. Ibid., pp. 160–61.

70. *Ps WA*, 440.

71. See, for example, Karl Barth, *The Epistle to the Romans*, translated from the 6th German ed. by E. C. Hoskyns (Oxford: Oxford University Press, 1933), p. 211.

72. Ibid., p. 109.

73. Ibid., p. 211.

74. Marcel, *Metaphysical Journal*, p. 161.

75. M. Buber, *I and Thou* (New York: Charles Scribner's Sons, 1958), p. 78.

76. The first sentence is in the translation by Pears and McGuinness; the second is my translation.
77. *Ps WA*, 448.
78. *Ps WA*, 447–48.
79. See *Ps WA*, 332–43.
80. *Ps WA*, 451.

Notes to Chapter 3

1. *W*, 641.
2. *W*, 470.
3. *W*, 470.
4. *Einführung*, 54. My translation. Manheim's translation of this passage appears in *Wisdom*, 56–57.
5. *Einführung*, 56/*Wisdom*, 58.
6. *Ph*, III, 153/134.
7. *Ph*, II, 279/243.
8. *Ph*, II, 281–82/245. My variant translation of the following:
Als daseiendes Leben suchen wir Sicherheit; wir verzweifeln an der Unmöglichkeit. Der Glaube aber vermag auf Sicherheit in der Erscheinung zu verzichten. Er hält in aller Gefahr an der Möglichkeit fest; er kennt in der Welt weder Sicherheit noch Unmöglichkeit.
9. *Gr Ph*, 156/*Gr Ph*, I, 52.
10. *Ph Gl Off*, 383/*Ph F Rev* 254. My italics.
11. Ibid.
12. See 2 Timothy 4:8.
13. *Ph*, II, 277/241–42.
14. See *Ph*, II, 276/241 and 279/243.
15. *W*, 1000.
16. Ibid.
17. Book XXI, 1361–62.
18. *W*, 1000.
19. 1. Corinthians 13:13. Goodspeed translation.
20. *Kleine Schule*, 138/*Everyman*, 98. My variant translation.
21. See *Ph*, III, 102 ff.
22. *Ph*, I, 255/263.
23. *Ph*, I, 260/267. My variant translation.

Notes to Chapter 4

1. *W*, 654 ff.
2. *The Sickness Unto Death* (Garden City, New York: Doubleday & Co., Anchor Books, 1954 and Princeton, New Jersey: Princeton University Press, 1941), pp. 176–77.

3. *Ph*, III, 117. My translation. For Ashton's see *Ph*, III, 103.

4. See *Ph*, III, 116−17/102−3, and 120−21/106−7.

5. *Ph*, III, 116. My translation. For Ashton's see *Ph*, III, 102.

6. See *Ph*, II, 416−17/361−62; and *W*, 739 ff.

7. See *Ph*, III, 117/103.

8. *Ph*, II, 418/362−63.

9. See *Ph*, II, 235 ff./206 ff; and *W*, 666 ff.

10. *Ph*, II, 234/205.

11. *Ph*, II, 234/206. My translation.

12. *Ph*, II, 243/212−13. My translation of the following:
Der Kampf ist auf den letzten unoffenbaren Sinn in Ursprung und Ende
gerichtet, aber dadurch, dass er sich in den augenblicklichen Situationen
und Zwecken bewegt, daher am konkret Gegenwärtigen sich abspielt und
das Geringste nicht als zu gering achtet.
Ashton, no doubt, misinterprets this passage in rendering it as follows:
It is a fight over the last, hidden meanings of the source and the end, but
it is waged in the purposes and situations of the moment and thus deals
with concrete, present things, without discounting the least of them.

13. *Ph*, I, 256/263.

14. *Entmyth*, 59/*Myth*, 57.

15. *Entmyth*, 111/*Myth*, 109.

16. See *Ph*, II, 439/380−81.

17. *Ph*, II, 440/381−82.

18. *Ph*, II, 245−46/215.

19. Schilpp, *Jaspers*, 784/787. My variant translation.

20. See, for example, *U Z Gesch*, 282−83/*History*, 221.

21. *Ph Gl Off*, 487−88/*Ph F Rev*, 328. I have changed Ashton's translation
slightly. Ashton's translation, in turn, differs from the official translation of
Barth's *Church Dogmatics;* in the official version this passage appears in vol.
III, pt. 4, pp. 479−80.

22. *Ph Gl Off*, 488/*Ph F Rev*, 328−29. My variant translation.

23. *Ph*, III, 122. My translation; for Ashton's see *Ph*, III, 107.

24. Paris, 1947, p. 391. My translation of the following passage:
Ce soupçon que Jaspers ait malgré lui ruiné l'idée de Transcendence avec
celle Dieu, le croyant peut le partager avec l'athée. Le philosophe qui
démasque les mythes et les courtise tous n'est-il pas un Don Juan de la
religion, qui perd d'ailleurs l'étroitesse de l'existence et l'intensité de la foi
pour avoir voulu embrasser "le monde des chiffres," depuis les mythes du
Karman jusqu'à la peinture de Van Gogh, en passant par la théologie
trinitaire. . . . Il pense qu'une philosophie intégrale de l'existence dans le
monde et devant Dieu n'est possible qu'à partir d'une conciliation
spécifique qui est l'essence de la religion.

25. Paul Ricoeur, "Philosophie und Religion bei Karl Jaspers"/"The Relation of Jaspers' Philosophy to Religion," Schilpp, *Jaspers*, 633/638−39.

26. *Ph*, II, 434/377. The last clause of this passage is translated by me; in
the original it reads: "aber als sich fremd in der anderen Ursprünglichkeit des
Glaubens." Ashton translates this as: "but alien to me in the originality of the
other faith."

27. Paul Ricoeur, "Philosophie und Religion bei Karl Jaspers," Schilpp,
Jaspers, 627/633.

28. Hans Urs von Balthasar, "Martin Buber and Christianity," in P. A.
Schilpp and M. Friedman, eds., *The Philosophy of Martin Buber* (LaSalle,
Illinois: Open Court Publishing Co., 1967), p. 343.

29. *Ph*, III, 123. My translation; for Ashton's see *Ph*, III, 108.

30. M. Buber, *I and Thou* (New York: Charles Scribner's Sons, 1958), p. 75.

31. Ibid., p. 11.

32. "Das Problem des Menschen," in Martin Buber, *Werke, Erster Band, Schriften zur Philosophie* (Munich and Heidelberg: Kösel Verlag and Verlag Lambert Schneider, 1962), p. 406.

33. Ibid.

34. See M. Friedman, *Martin Buber, The Life of Dialogue* (Chicago: University of Chicago Press, 1955), pp. 20–21; H. Bergman, "Martin Buber and Mysticism," in Schilpp and Friedman, *Martin Buber*, pp. 299–300; Martin Buber, "The Faith of Judaism," in W. Herberg, ed., *The Writings of Martin Buber* (New York: Meridian Books, 1956), pp. 254–55.

35. Herberg, *Writings of Buber*, p. 254.

36. Ibid., pp. 255–56.

37. "Reply," in Schilpp and Friedman, *Martin Buber*, p. 744. My variant translation of the original which appears in the German version of the work, p. 638.

38. *Ph Gl Off*, 340–41/*Ph F Rev*, 225. My variant translation of the following:

> Das Übersinnliche, Überseiende, Überrationale der Transzendenz wird in der Chiffer des persönlichen Gottes zum Du . . . mit dem er reden kann, zu dem er beten kann, zu dem er in der Verzweiflung des unbegreiflichen Unheils ein Begreifen heischt. Dieses mächtige Begehren, in Gottes überwältigender Allmacht die leibhaftige Realität des Du zu gewinnen, war nirgends in der Welt mächtiger als bei den Juden. Von dort her wurde es bestimmend für das Abendland.

Ashton translates this as follows:

> It is the experience of Transcendence-supersensory, beyond reason, above Being, yet turned into a 'Thou' by the cipher of the personal God . . . a Thou that man can talk to, pray to, appeal to for understanding when inconceivable evil drives him to despair. Nowhere in the world has the urge to turn God's overwhelming omnipotence into a tangibly real Thou been stronger than among the Jews. It was they who bequeathed it to the West.

39. *W*, 546–47.

40. *W*, 971.

41. *W*, 546 ff.

42. *W*, 587 ff.

43. *W*, 972.

44. *Ph*, II, 66/60–61.

45. *Ph*, II, 66/60. Jaspers says: "Das Schwermachen gilt aber allein in bezug auf die eigentlichsten Gründe des Entscheidens im Gehalt der Entschlüsse." This means literally: "However, making things tough is valid only with respect to choice's true foundation within the substance of decision."

46. "Zur Geschichte des dialogischen Prinzips," in Buber, *Werke, Erster Band*, pp. 301–2. For M. Friedman's English translation of this passage see M. Buber, *Between Man and Man* (New York: Macmillan Co., 1965), pp. 219–20. This paper originally appeared in 1954 as a postscript to a collection of Buber's writings on the dialogical principle. Now it appears under the title given op. cit., pp. 291–305. All quoted passages from it are in my translation.

47. In English translation this work appeared under the title *The Perennial Scope of Philosophy*; see Appendix 1, item 65.

48. Buber, "Zur Geschichte," p. 302. In M. Friedman's translation see *Between Man and Man*, p. 220.

49. *Ph*, II, 315 ff./274 ff.

50. *Ph*, II, 315–16/274–75.

51. Buber, "Zur Geschichte," p. 300. In M. Friedman's translation see *Between Man and Man*, p. 217.

52. "The Philosopher Replies," in Schilpp and Friedman, *Martin Buber*, p. 744.

53. Ibid.

54. See note 37 above.

55. Emil Brunner, "Judaism and Christianity in Buber," in Schilpp and Friedman, *Martin Buber*, p. 318.

56. Martin Buber, *Two Types of Faith* (New York: Harper & Row, 1961), p. 37.

57. Buber, *Two Types of Faith*, p. 12.

58. Buber, *Two Types of Faith*, p. 13. My variant translation of a passage appearing in the original in Buber, *Werke*, vol. I, p. 658.

59. Brunner, "Judaism and Christianity," p. 313.

60. Karl Barth, *Kirchliche Dogmatik*, vol. III, pt. 2, p. 333.

61. Ibid., p. 334; Barth's own emphasis.

62. Buber, "Zur Geschichte" p. 304. In Friedman's translation see *Between Man and Man*, p. 222.

63. Buber, "Zur Geschichte," p. 305. In Friedman's translation see *Between Man and Man*, p. 223.

64. Ibid.

65. Ibid. In Friedman's translation see *Between Man and Man*, pp. 223–24.

66. "The Philosopher Replies," in Schilpp and Friedman,, *Martin Buber*, pp. 742–43.

67. *I and Thou*, pp. 16–17.

68. "Postscript" (1957) to Buber, *I and Thou*, p. 137.

69. This was indicated in a conversation between Jaspers and me in 1963.

70. *Ps WA*, p. xii. My translation.

71. *Ph*, I, 321/319. My translation of "Unterwerfung und Nachahmung," which Ashton translates as "to make us bow and emulate."

72. *Ph*, III, 31. My translation; for Ashton's see *Ph*, III, 28–29.

73. *Ph*, II, 272/237–38. Except for one phrase, Ashton's translation was retained. In the place of the first occurrence of "a thou," Ashton has "another person"; the original is "ein Du."

Notes to Chapter 5

1. *W*, 767.

2. English version quoted from *The Grand Inquisitor on the Nature of Man*, translated by C. Garnett (Indianapolis and New York: The Library of Liberal Arts, 1948), pp. 30–31. Jaspers's quotation appears in *W*, 777.

3. Cf. *W*, 584 ff., 820−21; *Ph & W*, 46/38.

4. *W*, 585−86.

5. *W*, 864.

6. *W*, 770.

7. "Freedom and Authority," *Ph & W*, 47/39. My variant translation. In Ashton's translation a sentence is missing.

8. On the tension between authority and freedom, see especially *W*, 797 ff.

9. *W*, 747.

10. *W*, 768.

11. See *Ph*, I, 307−8/307, and *W*, 797−98.

12. *W*, 799.

13. *W*, 804.

14. "Freiheit und Autorität" ("Liberty and Authority"), *Ph & W*, 47/39.

15. Cf. *W*, 781 ff., 816−17; *Ph & W*, 44−45/36−37.

16. *W*, 782.

17. Cf. *W*, 782 ff.

18. *W*, 783.

19. *W*, 817.

20. Ibid.

21. *W*, 815.

22. *W*, 818.

23. In German: *Instanz.*

24. *W*, 815. See also *W*, 841 ff.

25. "Freedom and Authority," *Ph & W*, 47.

26. See the section on "Power and Political Freedom" in *U Z Gesch/History*, particularly 209 ff./163 ff.

27. *U Z Gesch*, 210/*History*, 164. See also *Ph & W*, 59−60/51−52.

28. See *W*, 823 ff.

29. *W*, 889 ff.

30. *W*, 793−94.

31. *W*, 813.

32. Ibid.

33. See especially *W*, 748−66.

34. *W*, 831.

36. See *W*, 801.

37. *W*, 831.

38. *W*, 748−49.

39. *W*, 750−51. About "Sacrifice" (*Opfer*) see *W*, 882 ff.

40. *W*, 759.

41. *W*, 765.

42. *Ph*, I, 310−11. My translation. In the English version, see *Ph*, I, 310.

43. About the relation of philosophy and heritage see especially *Ph*, I, 285 ff./287 ff., 307 ff./307 ff.; *Ph*, II, 395 ff./344 ff.; *Ph*, III, 10 ff./10 ff.; and *W*, 167 ff., 130 ff., 797 ff., 908 ff.

44. "Philosophische Autobiographie" ("Philosophical Autobiography") in Schilpp, *Jaspers*, 62/76. A more elaborate account of this episode appears in *Sch & W*, 87−88.

45. *Ph*, I, 312. My translation. In the English version see *Ph*, I, 311.

46. Hannah Arendt, "Karl Jaspers: Bürger der Welt"/"Karl Jaspers: Citizen of the World" in Schilpp, *Jaspers*, 535/541−42; italics are mine.

Notes to Chapter 6

1. *Ph Gl Off*, 150/*Ph F Rev*, 90. The slight alterations from Mr. Ashton's translation are mine.

2. Ibid.

3. *W*, 839. In the original: "Die eine Wahrheit haben wir nicht und werden wir nicht haben—und die Wahrheit kann nur eine sein."

4. See below chap. 7, sec. vii.

5. See "Kierkegaard" in *An & Pol*, 299; and *Ph Gl Off*, 469/*Ph F Rev*, 315.

6. *Ph Gl Off*, 469/*Ph F Rev*, 315.

7. *Ph Gl Off*, 294/*Ph F Rev*, 192.

8. *Gr Ph*, 275–76/*Gr Ph*, I, 143; emendations of the Manheim translation are mine.

9. *Die Schuldfrage*, 92 ff./*The Question of German Guilt*, 118 ff.

10. *Atom*, 318 ff./*Mankind*, 231 ff.

11. *Wohin treibt die Bundesrepublik?*, 279–80. The section in which this passage appears is not included in the English version (*The Future of Germany*).

12. *U Z Gesch*, 285/*History*, 223.

13. See below, chap. 5.

14. *W*, 660. The original reads:
In der Existenz ist der Glaube und ist die Verzweiflung. Beiden gegenüber steht das Verlangen zur Ruhe der Ewigkeit, wo Verzweiflung unmöglich und Glaube Schauen, d.h. vollendete Gegenwart der vollendeten Wirklichkeit selbst geworden ist.

15. See Schilpp, *Jaspers*, 821–22/838.

16. Ibid; see also *Vn & Wvn* 49–50/*Rea & Anti*, 63–64.

17. The ensuing passages of the chapter, dealing with the concept of reason, draw mainly on two sections in *Von der Wahrheit*. The first (pp. 113 ff.) is, to a great extent, a reiteration of a section of the second lecture in *Vn & Ex/Rea & Ex*; the second is on pp. 966 ff.

18. The method of transcending is subject to extensive discussion in a variety of contexts in both the *Philosophie* (1932) and *Von der Wahrheit* (1946), but especially in the former. The ensuing passages refer in the main to *Ph*, I, 32–52/76–89; and *Ph*, III, 36 ff./33 ff. See also below, chap. 7, sec. ii.

19. Jaspers's treatment of 'catholicity' appears in *Von der Wahrheit*, pp. 832–68; our present section is based mainly on this treatment. Unlike many other concepts which are characteristic of Jaspers, 'catholicity' is seldom explicitly mentioned in his works. However, it is indispensable and its conception very much present in many of his writings, particularly in his discussions of the ecclesiastical mode of faith and of the nature and danger of totalitarianism.

20. *W*, 832; see also *W*, 118.

21. See *Ph & W*, 14/9.

22. See *W*, 839–40.

23. *W*, 848.

24. *W*, 843. My translation of the following:
Im rationalen System wird ein Ganzes gedacht, in dem alles was möglich ist, seinen Platz . . . aber auch . . . seine Begrenzung hat.

Es wird nichts ausgelassen, nichts absolut bekämpft, sondern alles zugelassen, aber so, dass es, statt das Ganze zu sprengen, als Glied ihm dient. . . . Gesucht [wird daher] gegen alles Entweder-Oder das Sowohl-Als-auch, gegen die ausschliessende Entschiedenheit das Versöhnende. Ausschluss erfolgt nur gegen alles, was das Prinzip der Totalität sprengen will, gegen jede Radikalität, die statt sich einzugliedern zum Ketzertum wird. In allem ist Wahrheit, wenn man es nur recht auffasst. In allem ist Unwahrheit, wenn es im Eigenwillen sich selber durchsetzen will.
25. *W*, 845. The original reads:
Im praktischen Verhalten gilt das Prinzip: unter der Bedingung der Anerkennung des Zentrums der katholischen Macht und der Entscheidung . . . wird bis zum Äussersten zugelassen eine Entfaltung im Besonderen, ja im Willkürlichen, im Aberglauben, in moralischer Laxheit. . . . Überall gibt es Entschuldigungen, wenn der Täter und Denker nur im Prinzip dem Ganzen gehorcht und sich eingliedert. Überall dort aber gilt erbarmungslose Ablehnung, wo ein Keim innerer Auflehnung fühlbar ist, und mag diese aus hohem Enthusiasmus, hingebender Liebe, ethisch unbedingtem Wesen entspringen.
26. Ibid. The original is as follows:
Im politischen Verhalten der Führer der Katholizität gilt ein uneingeschränkter empirischer Realismus. Ein Spielenlassen der faktischen Mächte nach dem alleinigen Gesichtspunkt, wie sie als Faktoren zur Aufrechterhaltung und Festigung der katholischen Autorität im Dasein dienlich sind.
27. *W*, 842.
28. *W*, 833 note.
29. *W*, 839.
30. *W*, 844.
31. *Gr Ph*, 46—47/*Gr Ph*, I, 7.
32. Jaspers has written on all three a number of times. For the present context the most germane treatment of Marxism and Freudianism appears in the first of three lectures of his *Reason and Anti-Reason*.
33. See *W*, 836 ff.
34. *W*, 836. My translation.
35. *W*, 850.
36. *W*, 849.
37. *W*, 836 and 849.
38. *W*, 2.
39. *W*, 846.
40. *W*, 842. Italics are mine; the original reads as follows:
Gegen die eine Autorität richtet sich der philosophische, den Anspruch dieser Katholizität immer wieder durchbrechende Gedanke der Vernunft. . . . In der Realität ist die Autorität zu bestimmter Gestalt geworden. Sie ist in die Unlösbarkeit der Daseinsverstrickungen getreten. Daher ist sie wahr in dem Aufschwung der sie ergreifenden und schaffenden Bewegung, unwahr in der eine endlose Dauer verlangenden Fixierung. Sie hat mit ihrer Verwirklichung sogleich auch den Keim der Unwahrheit in sich, ohne den kein zeitliches Dasein ist. Daher muss sie sich bewegen in der ständig noch notwendigen Aufhebung ihrer Unwahrheit. Da diese aber nicht beiläufig ist, nicht blosse hinzukommende Trübung, sondern schon im Kern der ersten Verwirklichung liegt, so ist die Bewegung unaufhörlich. Solange die Bewegung ist, ist Wahrheit; sobald die Bewegung aufhört, ist nur noch Unwahrheit.

41. *W*, 833.
42. *W*, 867.
43. *W*, 866.
44. *W*, 867−68. My translation of the following:
Die Mannigfaltigkeit der Menschen, die Wesensverschiedenheit und die
Rangferne der Existenzen, die Weisen ihres Chiffernlesens, ihre Haltung
zum Tode, was ihnen Gott ist,—das alles kann sich nur bei Freiheit ausser-
halb der überwölbenden Kuppel unbedingter Katholizität lauter zur Wahrheit entfalten.
45. *W*, 858.
46. *W*, 861.
47. Ibid.
48. *W*, 861−62. My translation of the following:
Aber der Gegensatz ist auch so, dass, von der Vernunft her gesehen, das
andere, die Katholizität, in der Welt erhalten bleiben muss und soll. Sie
muss vielleicht erhalten bleiben, weil die Geschichtlichkeit des Seins in
der Mehrzahl der Menschen nicht ohne die Illusion der Allgemeinheit
ihrer konkreten Gestalt verwirklicht werden kann. Sie *soll* erhalten
bleiben, damit die Klarheit des Wahren sich durch Vernunft im ständigen
Kampf mit dieser gefährlichsten, weil verführendsten Abgleitung wieder-
herstellen kann. Dass die Katholizität die Ausflucht ist für alle Menschen,
denen Vernunft in ihrer offenen Geschichtlichkeit nicht tragbar ist, das
zwingt die Vernunft selbst zur Anerkennung, ja zum Mitmachen in der
Welterscheinung, zumal wenn die Katholizität politisch allmächtig wird,
wie die Kirche in früheren Jahrhunderten und wie vielleicht ein neuer
anderer unchristlicher Katholizismus in kommenden. Die Frage ist dann
nur, wo für den in Vernunft Lebenden im Konfliktsfalle der Vorrang
liegt. Nicht das Mitmachen von Formen, Riten, Sprechen entscheidet,
sondern die Wahl in konkreter Kollision.
49. Jean Paumen, *Raison et existence chez Jaspers* (Brussels: Édition du
Parthénon, 1958), p. 279. My translation of the following:
Il n'importe plus que de savoir si nous optons pour le point de vue de la
catholicité . . . ou si nous optons pour le point de vue de la raison. . . .
Elle n'est pas seulement l'opposition la plus profonde; elle est aussi
l'opposition la plus vaste. Il n'est rien, dans notre pensée ou dans notre
action, qui ne l'illustre out qu'elle n'affecte.
50. Ibid. In this passage Paumen refers to *W*, 991 ff. The original is as follows:
Contre la catholicité, Jaspers . . . opte pour la raison. Optant pour la
raison, il opte . . . pour l'amour. Comme la raison, l'amour, en nous
ouvrant aux êtres et aux choses, nous ouvre à nous-mêmes. L'amour coincide avec la raison; il est l'âme de la raison.

Notes to Chapter 7

1. See *U Z Gesch*, 280 ff./*History*, 219−20.
2. *Einführung/Wisdom*, chap. IV; *Ph Gl*, 32 ff./*Scope*, 34 ff. See also *W*,
643−44 and 897.

3. *Einführung/Wisdom,* chap. V; *Ph Gl,* 34/*Scope,* 36−37. Bracketed addition supplied.

4. *Einführung/Wisdom,* chap. VII; *Ph Gl,* 34 ff./*Scope,* 37 ff. My translation. In the original this proposition reads: "Die Welt hat ein verschwindendes Dasein zwischen Gott und Existenz." This is translated by Manheim in *Scope* as: "The world is an ephemeral stage between God and existence." A year later in *Wisdom,* Manheim offers this translation: "The reality of the world subsists ephemerally between God and existence." Both are wrong: Manheim hesitates when translating "hat . . . Dasein" literally, i.e., "has . . . reality." No doubt "to have reality" is an unusual phrase in English, but no more so than in German. Let us discount altogether the fantastic first version where this is construed as identifying the world as a "stage" (of reality?) between God and self. Yet even the better second rendering orders the world as a reality among realities, locating it between that of God and that of self and, incidentally, characterizing this located reality as being of short duration, i.e., "ephemeral." Yet Jaspers was not concerned about giving an ontology of the world. Not the world's reality but the function of this reality is the topic of the proposition, i.e., its function for the relation of God and self. This relation is, in principle, immediate and with regard to this immediacy the world, as mediating actuality, is "evanescent." This meaning can be shown by reversing the sequence of the sentence: "[In the relation] between God and Existenz the world's reality is evanescent."

Yet we cannot reverse the sentence, because it must carry a further meaning, namely that in the self's effort to realize the immediacy of its relation to God the world interposes itself as the inevitable and indispensable actuality mediating this immediacy. In order that both meanings be shown, it is necessary to make reference to the world's reality (more correctly, 'existence', i.e., *Dasein*) not *per se* but in its functional role; and this is accomplished by speaking of "having" reality relative to the relation of God and Existenz.

5. *Einführung/Wisdom,* ch. VI.

6. Ibid.

7. Hannsjörg A. Salmony, *Johann Georg Hamanns Metakritische Philosophie* (Zollikon: Evangelischer Verlag, 1958), pp. 152−64.

8. See Xavier Tilliette, *Karl Jaspers: Théorie de la vérité, Métaphysique des chiffres, Foi philosophique* (Paris: Aubier, 1960), Pt. II.

9. Ibid., pp. 167−68.

10. Urs Richli, *Transzendentale Reflexion und Sittliche Entscheidung. Zum Problem der Selbsterkenntnis der Metaphysik bei Kant und Jaspers, Kantstudien,* Ergänzungsheft 92 (Bonn: 1967), pp. 145 ff.; see also p. 149.

11. Immanuel Kant, *Critique of Judgment,* trans. J. H. Bernard (New York: Hafner Publishing Co., 1951), p. 143. The original can be found in Academy Edition, vol. V, p. 301.

12. Hugo von Hofmannsthal, "Ein Brief," *Gesammelte Werke,* vol. 8, *Prosa II* (Frankfort on the Main: S. Fischer, 1951), p. 18. See H. v. Hofmannsthal, "The Letter of Lord Chandos," *Selected Prose,* trans. M. Hottinger and T. J. Stern (New York: Pantheon Books, 1952), p. 138.

13. Hofmannsthal, *Gesammelte Werke, Prosa II,* p. 102.

14. See, for example, *Einführung,* 11−12/*Wisdom,* 9 ff.

15. These references can be found in the section of the projected *Methodenlehre* dealing with *Metaphysisches Verstehen.* They are to *Die symbolische Kunstform,* pt. II, sec. 1 of Hegel's *Aesthetik,* "Of beauty as the Symbol of morality," sec. 59 of Kant's *Critique of Judgment,* the chapter on 'symbol' in Vischer's *Kritische Gänge,* vol. IV, and to the four marks of 'sym-

bol' in Tillich's early article "Das religiöse Symbol," *Blätter für Deutsche Philosophie*, vol. I, 1928. It should be noted that the reference to Kant's third *Critique* is not to the cited use of 'cipher' (*Chiffreschrift*).

16. *Ph*, III, 43 ff./39 ff.
17. *Ph*, III, 54 ff./49 ff.
18. *Ph*, III, 63 ff./57 ff.
19. Schilpp, *Jaspers*, 62/75.
20. *Ph*, III, 66/59.
21. *Einführung*, 43/*Wisdom*, 45. My variant translation. The original reads: "Freiheit und Gott sind untrennbar. Warum? Ich bin mir gewiss: in meiner Freiheit bin ich nicht durch mich selbst, sondern werde mir in ihr geschenkt, denn ich kann mir ausbleiben und mein Freisein nicht erzwingen."
22. *Ph Gl Off*, 158/*Ph F Rev*, 95.
23. Schilpp, *Jaspers*, 31/42.
24. *The Sickness Unto Death* (Garden City, New York: Doubleday & Co., Anchor Books, 1954 and Princeton, New Jersey: Princeton University Press, 1941), pp. 146–47.
25. See *Ph*, III, 68–127/61–112.
26. See *Die Geistige Situation der Zeit*/*Man in the Modern Age*, pt. VI.
27. *Ph*, III, 82. My translation. For Ashton's see *Ph*, III, 73.
28. *Ph*, III, 66. My translation: For Ashton's see *Ph*, III, 59.
29. *Republic*, II, 377e.
30. Ibid., III, 389a.
31. See *U Z Gesch*/*History*, pt. I.
32. See *U Z Gesch*, 21/*History*, 3.
33. *Gr Ph*, 304–5/*Gr Ph*, I, 165.
34. *Ph*, III, 131 ff./115 ff.
35. *Ph*, III, 134 ff./117 ff.
36. *Ph*, III, 130–31/114–15.
37. *Ph*, III, 131. My translation; for Ashton's see *Ph*, III, 115.
38. *Entmyth*, 39/*Myth*, 39. See also *Einführung*, 84–85/*Wisdom*, 88–89.
39. *U Z Gesch*, 169/*History*, 131.
40. *Ph Gl*, 126–27/*Scope*, 138–40. My variant translation.
41. *Ph Gl*, 127/*Scope*, 140. My translation.
42. *Einführung*, 85/*Wisdom*, 90.
43. *Ph Gl*, 150–53/*Scope*, 166–68. My variant translation.
44. *Ph*, I, 51/88; *Ph Gl Off*, 213/*Ph F Rev*, 136.
45. For example, *Einführung*, 46/*Wisdom*, 48; *Ph Gl Off*, 213, 385/*Ph F Rev*, 136, 255; *W*, 693.
46. *Ph Gl Off*, 483. My translation; brackets provided for clarification. Ashton omitted from his translation the small paragraph from which this passage is taken. It belongs to a section which appears in *Ph F Rev*, 325. The original is: "Der philosophische Glaube will in den nahen Göttern als Chiffern niemals den fernen, allein wirklichen Gott verlieren, dann aber den fernen Gott in den nahen Chiffern lebendig erfahren."
47. See *Ph*, I, 51–52/88–89; *Ph Gl Off*, 389/*Ph F Rev*, 258.
48. *Ph Gl Off*, 387/*Ph F Rev*, 256. My translation.
49. Ibid. My translation.
50. *Ph Gl Off*, p. 213. My translation. The original is: " . . . an der der Mensch, weil er den Gottesgedanken durch das 'nicht' denkt, die Wirklichkeit Gottes ineiner geschichtlichen Existenz ungreifbar erfährt." Ashton, *Ph F Rev*, p. 136, translates it in this way: " . . . man—approaching the thought of God by way of a 'not'—can incomprehensibly experience the divine reality in

his historic Existenz." Clearly it is not the experiencing which is incomprehensible, as Ashton would have it, but the actuality of God.

51. *Ph Gl Off*, 399/*Ph F Rev*, 265. My variant translation.

52. *Ph Gl Off*, 390/*Ph F Rev*, 259.

53. See *Summa Theologica*, pt. I, q. 13, art. 2.

54. Ibid., art. 2.

55. Ibid., art. 2.

56. Ibid., art. 5.

57. Ibid., art. 2.

58. Ibid., art. 5. "Et hoc est tam contra Philosophos, qui multa de Deo demonstrative probant."

59. Ibid., art. 12.

60. *The Guide for the Perplexed*, pt. I, chap. 2.

61. Ibid., chap. 50.

62. See ibid., the prayer at end of chap. 57.

63. Ibid., chap. 52.

64. Ibid., chap. 58.

65. Ibid., chap. 53.

66. A. Lichtigfeld, the well-known interpreter of Jaspers from Witwatersrand University in Johannesburg, presented a like-minded apposition of Jaspers and Maimonides in a paper read at the Fourteenth International Congress of Philosophy in Vienna, September 1968. An abstract of this paper appears in the *Proceedings* of the Congress, vol. V (Vienna, 1970), pp. 487 ff.

67. *Einführung*, 43/*Wisdom*, 45. My variant translation.

68. See *Ph*, III, 73–74, 79.

69. *Ph*, I, 302/303. My translation. The original reads as follows:
Die Gottheit sagt nichts direkt, aber durch diese Möglichkeit der Freiheit scheint sie zu sprechen, nämlich zu fordern, dass ihr uns unbegreiflicher Wille erfüllt werde, aus dem sie den Menschen unabhängig machte, damit er in eigener Verantwortung über sich selbst entscheide und darin seine Würde habe.
Ashton's translation changes several meanings and eliminates an essential item in Jaspers's complicated structure of connections. He translates this passage as follows:
The Godhead says nothing directly, but through this chance of freedom it appears to speak, to demand that its—for us—unfathomable will be done, that man use the independence it gave him, that he make his own decisions on his own responsibility and derive his human dignity from so doing.

70. *Ph*, II, 272/237.

71. See *Ph*, I, 302–3/303; *Ph*, II, 327/284–85.

72. See *Ph*, III, 164/144; *Ph Gl Off*, 176/*Ph F Rev*, 110.

73. *Ph*, III, 165. My translation. For Ashton's see *Ph*, III, 144–45. Ashton mistranslates the metaphor of the tension of Existenz *toward* the hidden transcendence as the tension *between* Existenz and the hidden transcendence.

74. *Ph*, III, 165 ff./145–46.

75. *Ph*, III, 327/285. My translation. The original reads as follows:
In dieser Angewiesenheit auf sich selbst ist die Erscheinung der Existenz schwankender, zweideutiger, kraftloser als die Erscheinung der in objektiven Gebundenheiten gesicherten und bejahten Existenz; denn bei der Schwäche unseres Wesens ist in der Freiheit die grössere Gefahr durch Zweifel und Verzweiflung; Freiheit bleibt ein Wagnis.
Ashton translates this as follows:

In this dependency upon ourselves the appearance of Existenz is more wavering, more ambiguous, less vigorous than the appearance of an Existenz secured and affirmed in objective ties; for to our feeble nature freedom means the greater threat of doubt and despair. Freedom remains a risk.

76. *Ph*, III, 127. My translation. For Ashton's see *Ph*, III, 111.

77. *Ph*, III, 152. My translation. The original reads: "Philosophische Existenz erträgt es, dem verborgenen Gotte nie zu nahen. Nur die Chiffreschrift spricht, wenn ich bereit bin für sie." Ashton translates this as (*Ph*, III, 133): "Never to approach the hidden God directly is the fate which a philosophical Existenz must bear. Only the ciphers speak, if I am ready."

78. *Ph*, II, 327/285. My translation of: "Existenz erfährt von der Gottheit indirekt nur so viel, als aus eigener Freiheit ihr wirklich wird." Ashton translates this as: "What Existenz indirectly learns about the deity is no more than it will realize out of its own freedom."

79. See for example, *Ph*, I, 4 ff./47 ff.; and *Ph Gl Off*, 33—34/*Ph F Rev*, 7.

80. See *W*, 255—56; and *Ph Gl Off*, 156/*Ph F Rev*, 94.

81. See *Ph*, II, 15—16/15—16; *W*, 257; *Ph Gl Off*, 156—57/*Ph F Rev*, 94.

82. *Ph*, III, 141—50/123—31.

83. *Ph*, III, 16. My translation of the following (for Ashton's see *Ph*, III, 16): "Der Gegenstand, welcher Symbol ist, ist *nicht* festzuhalten *als* daseiendes Wirklichsein der *Transzendenz*, sondern *nur als ihre Sprache* zu hören" (Italics in the original).

84. This has also been noted by Tilliette, *Karl Jaspers: Théorie, Métaphysique, Foi*, p. 185.

85. *W*, 256.

86. See his interpretation of Kant in *Ps WA*, 446 ff.

87. *W*, 1030—31. The original reads as follows:
Die Welt und alles, was in ihr vorkommt, ist Geheimnis. . . . Philosophie erhellt das Geheimnis und bringt es ganz zum Bewusstsein. Sie beginnt mit dem Staunen und steigert das Staunen. . . . Dann zeigt die Welt im Ganzen und jeder Zug in ihr die unendliche Tiefe. . . . Dies Geheimnis ist wesentlich; in ihm spricht das Sein selbst. . . .
Unser Staunen reisst uns hin, durch die Welt hindurch uns hineinzustürzen in die Transzendenz. Aber wir bleiben in der Welt und finden uns wieder, nicht in der Transzendenz, sondern in gesteigerter Gegenwärtigkeit. Was immer für uns ist, wird uns mehr, als es zunächst schien. Es wird durchsichtig, es wird Symbol.

88. *W*, 401 ff.

89. *Ph*, III, 141/124. Ashton speaks here of "conscious symbolism."

90. Ibid. My translation.

91. *W*, 1032; Jaspers says: "Das Sein ist keine zweite Realität, die hinter den erkennbaren Realitäten steckt."

92. See *Ph*, III, 145—46/127—28.

93. *W*, 1032.

94. See *Ph*, III, 144 ff./126 ff.

95. *Ph*, III, 146—47/128—29.

96. *Ph*, III, 146. My translation. For Ashton's see *Ph*, III, 128.

97. See *Ph*, III, 146/128.

98. *Ph*, III, 148—49. In the original this reads:
Als Möglichkeit der Aneignung wird sie [die Chiffre] erst im Augenblick geschichtlicher Gegenwart der Existenz für diese in unübertragbarer und

für sie selbst unwissbarer Weise eindeutig. Diese Eindeutigkeit ist in der Unvertretbarkeit der für diese Existenz erfüllenden Transzendenz.
Ashton translates this as follows (*Ph*, III, 130):
Not until an Existenz is historically present will the possibility of adoption become unequivocal for that Existenz, in a way that is nontransferable and unknowable for the Existenz itself. The unequivocality lies in the fact that nothing substitutes for the transcendence that fulfills this Existenz.
The difficulty the translator faces here is how to translate *eindeutig (having one meaning)* in its present contraposition to *vieldeutig (having many meanings)*. Both words are here also related to *deuten*, i.e., *interpreting* or *determining meaning*. Ashton opts for *unequivocal*. While this translation is possible without disturbing the thought that Jaspers expresses, *singular in meaning* seems to me to be much more to the point.
  99. *Ph Gl Off*, 157–58. Strangely enough, this passage was omitted by Ashton in the English translation. In the original version it is as follows:
Wir ziehen das Wort Chiffer dem Worte Symbol vor. Chiffer bedeutet "Sprache," Sprache der Wirklichkeit, die nur so gehört wird und angesprochen werden kann. Symbol dagegen bedeutet eine Vertretung für ein Anderes, auch wenn dieses nur im Symbol und auf keine andere Weise da sein kann. In Symbolen sind wir meinend auf das Andere gerichtet, das dadurch Gegenstand wird und in diesem gegenwärtig ist. Aber Symbole können Moment der Chiffernsprache werden. Dann sind sie hineingenommen in die Bewegeng des Denkens auf die Transzendenz hin oder von ihr her. Dann verlieren sie ihre verführende Substantialität, aber versinken auch nicht in die Blässe "blosser Symbole."
  100. *Ph*, III, 146–47/128–29.
  101. *W*, 1033.
  102. Ibid. In German this passage reads as follows:
Das Bedeuten der Chiffern ist nicht so, dass ein Gegenwärtiges ein Abwesendes, ein Diesseitiges ein Jenseitiges bedeute. . . . Chiffersein ist ein Bedeuten, das nichts Anderes bedeutet. . . .
. . . Die Chiffer ist das unendliche Bedeuten, dem keine bestimmte Bedeutung gemäss ist, die vielmehr in der Deutung selber eine unendliche Bewegung des Deutens fordert. Das Deuten ist . . . selber ein gleichnishaftes Tun, ein Spiel. Deuten ist unmöglich: das Sein selbst ist gegenwärtig, die Transzendenz. Sie ist namenlos. Reden wir davon, so brauchen wir unendliche Namen und heben sie alle wieder auf. Das, was bedeutet, ist selber Sein.
  103. Tilliette, *Karl Jaspers: Théorie, Métaphysique, Foi*, p. 70.
  104. *Ph*, III, 149. My translation. For Ashton's see *Ph*, III, 131.
  105. *W*, 519.
  106. *W*, 300–301.
  107. *Ph Gl Off*, 183/*PhF Rev*, 115. My variant translation.
  108. *W*, 1049.
  109. *Entmyth*, 23/*Myth*, 20. My translation.
  110. *Entmyth*, 47/*Myth*, 47. My translation; brackets supplied.
  111. Ibid. My translation.
  112. *Entmyth*, 63/*Myth*, 61.
  113. *Entmyth*, 91/*Myth*, 87.
  114. *W*, 1054. The following is the passage in the original:
Das Entscheidende ist je einmalig, kann nicht allgemein vorweggenommen

werden. Es wäre ein Irrtum, zu meinen, mit dem Hinweis auf Grund und Weise der philosophischen Bewegung sei schon eine Erfüllung gegeben, sei ein Programm aufgestellt oder sei gar das Seinsbewusstsein in seinem Gehalt vermittelt. . . . Auflockerung der Möglichkeiten . . . ist nich Vermittlung der Substanz. . . . Philosophie erweckt, macht aufmerksam, zeigt Wege, führt eine Strecke weit, macht bereit, lässt reif werden, das Äusserste zu erfahren.

115. *Ph*, III, 151. My translation. For Ashton's see *Ph*, III, 132.

116. *Ph*, III, 151. My translation. For Ashton's see *Ph*, III, 133.

117. *Ph*, III, 153/134.

118. See *Ph*, III, 225–26/197 ff.

119. *Ph*, III, 223. My translation; for Ashton's see *Ph*, III, 196.

120. *Ph*, III, 227/200.

121. MacNeice translates these lines as: "He only earns his freedom and his life/Who takes them every day by storm."

122. *Ph*, III, 228–29/201.

123. See *Ph*, III, 230 ff./202 ff.

124. *Ph Gl Off*, 195/*Ph F Rev*, 125. My translation of the following: Interpretation findet ihre Grenze, wo die Sprache aufhört. Sie vollendet sich im Schweigen. Aber diese Grenze ist selber nur durch Sprache da. . . . Dieses Schweigen ist nicht Verschweigen von etwas, das ich weiss und sagen könnte. Es ist vielmehr . . . dans an der Grenze des Sagbaren erfüllte Schweigen.

Ashton translates this as follows:
The end of language is the limit of interpretation. It is completed in silence. But the limit itself exists by language alone. . . . This kind of silence is no suppression of something I know and could say. . . . It is a fulfilled silence at the limits of what men can say.

125. A discussion of Jaspers's extensive treatment of the tragic exceeds the scope of this chapter. See his *W*, 915–60; this section appeared in English under the title *Tragedy is Not Enough* (see Appendix 1, item 77).

126. *W*, 896. This is the text in the original:
Es ist genug, dass Gott ist. Angesichts aller Furchtbarkeit der Welt . . . angesichts der Zerstörung . . . durch erbarmungslose Eroberer . . . in dieser Hoffnungslosigkeit für den Einzelnen und für den Staat war es einigen Juden . . . genug, dass sie des Daseins Gottes gewiss waren. Dieser Menschen Trost in allem Verzweifeln, ihre Sicherheit in ratlosen Lagen, ihr Jubel im Seinsbewusstsein war allein dieses: Gott ist. . . . In dieser Gewissheit wollte der Mensch nichts mehr für sich.

127. *Ph Gl Off/Ph F Rev* (1962).

128. See *Ph Gl Off*, 385–428/*Ph F Rev*, 255–85.

129. *Ph Gl Off*, 417/*Ph F Rev*, 276.

130. *Ph Gl Off*, 425/*Ph F Rev*, 283. My variant translation of the following: Im Transzendieren über alle Chiffern, hinaus nicht nur über die Welt, sondern über die Wirklichkeit unserer Existenz im Dasein, gelangen wir in die grosse Leere, in das All, das Nichts ist, in die Fülle, die ohne Offenbarung bleibt.

Ashton translates "die Wirklichkeit unserer Existenz im Dasein" as: "the reality of our Existenz in existence."

131. Ibid.

132. The meaning of these lines, i.e., "All that is transient is but a symbol," is missed in MacNeice's translation: "All that is past of us was but reflected."

133. See end of *Faust* II, act I, scene I. In MacNeice's translation: "Reflected colour forms our life forever." The use of "our" is misleading. What Goethe has Faust say here is that we do not have life at its source but in its reflection; however this reflection is colorful.

134. Tilliette, *Karl Jaspers: Théorie, Metaphysique, Foi*, p. 160.

135. "Reply," in Charles W. Kegley and Robert W. Bretall, eds., *The Theology of Paul Tillich* (New York: Macmillan Co., 1961), p. 334.

136. Paul Tillich, *Systematic Theology*, vol. I (Chicago: University of Chicago Press, 1951), pp. 238–39.

137. "Reply," in Kegley and Bretall, *The Theology of Paul Tillich*, p. 334.

138. Tillich, *Systematic Theology*, vol. I, p. 15.

139. John Herman Randell, Jr., "The Ontology of Paul Tillich," in *The Theology of Paul Tillich*, ed. C. W. Kegley and R. W. Bretall, p. 161.

140. "Reply," in Kegley and Bretall, *The Theology of Paul Tillich*, p. 335.

141. Tillich, *Systematic Theology*, vol. II, p. 9.

142. Richli, *Transzendentale Reflexion und Sittliche Entscheidung*, p. 146.

143. Tillich, *Systematic Theology*, vol. II., p. 9.

144. Martin Buber, "Zur Geschichte des Dialogischen Prinzips," in *Werke*, vol. I, pp. 302–3.

145. Ibid., p. 300.

146. "Answer" in Schilpp, *Jaspers*, 780–81/783. My variant translation; brackets provided.

Notes to Chapter 8

1. See *Ps WA*, 232 and 247–48.

2. *Ph Gl Off*, 309–84/*Ph F Rev*, 203–55.

3. See "Der philosophische Glaube angesichts der christlichen Offenbarung" in *Philosophie und christliche Existenz: Festschrift für Heinrich Barth*, ed. G. Huber (Basel and Stuttgart: Verlag Helbing & Lichtenhahn, 1960); and *Chiffren der Transzendenz*, lectures 2 and 3 (see Appendix 1, item 9).

4. See M. K. Malhorta, "Die Philosophie Karl Jaspers' und die indische Philosophie," *Zeitschrift für Philosophische Forschung*, XV, pp. 363–73.

5. *Ph*, II, 170/150–51. My variant translation.

6. *W*, 532.

7. Ibid. See also *Ph Gl Off*, 322/*Ph F Rev*, 212.

8. *Ph*, II, 171/151. My variant translation of "Gut und böse sind also nicht inhaltlich bestimmbar, sondern alle inhaltlichen Möglichkeiten beiden eigen. Es sind nicht bestimmte Werke als solche gut oder böse." Ashton translates this as: "Good and evil are thus not definable by substance. All substantial possibilities lie in both. Not certain works as such are good and evil."

9. *Ph Gl Off*, 322.

10. *Ph F Rev*, 212.

11. Martin Buber, *Good and Evil* (New York: Charles Scribner's Sons, 1953), p. 77.

12. Martin Buber, *I and Thou* (New York: Charles Scribner's Sons, 1958), p. 52. My variant translation.

13. Ibid., p. 51.

14. Ibid., p. 46. My variant translation.

15. See *Grundlegung zur Metaphysik der Sitten*, 393.

16. *Ph*, II, 171/151.

17. Jowett translation.

18. *Gr Ph*, 257/*Gr Ph*, I, 130. Where Manheim says "fundamental knowledge," I translate "original knowledge"; the original is *ursprüngliches Wissen*.

19. *Gr Ph*, 256/*Gr Ph*, I, 129. My variant translation.

20. *W*, 532. My translation.

21. *Ph Gl Off*, 321/*Ph F Rev*, 211. Variants in the translation provided. Kant's distinction appears in *Critique of Practical Reason*, 117 ff. (Academy Edition pagination).

22. See especially *Ph*, II, 346/303–4; *W*, 535–36; *Ph Gl Off*, 320/*Ph F Rev*, 211; and *Chiffren*, 24.

23. *W*, 991.

24. *W*, 997.

25. See *Ph*, II, 346–47/304.

26. See *W*, 534–35; *Ph Gl Off*, 321–22/*Ph F Rev*, 212; *Chiffren*, 25; and, above all, "Das radikal Böse bei Kant" in *R & A*, 90 ff. Concerning the political import of the last mentioned study see Jaspers's "Reply" to Eduard Baumgarten's "Für und wider das radikale Böse"/"The 'Radical Evil' in Jaspers' Philosophy," both in Schilpp, *Jaspers*.

27. I. Kant, *Religion within the Limits of Reason Alone*, Academy Edition, pp. 28 ff.; in English: T. M. Greene and H. H. Hudson, trans. (New York: Harper & Brothers, 1960), pp. 21 ff. Kant says, "Man is Evil by Nature." He explains that what he means by this is "that evil can be predicated of man as a species; not that such a quality can be inferred from the concept of his species." Since this has not been properly regarded, Kant has been misunderstood—from his time to the present—as considering man to be by nature diabolical. Careful readers and interpreters of Kant have had to take great pains to correct the mistakes in the understanding of Kant's views on man's evil. See, for example, Jaspers's "Reply" to Baumgarten's contribution to Schilpp, *Jaspers*, 848/864, and his *Chiffren*, 25. See also the Introduction to the English translation of Kant, op.cit., by John R. Silber, "The Ethical Significance of Kant's *Religion*", pp. cxi ff.

28. Kant, *Religion within the Limits of Reason Alone*, Academy Edition, pp. 29–30; in English, pp. 24–25.

29. Kant, *Religion within the Limits of Reason Alone*, p. 30. My translation. See Greene and Hudson translation, p. 25.

30. *Ph Gl Off*, 321/*Ph F Rev*, 212. The emendations of Ashton's translation are mine. See also *R & A*, 93–94; *W*, 534–35; *Chiffren*, 25.

31. See *Chiffren*, 24.

32. *W*, 537.

33. See *W*, 536.

34. *Ph*, II, 197/172.

35. See S. Kierkegaard ("Anticlimacus"), *The Sickness Unto Death*.

36. See note 12 above.

37. *Ph Gl Off*, 319/*Ph F Rev*, 210.

38. *Ph Gl Off*, 317/*Ph F Rev*, 209.

39. See *Ph Gl Off*, 311 ff./*Ph F Rev*, 205 ff.; also *Chiffren*, 21.

40. See *Ph Gl Off*, 310–11/*Ph F Rev*, 204–5.

41. *Ph Gl Off*, 323/*Ph F Rev*, 213. Brackets provided. My variant translation of the first two sentences: "Liegt die Schuld für das Schuldigwerdenkönnen oder gar für das Schuldigwerdenmüssen des Menschen vor ihm in einem anderen? Wer ist dann schuld? . . ." Ashton's remarkably incorrect translation reads: "Is something else to blame for permitting, indeed forcing man to bear guilt? And if so, what? . . ."

42. See *Grundlegung zur Metaphysik der Sitten*, Academy Edition, p. 446.

43. *Ph*, II, 199–200/173–74. My variant translation.

44. Ashton translates this sentence as: "It is in the origin of my self-being that I mean to encompass the necessities of natural and moral laws, and it is there that I feel I have not created myself." The original reads: "Grade im *Ursprung* meines Selbstseins, indem ich die Notwendigkeiten des Natur- und Sollensgesetzes zu über-greifen meine, bin ich mir bewusst, mich *nicht* selbst geschaffen zu haben."

45. *Ph Gl Off*, 323/*Ph F Rev*, 213.

46. *Ph Gl Off*, 324/*Ph F Rev*, 213.

47. Ibid.

48. *W*, 903.

49. See *W*, 899.

50. See *Ph*, III, 76–77/68; and *Ph Gl Off*, 232 ff./*Ph F Rev*, 149 ff., and 330–31/218–19.

51. See *Ph*, III, 76/68; *Ph Gl Off*, 325/*Ph F Rev*, 214–15; *W*, 900.

52. See *Ph Gl Off*, 327/*Ph F Rev*, 216.

53. See *Ph*, I, 73/109; *Ph Gl Off*, 361 ff. and 460–61/*Ph F Rev*, 239 ff. and 308–9.

54. See *Ph*, III, 72/64–65; *Ph Gl Off*, 455 ff./*Ph F Rev*, 305 ff.

55. See *Ph Gl Off*, 363 ff./*Ph F Rev*, 240 ff.

56. *Ph Gl Off*, 367/*Ph F Rev*, 243.

57. *Ph Gl Off*, 366/*Ph F Rev*, 242. My variant translation.

58. See chap. 4.

59. See, for example, *Ph*, III, 215 ff./189 ff.

60. See *Ph*, II, 105 ff./93 ff.

61. Ibid. and *Ph*, III, 81/72.

62. *Ph Gl Off*, 378/*Ph F Rev*, 250.

63. *Ph*, III, 78/70.

64. See Kant's "Über das Misslingen aller philosophischen Versuche in der Theodicee," 1791 ("On the Failure of All Philosophical Essays at Theodicy").

65. Concerning Jaspers's treatment of predestination see especially *Ph*, III, 77 ff./69 ff.; *W*, 901; *Ph Gl Off*, 351 ff./*Ph F Rev*, 232 ff.; *Chiffren*, 32–33.

66. *Ph Gl Off*, 361/*Ph F Rev*, 238.

67. *Ph*, III, 77/69.

68. *Ph Gl Off*, 337/*Ph F Rev*, 223.

69. *Ph Gl Off*, 340. My translation. For Ashton's abbreviated version see *Ph F Rev*, 224.

70. Ashton translates this as: "He is in earnest about God as the cause of all things, and thus of his own experience." Jaspers says no such thing, as can be seen from the original: "Er beansprucht die Ursprünglichkeit seiner eigenen Erfahrung ernst zu nehmen."

71. *Ph Gl Off*, 348/*Ph F Rev*, 229.

72. *Ph Gl Off*, 344/*Ph F Rev*, 227.

73. Saint Gregory the Great, *Morals On the Book of Job*, vol. III, pt. II, (Oxford: J. H. Parker, 1850), p. 669.

74. Ibid., p. 667.
75. *Ph Gl Off*, 348/*Ph F Rev*, 230.
76. *Ph Gl Off*, 351. My translation. For Ashton's version see *Ph F Rev*, 231.
77. *Ph Gl Off*, 344/*Ph F Rev*, 227.
78. See *Ph Gl Off*, 340–41 and 346/*Ph F Rev*, 225 and 228.
79. J. I. Loewenstein's contribution to Schilpp, *Jaspers* is one of the best accounts of Jaspers's relation to Judaism.
80. See *Ph Gl*, 90/*Scope*, 100–101.
81. *Ph Gl Off*, 347/*Ph F Rev*, 229.
82. See for example *Ph Gl/Scope*, chap. IV.
83. *Ph Gl Off*, 383/*Ph F Rev*, 254.
84. See *Ph Gl Off*, 196 ff./*Ph F Rev*, 125 ff.
85. *Ph Gl Off*, 373/*Ph F Rev*, 247. My variant translation.
86. See *Ph Gl Off*, 374–75/*Ph F Rev*, 248.
87. *Critique of Practical Reason.* Academy Edition pagination 147–48. L. W. Beck translation.

Notes to Chapter 9

1. *Gr Ph*, 233/*Gr Ph*, I, 111. My variant translation.
2. *Gr Ph*, 46 ff./*Gr Ph*, I, 6 ff.
3. Manheim, in his translation, calls the members of the first main group the "Paradigmatic individuals." The original is "die massgebenden Menschen."
4. *Gr Ph*, 55.
5. *Gr Ph*, 231/*Gr Ph*, I, 109.
6. *W*, 192. For more about the 'ingenuous synthesis' see the Introduction.
7. *Gr Ph*, 619/*Gr Ph*, II, 3. My variant translation.
8. *W*, 744. My translation.
9. *Gr Ph*, 232–33/*Gr Ph*, I, 109–10. My variant translation.
10. Richard Wisser coined this phrase in apt reference to Jaspers. See his "Ein Philosoph denkt sich frei," *Zeitschrift für Philosophische Forschung*, vol. 17, 1963, pp. 284–96.
11. Op.cit., Bonn, 1965.
12. *Faust I*, ll. 1801–2. Quotations are from the Artemis edition.
13. Ll. 1803–5.
14. Ll. 1587–92.
15. Ll. 1605–6.
16. L. 1806.

Index

A *See also* reference at the end of an entry refers to the entire entry.
A parenthetical *see also* within a subentry refers just to the subentry.

Abelard, 216
Abraham, 61, 112
Absolute, 128
  inevitability of positing some-
  thing as absolute, 27
Absoluteness
  historic and universal abso-
  luteness, 136
Absolutism, 6
Absolutization, 66, 120f., 123,
  150, 166, 205f. *See also* Cipher,
  Freedom, Intellect, One truth,
  Reason, Transcendence, World
Abstraction
  Aristotelian epistemology, 43, 48.
  See also Intuition
Action, 58, 72, 102, 128, 130, 134
  action as form of testimony, 19,
  69
  religious action, 84. *See also*
  Thought
Activity, 118
Actuality
  concrete actuality, 148
  transcendent ground of actuality,
  148. *See also* Concrete, Faith
Actualization. *See* Freedom
Agnosticism. *See* Ignorance
All and nothingness, 171
Analogy, 21, 147
  Aquinas' theory of analogy, 153f.
  knowledge of God's essence as
  analogy, 154. *See also* Cipher,
  Predication
Analysis, 24
Anscombe, G.E.M., 49
Anselm, Saint, 47f., 54, 240nf.,
  243n
Cur Deus Homo? 48
Proslogium, 47
Antinomy, Antinomies, 16, 240n
Anti-Semitism. *See* Jews
Appearance, 157f., 211. *See also*
  Being in itself and in its appear-
  ance
Aquinas, Thomas, 132, 154f., 197,
  216, 217, 218, 240nf., 244n
  comparison with Wittgenstein, 50

negative theology, 153f.
philosophy as understood by
  Thomas, 154
refutation of Anselm, 47f., 54
Thomas and Maimonides, 154f.
  See also Analogy, Faith, God
Arbitrariness, 102
Arendt, Hannah, 104, 116
Argument, 19
Aristotle, Aristotelianism, 43, 132,
  154, 216, 217, 219
De Caelo, 210
Art, 5, 19, 63, 138, 166
  art and decision, 57
  art and faith, 57
  art and mysticism, 57
  art and situationality, 57
  art and time, 57
Asceticism
  Indian asceticism, 55
Ashton, E. B., 142n, 240n, 241n,
  246n, 247n, 250n, 254nf., 256n,
  257n, 258n, 261n
Assurance of transcendence. *See*
  Cipher, Transcendence
Atemporality. *See* Time
Atomic annihilation, 122
Atonement, 47
Attribution
  modes of attribution, 155. *See*
  also God
Augustine, 36, 132, 198, 209, 214,
  215, 216, 217, 220, 222
Authoritarianism, 197
Authority, 16, 21, 37, 101ff., 118,
  123, 149
  antagonism of authorities, 107
  approval and opposition, 103
  authority and catholicity, 70,
  129, 131, 132
  authority and conscience, 76
  authority of cultural goods, 101
  authority and dogma, 108
  authority of heritage, 101
  authority as indispensable, 103
  authority is human, 105, 119
  authority of law, 109
  authority not absolute, 105f.